La Vie en Rosé

By the same author

Extremely Pale Rosé

La Vie en Rosé

—

JAMIE IVEY

Weidenfeld & Nicolson
LONDON

First published in Great Britain in 2007
by Weidenfeld & Nicolson

1 3 5 7 9 10 8 6 4 2

Text © Jamie Ivey 2007
Illustrations © Neil Ashworth 2007

A CIP catalogue record for this book
is available from the British Library.

ISBN 978 02978 5228 5

Typeset by Deltatype Ltd, Birkenhead, Merseyside

Printed in Great Britain by Mackays of Chatham Ltd
The Orion Publishing Group's policy is to use papers that
are natural, renewable and recyclable products and made
from wood grown in sustainable forests. The logging and
manufacturing processes are expected to conform to the
environmental regulations of the country of origin.

Weidenfeld & Nicolson

The Orion Publishing Group Ltd
Orion House
5 Upper Saint Martin's Lane
London, WC2H 9EA
An Hachette Livre UK Company

www.orionbooks.co.uk

For our parents

Contents

I

An Alpine Experience

In the centre of Aix-en-Provence, just off the main shopping street, is a quiet cobbled square. A few tables and chairs shelter under faded green umbrellas, and an old building horseshoes round them. Two circular basins, one mounted on top of the other, overflow with water, and next to this fountain, our good friend Peter Tate stood talking to an artist. They made an unusual couple, different in build but united by their similar age – I guessed the artist was in his sixties – and slightly unkempt look. Peter's panama hat was crumpled from the road and he wore an old sun-bleached shirt, which lay open at the neck, revealing a nut-brown chest. His large-rimmed sunglasses had recently broken and so he held them to his eyes like a pair of oversized theatre glasses. The artist wore a beige suit, which hung in drapes from his slight frame. Like Peter, he was unshaven and had tufts of hair exploding from his ears and above his eyes.

They were examining a series of canvases that showed the square at different times of day. In one painting, the artist had depicted a crowd of café customers peering inwards, perhaps curious how the dilapidated building that enclosed the square could be so arresting. And in another, nothing but the sun crossed the courtyard and he'd concentrated on how the light dallied on the crumbling red brick and projected through the slats of the shutters.

My wife, Tanya, and I took a seat in the nearby café. We knew from experience how long the conversation could last. Ever the enthusiast, Peter was twirling his damaged sunglasses in the air, discussing the mixture of colours used – the burnished ochre, brittle green and lush azure blue – and so we ordered drinks and began to reminisce about our summer.

Tanya, Peter and I had been challenged by a vigneron to find France's palest rosé and our quest had begun nearly seven months ago. Things had started badly when the Parisian wine collector François Gilbert had declared that pink wine was 'fit only to be drunk with a curry'. Undeterred, we'd visited hundreds of vignerons, discovered a rosé laboratory, played in a boules tournament and nearly lost our lives in an encounter with a herd of Corsican cows. In the process, we'd discovered that rosé was beginning to be taken seriously by the French wine establishment.

Vignerons were making better and better pink wines, and the market for them was growing rapidly. Competitions such as the annual Concours Mondial de Rosé in Cannes were helping to raise winemaking standards and promote the image of pink wine, and old prejudices about drinking rosé with food were gradually being broken down by the emergence of gastronomic rosés such as Domaine Ott, which was nearly always present on the *carte des vins* at top restaurants. A decade ago sommeliers would have looked away with disdain if a customer ordered rosé; now they were more likely to eulogise about pink wine.

It also helped that rosé had become trendy. Once derided by chauvinists as a woman's drink, it was now unashamedly sipped from straws at nightclubs by young Lotharios. It was drunk by both sexes with almost any meal in the sun, and the French even seemed to think it had mystical powers, maintaining that despite an alcohol percentage equivalent to other wines, you could drink as much rosé as you liked and still drive. And after travelling for six months, somehow, almost inconceivably, we'd managed to win our bet and arrive at the mid-September harvest party with a paler rosé than Château Etienne.

Then came the hardest part – going home. Instead of returning immediately to England, we'd lingered in the south for two further weeks, unwilling to admit our summer was at an end. On our journey we'd met a psychoanalyst who'd cryptically advised, 'People on a quest only think they know what they are looking for.' At the time I'd dismissed it as the type of psychobabble lapped up by patients on couches, but the more we'd travelled, the more I'd realised how trapped I felt by my life in London. Tanya had always wanted to live in France, but I'd dismissed it as a romantic but impractical notion. Now, at the end of our trip, as the leaves of the vines had turned golden red, I'd started to hope it might be possible.

But the mistral was no respecter of dreams. It gusted ever harder, sweeping the chill air from the Alps down the Rhône Valley and battering the windowless houses of the *gardiens* in the Camargue. Although we'd defiantly remained dressed in shorts and T-shirts, the locals had changed to their winter wardrobe – fleeces zipped up to the neck and, among the elderly, even the odd fur coat.

On the terraces of restaurants, the fans were wheeled away and replaced by heaters shaped like tall mushrooms with glowing orange underbellies. The roads gradually emptied and the rain began to fall. In the countryside, which had been a tinderbox all summer, the villagers were relieved to be able to light fires in their gardens to burn the drenched autumnal leaves. And it was this smell of wet smoke carried on cold early-morning air that finally broke our resolve. It reminded us of England, of fireworks and the encroaching darkness of winter. And so, with no reason to stay in the south and an ever-emptying bank balance, we finally had to head home. After, that is, one final, fateful day in Provence.

It was 2 October and we'd chosen to stay in Aix, the ancient capital of the region, birthplace of Cézanne and a city that had lured figures as diverse as Zola, Picasso and Churchill to share the shade of its leafy central street – the Cours Mirabeau. All we'd asked of Aix was one final echo of the summer, an opportunity to sit in a square in the sun and in Peter's case to enjoy one last luxurious meal. We knew exactly what he wanted – foie gras with a fig confit, and a *médaillon de veau aux morilles* – because he'd been talking about it all day.

So far the city had obliged. For much of the morning low cloud had sped across the sky, but as we'd wandered amid the narrow streets of Aix, fingers of sunlight had begun to reach down the old walls, stretching towards the fountains and re-claiming the squares. For the first time in a week the sun had burnt off the remaining cloud, and now, as we sipped rosé in the cobbled courtyard, watching as Peter and the artist haggled, Tanya's unwavering nose for the smells of the Mediterranean discerned the sticky scent of pines.

Eventually a deal was concluded and Peter returned with a small canvas for his wife. 'It's for Jenny,' he said, as he showed us the brightly coloured picture, a mirror of the view we'd enjoyed as we sat down an hour ago.

Although it was late afternoon, it was still hot enough for us to seek the shade as we began to look for somewhere to eat. All around us restaurateurs were closing up, stacking chairs on top of each other and chaining them together. Iron shutters were drawn over the shopfronts, revealing florid graffiti – cartoon characters on skateboards leaping between the roofs of houses, and surfers cruising the universe as stars exploded around them. Peter kept stopping and peering into the dimly lit interiors of potential restaurants. In hope rather than expectation he tried the door of each new candidate. 'Another that's closed on Monday night,' he said before leading us onwards.

Eventually Tanya accosted a café owner who was closing up

for the day and asked for directions to the nearest open restaurant. The man simply shrugged. A cigarette hung from his mouth and the end was bent like a paperclip around his lower lip. '*Quand il n'y a pas de pêche, il n'y a pas de pêcheurs.*' Extinguishing the stub of his Gaulois, he turned off the lights, locked the door and walked off down the street, trailing smoke from a newly lit cigarette.

And so, on our last night in the south, in one of the most cosmopolitan cities in France, with the sun still warming the cobbled streets, and the residents casting open their shutters for one final time before winter closed in, we sat down to eat in a fondue restaurant. We'd passed through several idyllic locations for a meal – pretty squares lit by lazy evening light – but it was a Monday, it was October, and all the tourists – or the 'fish', as the café owner had called them – had gone home. So, it seemed, had the restaurateurs of Aix, except that it is for the owner of the Matterhorn, who, thankfully for us, was Swiss and apparently unaware of the French habit of closing on Mondays.

From the outside the Matterhorn looked like a ski chalet. It had a cambered, sloping roof of the type ideal for preventing a heavy build-up of snow. There were rows of geraniums in window boxes and a small speaker which piped yodelling voices into the street. Inside, thick varnished beams ran the length of the ceiling, the walls and floors were constructed from planks, and the kitchen – located of course behind a wooden partition – poured steam into the room. With beads of perspiration running down our foreheads, we chose a long wooden table underneath a large clock.

'We're a burning brazier short of a sauna,' said Peter, as he studied the menu.

But instead of finding red–hot coals in the corner, one of the walls had been hollowed out and made into an aviary. Behind a sheet of glass, there were about fifteen small finches, ranging in colour from brilliant yellow to sea blue. They had little flashes of red or orange under their wings, and tiny inquisitive beaks that pecked at the seed scattered across the floor. The back of the aviary consisted of a painted Alpine scene: cows with heavy bells dangling from their necks, cable cars heading up to glacier-capped mountains, and what appeared to be a real waterfall tumbling through the lower meadows.

'Well, isn't this wonderful,' said Peter, wiping sweat from his forehead and pretending not to notice a yellow finch cannoning into the glass partition as he ordered rosé from the lederhosen-clad waiter.

A plate of dried and finely sliced mountain ham arrived, followed by a whole *saucisson* together with a serrated knife and chopping board. There were gherkins and small pickled onions and slabs of thick white bread, all washed down by a bottle of Dôle Blanche mountain rosé. The main course was a cheese fondue, an enormous pot of bubbling Gruyère served with hunks of bread, potatoes and mushrooms. Steam poured from the pot into our faces, and soon a maze of cheese trailed and looped across the table.

As we neared the bottom of the fondue, the waiter arrived with more bread, an egg and a shot of schnapps. He cracked the egg into the pot, gave a quick stir and then doused the contents with the schnapps. The cheese and egg combined into a deliciously rich omelette, which we scooped on to pieces of bread as we discussed our route home. Tanya wanted to make a detour and spend a night by the shores of Lake Annecy, enjoying the clear Alpine air before returning to London, and Peter had prepared a list of Burgundy producers to visit as we headed through the Côte d'Or, via Gevrey-Chambertin and Marsannay to Calais.

As the cheese fondue was cleared away I loosened my belt by one notch. I assumed it was time for bed, unless of course we could find anywhere open for a nightcap. I was wrong. A complicit smile spread across Peter's face as the waiter arrived

[6]

with another bottle of rosé and swapped one bubbling pot for another. Trays of fruit arrived on the table – segmented oranges and apples and slices of banana and even melon.

I was given a fresh fondue fork and peered into the pot. Thick, viscous chocolate erupted in small bubbles. It was probably nearly 70 degrees inside the Matterhorn and our T-shirts were wet with sweat, but next to us in the aviary small finches swooped in front of a snowy landscape and perched on toy cable cars. The clock above our table struck ten and two small figurines emerged from the interior and performed a twirling dance.

Peter topped us all up with rosé and then leant conspiratorially over the table. 'I've got a little idea,' he began.

These were ominous words. Tanya and I were both aware that Peter had been involved in some crazy business projects in his time, like shipping three-dimensional chessboards from Thailand. The boards had more levels than a wedding cake, and the pieces had a varying ability to leap horizontally and vertically between squares. At the time the nation was entranced with the Rubik's Cube and Peter had backed this new form of Thai chess as the next craze to sweep the country. Unfortunately, a week after the import contract was agreed, a grand master demonstrated that it was impossible to achieve a three-dimensional checkmate. Over the following years hexagonal pool tables, rubber-duck bath radios and night-sight driving goggles joined the chessboards in the loft of his house.

Given this chequered track record as an entrepreneur, we should have known better than to listen to his latest idea, but in our defence, there can be few people in the world as persuasive and enthusiastic as Peter after a few bottles of rosé, so Tanya and I huddled closer.

'We've met some wonderful vignerons, tasted more French rosés than any snooty sommelier, and rosé is booming in France – people love it.' Peter beamed at us both, relishing the suspense he was creating.

'So?'

'Well, we can return to London for good or ...' We were seated so close to the table that Peter was able to put his arms round both of us. Giving each of our shoulders a squeeze, he somehow seemed to fix us both in the eye at the same time. '... we could come back next year and sell rosé.' He rocked back on his chair in glee, but seconds later as he swung towards the table he was suddenly earnest. 'Think about it. We'll give local people the chance to drink rosé from all over France – clairet and Marsannay, Corsican *gris* and *vin de sable*, Bellet and Tavel. Wines they've never had a chance to taste before.'

'How?' I asked.

'Well, there's the genius of it,' said Peter, still enjoying the suspense and making us wait as he swallowed a chocolate-covered slice of banana. 'We'll create our own rosé bar. All we need is some outside space, five or six sets of tables and chairs, a blackboard with our wine list and some ice buckets.'

'But we would need an alcohol licence,' I resisted, 'and since this is France, probably a hundred other licences as well.'

'Not,' continued Peter, as he triumphantly twirled a piece of apple on his fondue fork, 'if we partner with a bar that already has a licence. Then we can learn the tricks of the trade and later, when the time's right, we can establish our own bar.'

'We'll call it La Vie en Rosé,' burst out a delighted Tanya, 'the world's first rosé bar.'

'Marvellous,' said Peter, banging the table excitedly.

For the next hour we fought the heat and our full stomachs, dipping fruit into the fondue, sipping rosé and plotting the future. Each time I placed a practical hurdle in our path it only seemed to encourage Tanya and Peter.

They visualised their perfect French bar – the glasses hanging from racks above the head of the barman, the raisin-faced old man with a baseball cap pulled low over his eyes sipping beer and watching his own reflection in the mirror. The trophies for boules and rugby arranged above the cigarette stall, and a small television mounted high on the wall showing the Tour de France. There would be a large set of double doors opening out on to a terrace with tables and chairs that bathed in the cool air underneath a row of plane trees. And as they described how each day we would chalk up a daily selection of our wines on a blackboard, I gradually became hooked. It should have been an unrealisable dream, but in the sweaty deliria of the fondue restaurant-cum-sauna, it was all too plausible.

The next morning, however, our heat-baked brains had recovered and reality had begun to intrude. How would we, three foreigners, two of whom spoke little or no French, persuade anyone to let us take over half of their bar? It was like Peter agreeing to share his foie gras with a fellow diner. The idea was ludicrous. But before I could properly voice my doubts, Peter was off: 'Come on, what do we have to lose?'

The sun once again warmed the walls of the old town, and the streets were vibrant and busy. Aix seemed perfect for La Vie en Rosé. The tiny alleys were boutique-lined and prosperous. Ateliers sold canvases swathed in colour, and tiny delis offered rows of tapenades and oils. In a nearby shop, a butcher slowly laid out silver trays of his specialities – *pâté de canard, pâté aux olives, timbale de légumes, gratin de courgettes, gratin d'aubergines* and tomato confit.

Mixed in with the window-shopping French, there were plenty of American and English voices. We knew there was a twice-weekly market to lure the tourists to the old town and an annual opera and dance festival. And all around we could see our trump card, the world's biggest drinkers – students. They sat idly smoking on the steps of churches or stirring the dregs of an espresso. Aix had an estimated 40,000 of them. Surely rather than downing pints in the pub, French undergraduates could be persuaded to take a more aesthetic approach – to read Molière and sip rosé in the sunshine.

The logical place to start was the Cours Mirabeau. A row of cafés ran from the statue of good King René at the top of the tree-lined avenue down to the playful fountain at the end. Magnificent terraces spilled out on to the street, so that the tables and chairs appeared to mingle with the pedestrians and the stallholders. For an hour we slowly worked our way from bar to bar, trying to find an open-minded owner prepared to host us. But all we found were rebuttals: 'The manager has left to go on holiday'; 'Customers don't drink wine from outside Provence'; and 'We'd upset the local vignerons if we sold your wine.' In the process we learnt a new French expression – '*Allez*'. Translated literally, it meant 'Go away you've taken up enough of my time' but somehow it was delivered politely, almost as a compliment. By lunchtime we'd tried ten bars without success. People had listened to us, considered our proposition and then explained why it would never work. Finally they'd asked us to '*aller*' and so we had.

As we headed away from the Cours Mirabeau, the road opened on to a large square full of plane trees. Underneath these trees, a couple of traders had set up stalls. One table was loaded with mushrooms: trays of *girolles*, *morilles* and *cèpes*, all laid out in front of some cast-iron scales. The other was heaped with vegetables, French beans, courgettes and potatoes, still coated in dark, muddy earth. And in the corner of the square was a bar that late the previous evening we'd discussed approaching. It was set away from the main drag and almost hidden from pedestrians by the thick trunks and heavy foliage.

Long rows of chairs stretched from the bar towards the market traders. The chairs were arranged in twos in front of small circular tables, and a set of steps led up to the interior of the bar, handily splitting the outside terrace in half. It was dangerously easy to visualise spreading pink cloths across some of the tables and selling glistening glasses of rosé in the leaf-dappled sunshine.

As we entered and my eyes adjusted to the dark, I could make out a long, narrow room. Along one wall ran a bench scattered with cushions, and against the opposite wall was the bar itself. There was a coffee machine, four taps for beer, an extensive selection of spirits including several Scottish malt whiskies, an old ice-cream freezer that now held bottles of wine, and three or four stools in a row in front of the counter. On one of these stools sat an old Frenchman, not dissimilar from the raisin-faced individual we'd dreamt up last night. And just like our imaginary individual, this customer's baseball cap was pulled so low over his face that each time he took a sip of beer he had to bend the peak of his cap away from the lip of the glass.

The barman was a tall man with a heavy belly and a lazy manner. He slowly dried some glasses and pretended not to notice when we asked to see the owner. Finally we managed to elicit a response. '*Il n'est pas ici*,' he barked as if it was self-evident that the wet glasses in front of him merited more attention than us.

'*Quand il sera ici?*' Tanya persevered, explaining that we had an important business idea.

'*Lundi prochain.*' The barman shook the dirty wet cloth in our faces and turned on the radio.

But the word 'business' had awoken someone's interest. From a raised dais in the far corner of the room, a man shouted over to the barman. It was too dark to see his face, but we could make out a tightly cropped head of silver-grey hair and a pair of sunken eyes. A lethally quick French conversation ensued. Peter and I didn't have a chance of understanding it, and Tanya only managed to snatch the odd intelligible word from the air. But after a couple of minutes the man with the cropped grey hair raised his hand in the air and beckoned to us with two quick, jerky gestures.

Despite sitting down within a few feet of him, his features

were still shrouded in shadow. I could make out a narrow face and eyes that twitched quickly between us. In front of him was a half-full bottle of white wine and a silver tray piled high with oysters and crushed ice. His napkin was tucked into his shirt, and as he introduced himself as Hervé, the owner of the bar, he continuously slurped oysters, squeezing great slices of lemon over each mouthful until the taste was so tart that it made him grimace.

It was time to explain our idea. We talked about the growing popularity of rosé, and how we thought we'd identified a gap in the market. Hervé said nothing. He filled the plentiful silences by slurping yet more oysters and staring at us with a look of bewilderment. Finally having established our credentials, or lack of them, Tanya asked whether he'd consider letting us convert half of his terrace into a rosé bar, hurriedly adding that we would of course share the profits. The proposition was almost embarrassing.

Hervé, it appeared, was having similar thoughts, either that or he'd put too much lemon on his last oyster. In any event, as the full details of our proposal spilled hurriedly from our mouths, he suffered an almighty coughing fit. His eyes began to bulge and water. In the gaps between coughs he took huge swigs of white wine, but his face still turned an ugly blotchy red.

We'd finally blown it. We'd spent the whole summer trying to charm people with our wide-eyed innocence, and despite asking complete strangers where they thought we could find France's palest rosé, we'd so far escaped ridicule. But the concept of the English selling wine to the French was clearly too much. Hervé was not going to content himself with a gentle '*Allez*' – we were about to be laughed out of the bar.

When he calmed down, Hervé was still too dumbstruck to speak, but he did pour us all a glass of white wine. Tanya nudged me and a smile spread across her face.

Finally he spoke: 'It's a crazy idea.' The three of us nodded in agreement. I noticed that the barman was staring at us. He was drying the same glass over and over while his cigarette, resting in an ashtray right in front of him, smouldered unnoticed to a stub.

'My uncle makes rosé,' Hervé inexplicably continued, as I judged the distance to the exit. We would only have to endure ten seconds of laughter before we made it outside. 'As long as you sell my uncle's rosé, you can do it, but it will have to be next summer. You can start next May.' Hervé smiled a slightly uneasy smile.

'Next May is marvellous,' said Peter, 'absolutely marvellous.'

2

Two Roads Diverged in a Wood

W hat had begun as a surreal idea cooked up in the bottom of a fondue pot was suddenly a possibility. In May
next year we could be standing in the heart of Aix selling rosé.
Provided things went well, Hervé had said we could stay for the
whole summer. It was a delightful and also terrifying thought.
Just twenty-four hours ago I had been preparing myself to return
to London and resume my career as a lawyer. Tanya and I had
agreed that at some stage we wanted to live in France, but we'd
also resigned ourselves to the fact that for financial reasons this
might take some time. Now, as we followed the Rhône north
towards Orange, driving through apple orchards heavy with
fruit, I tried to picture the future opening up before us.

Our nascent rosé empire so far consisted of persuading a bar
to allow us to share its terrace. And if the concept worked in
Aix, we had the freedom to go wherever we wanted in France,
to buy our own bar amid the olive groves of the Luberon or
in the villa-dotted hills above Cannes and Nice. And when we
found the right place, where shifting our ice-kissed bottles of
pink wine was as easy as selling a bunch of lavender to Tanya,
we'd settle down and make our lives. But before next summer
unfolded, we had to return to London, to rent out or even
perhaps sell our flat, and to earn some money with which to buy

our stock of wine.

As we left Provence, the umbrella pines gave way to flat agri-culture plains and worries began to creep into my mind. Did the average consumer care what rosé they drank? Surely it just had to be cold, pink and served in the sunshine. And given the rampant regionalism of the French, would people from the south drink rosé from Sancerre? Most importantly, how much rosé would we need to sell in order to survive? The rosé season lasted as long as the sunshine. It probably began in May of each year and ran through to the end of September. How would we manage in the winter months?

They were sensible questions to which none of us had answers. And yet we were still clinging to our dream by the time we reached the vine-laced hills of Champagne. Autumn was slower to reach the north and the vines remained a resplendent green, dotted with the camper vans of the itinerant harvesters. The roads were clogged with the vignerons' tiny tractors, pulling trailers of freshly harvested grapes. By chance we passed the golden gates of Vilmart & Cie, the very first vineyard we'd visited on our trip. We stopped and tried to buy some rosé, but all last year's stock had been sold, and the vigneron, Laurent Champs, was out in the fields, supervising the first steps in making a champagne we hoped to be selling in La Vie en Rosé in the future.

For a summer we'd been immersed in the wine industry and we couldn't let it go easily. And so, by the time the wake of the ferry trailed back towards Calais and the cloud-shrouded coast of England came into view, we'd resolved that we'd be back for good the following summer.

'Sometimes in life you just have to go for it,' advised Peter cheerily, as we drove off the ferry. 'And if anyone tells you not to,' he said, roaring with laughter as the tyres of his car touched English soil for the first time in six months, 'f★★★ 'em.'

'So why do you want to return to the law?'

I was sitting in a large room in the corner of a modern office block on the fringes of the City. There were tropical plants, relaxing sofas and low glass tables spread with lifestyle magazines. I could have been in an expensive hotel, and in my experience this was a major warning sign. Any firm that tried to make you too comfortable did so for a reason: they never wanted you to go home.

Opposite me was one of the most unusual individuals I'd been interviewed by since our return to London. His name was Horatio Hanson. His scalp was bald and covered in blotchy brown birthmarks. Wisps of grey hair sprouted from around his ears, but he made no attempt to brush them across the top of his head. Instead he let the remnants of his hair project outwards, like a set of bizarre wings. The skin on his face was pale and clung tightly to his cheekbones. In repose, it gave him a slightly skeletal appearance, but when he smiled – and on first impressions he did so quite frequently – colour flooded into his face. But by far the most interesting element of Horatio's appearance was that he had teamed a pair of tailored beige shorts with a pinstripe jacket. The overall impression was quite confusing – the crazy hair, the pale skin counterbalanced by the warm smile and the more than quirky dress sense.

Untroubled by my silence, he repeated the question: 'Why do you want to return to the law?'

I hurriedly flicked through the rollerdeck in my head, hoping to come up with something vaguely convincing. The truth was that I didn't want to be a lawyer; in fact I couldn't think of anything worse than being a lawyer, but I needed some good quick money to help fund next summer. On our return Tanya had found a job as a freelance drama teacher, but a month later, in November, I was still bouncing from interview to interview trying to be convincing. In the end we'd blamed my continued failure on a disease we had christened flip-flop syndrome.

After a summer wearing only flip-flops, the skin on the heels of my feet had reverted to a baby-like softness, so my old office shoes gave me large, painful blisters. I winced as I walked into each new interview and I winced as I walked out. But flip-flop syndrome wasn't a purely physical disease – the blisters were an appropriate metaphor for my state of mind.

Settling back into life in London had been much harder than we had expected. I knew the city was going to be crowded and noisy, that pressing into the Tube every morning was always going to be uncomfortable after the open spaces of France. But living outside a society we'd grown up in allowed us to look afresh, and it was a disturbing experience. Amid the bustle and the rush was a sales onslaught that filled and defined lives, but which I'd scarcely registered before.

In my first ten minutes of TV since April, I'd been urged to buy the DVD of the summer's unmissable movie, which of course I had missed, pay by credit card for that evening's crunch football match, which would decide the destination of the Premiership a full eight months before the end of the season, and to build a conservatory on to my non-existent garden because – and this was in the second week of October – summer was just round the corner. And if there was anything I couldn't afford, I could always borrow some money from a gaggle of C-list celebrities imploring me to sign up with various loan companies.

It wasn't just the adverts and the billboards; it was the radio and the papers – everything was filled with this totally miss-able 'unmissable' nonsense. Just stepping outside our flat was disconcerting. We lived in an area of London nicknamed 'Nappy Valley', and in our absence it seemed to have undergone a further population explosion. The valley was now a canyon, and phalanxes of broad-hipped women wearing identikit clothes pushing identikit prams plagued the streets. We couldn't open our window without hearing a plummy conversation about the problems of ensuring that one-week-old Jack or Isabel made it into the right prep school.

And then there was the problem of seeing old friends. Trying to explain what had happened to us during the summer was not easy while crushed into the corner of a pub. Nearly everyone asked what it was like, but it was impossible to tell them and I am not sure they really wanted to know. There were new babies to discuss, career moves to be evaluated, and the all-consuming worry about the future health of the housing market. No wonder I had such a distracted air in interviews: I was thinking about possible cures for my syndrome.

'Never mind,' said Horatio Hanson, calling me back from my reverie to the modern office block and its low-slung sofas. 'It was a silly question. The truth is, nobody wants to be a lawyer.' He paused. 'Now I am going to hold up a sequence of coloured cards,' Horatio continued, ignoring the perplexed expression on my face, 'and in each instance I want you to tell me your favourite colour.'

I smiled. Things were getting very strange, but at least I didn't have to lie. I chose red, then green, then black and then yellow. Horatio rose from his chair with a grin on his face and patted me on the back before crossing to a cupboard and removing some more cards.

'Now I am going to show you a sequence of shapes and in each case I want you to complete the sequence. Are you ready?'

I nodded, inwardly despairing of ever finding a job. A succession of cards was flashed so quickly in front of me that I had no time to work out the correct order; instead I just answered instinctively: 'Square, square, triangle, rectangle, square.'

Horatio smiled again and sat back in the chair opposite me. 'Congratulations, Jamie, I pleased to be able to offer you a job.'

'That's it, the interview's over?' I asked incredulously.

'That's it. You can start on Monday.' He held open the door to show me out. 'Oh, and if you're curious about the shorts, I always put them on for interviews. I like to see how people react.'

I emerged bewildered into the sunshine. I'd just been employed by Hanson & Co. And although I didn't know it at the time, I was about to begin a job that I would really enjoy, working for the man who'd recently been featured in a newspaper article under the headline 'Is This the Best Boss in Britain?'

Once I was back at work, I quickly overcame flip-flop syndrome. The skin on the back of my heels hardened, and I became used to the designer-muck coffee and processed sandwich I had for lunch every day. They were comforting, even enjoyable. I caught myself gazing into showrooms, coveting a new widescreen TV and a surround-sound system. Tanya and I started going to the cinema, learning to suspend our disbelief and lap up the latest romantic pap from Hollywood. I even began to devour the property pages of all the papers, looking at the charts and graphs plotting the rise and fall of house prices. But at least I had a good excuse – we'd just put our flat on the market.

Tanya and I had done this with mixed emotions. By the time the festive season arrived our summer in France had nearly faded from memory, and although I hated to admit it, I had started liking my job. Life at Hanson & Co. was rarely boring. Rather than waste time with the pointless paper-pushing, introspection and the endless committees of other law firms – the client-pitch committee, the client-entertainment committee, the client-satisfaction committee – Horatio Hanson insisted on only one meeting a week. On Friday afternoon the entire staff of the office – we numbered about twenty – decamped to the sitting room of Horatio's house, which was just a two-minute walk from the office. There, we ate homemade sorbet sprinkled with black pepper – Horatio had a taste for unusual flavours – and discussed the successes and failures of the past week. It was man management as I'd never encountered it before, and the employee of the week, as voted for by the other staff, got a Flake and a sparkler in their sorbet.

Tanya was also enjoying her new job. It was fun working in an environment where her pupils were so excited about their weekly drama lesson that they hugged her on arrival. And while teaching the budding stars who pirouetted across the stage was interesting, the most rewarding element was developing the confidence of children who arrived too shy to speak – learning to unwrap the tightly crossed arms and tangled legs until these children embraced rather than retreated from the world.

So why were we trying to sell the flat? The simple answer was that while our life in Balham was stable and happy, we'd fallen in love with France the previous summer and couldn't shake the idyll of living and working in Provence. If we didn't have the courage to do it now, when we were young, then would we ever do it? My first instinct was to be cautious and just rent out our flat, particularly since we were only going to rent in Aix, but in the end Tanya persuaded me. We discussed what would happen if we found the perfect place to set up a bar in France and then didn't have the available funds to buy it. 'We'll kick ourselves,' said Tanya.

And she was right. I'd spent hours researching on the Internet and buying industry magazines for the bar and catering industry. I'd even managed to get hold of business plans for potential bars in the UK. Figures usually scrambled my brain, but I'd sat down and worked my way through the spreadsheets until I'd reached a rudimentary understanding. The conclusion I came to was that because of the uncertain nature of the bar business, borrowing was unusually expensive. The larger the cash sum we had available, the better, and this meant selling was the only realistic option.

Encouragingly, I also came across an article arguing that it was a good time to invest in bars in France. Pastis bars were struggling to attract the new generation of drinkers and were going under as a result. The author, an investment analyst, thought that anybody who got the formula right and successfully appealed to the youth market could roll out a brand in the country. The piece was aimed at big business, but it still had some relevance to our position.

When we eventually managed to get Hervé on the phone to confirm the arrangements for next summer, the last barrier to selling fell away. I tried to kid myself that if it didn't work out, we could always get back on to the London property ladder at a later date.

In the evenings and at the weekend, together with Peter, we pressed on with plans to make our living by selling rosé. Peter wrote to all the vignerons we'd visited the previous year and negotiated excellent prices for their wine. Tanya sourced pink-checked tablecloths and discovered some old iron pails that we could use as ice buckets. They looked as if they'd been bought at great expense in a French *brocante* – a flea market – but she'd found them for a fiver in a Balham corner shop.

We'd had several interested buyers view the flat, and our plan was to leave on 20 April – exactly a year to the day since we'd set off to find France's palest rosé. But in early April we suffered a setback, when Guy de Saint-Victor, the Béziers-based wine merchant who'd helped us so much the previous summer, arranged to meet us at the London Wine Fair.

'I am on stand A2, Jammie. But remember to look for me upstairs, Jammie – that is the VIP area. Even then you may struggle to find me. I am like one of your SAS commandos at wine fairs: I have to move quickly to make the deals. I am – how you say? – like a shadow.'

The London Wine Fair was laid out in a sprawling hall in the East London Docklands. As Peter, Tanya and I entered, we were each handed a thin-stemmed tulip-shaped tasting glass. Before us were over a thousand stands offering wine from all the major producing areas. And it was all free – Chablis, Sancerre, Pouilly Fumé, Australian Shiraz, New Zealand Sauvignon Blanc, the list was endless. Once we'd managed to resist the temptation to drink our way around the world, we looked, as instructed, for stand A2 in the upstairs VIP area. But rather than our French wine warrior, we found a party of Japanese chefs sampling pink champagne. Guy, it seemed, had commando-rolled away, and so some sushi and a glass of bubbly later we were back on the main floor.

Of course, with his trained eyes Guy spotted us first. 'I'm up here, Jammie,' he called from the mezzanine level of a stall in the centre of the hall. Guy's feet were at the level of our heads, and a small flight of steps led down to our floor, but a highly skilled wine warrior like Guy had his own way of descending. 'Hold on a second and I'll parachute down.'

When we'd last seen him, just outside Béziers, Guy had appeared tanned and comfortable in a pair of crumpled shorts and a bright-red shirt. Whereas now, in a loose-fitting suit and with his tie askew, he looked all wrong. 'It's only a disguise,' he whispered, as he greeted us with a broad smile. 'I am afraid it's very quiet today – it's a Friday and most of the French have decided to have a long weekend,' he said, as he guided us through the fair. 'No wonder our wine industry's in a mess.'

Guy stopped various producers and introduced us. We were offered some Hungarian pink Pinot Grigio at a knockdown price and a Lebanese rosé for under a euro a bottle. But the longer we spent with Guy and the more we explained about our plans, the more serious he became.

'Jammie, I don't think your business will work. No one is drinking any more in France. The country is as dry as the Sahara. It's depressed, no one has any money for wine, and the few that do are afraid to drink. It's all the government's fault: they've spent millions advertising the harmful effect of drink.

'It's true some of us still drink –' Guy winked '– but there are roadblocks on every street corner trying to catch drink drivers, so we have to drink at home. Anyway, Jammie, France is wrong for you, and you don't want to do business in the south – it's full of the Mafia. Pay up or it's bang, bang you are dead.'

And so it continued, reason after reason why La Vie en Rosé would struggle. Guy told us that the market in France was flooded with wine. 'People don't buy wine any more: they wait for vineyards to give it away. Take my advice, Jammie, set your bar up in London,' concluded Guy, before slipping into the shadows to make another deal.

What we needed was time. Time to evaluate what Guy had said to us, to reconsider our options and to make the right decision. But early the following week we received an asking-price offer on our flat, with a request from the prospective buyer that we take the flat off the market that day and complete the sale by the end of the month. We stalled for a couple of days, only too aware that our buyer was becoming less and less keen. On Thursday afternoon he issued an ultimatum: he wanted an answer by Monday or he'd walk away from the deal. It was a buyer's market and if we wanted to go to France with cash in our pockets, then we couldn't afford to ignore the offer.

We recalled our experiences of the previous summer. The Côte d'Azur had been packed with people driving flash cars, wearing expensive clothes and spending money wherever they went. There had been no sign of a downturn. Some bar owners had moaned that there were fewer tourists than the year before, but this was probably just the 'glass is half empty' attitude of the London taxi driver. I convinced myself that my doubts were just natural anxiety and that despite Guy's advice we had to go ahead. To reassure myself still further, I reread the article about the failing pastis bars and the opportunities for new bars that appealed to the younger generation. It was written by an investment analyst at a well-known French bank and was supported by extensive facts and figures. Surely these were more trustworthy than Guy's gut feeling.

And then there was Peter's inimitable view. He'd listened

to Guy and then, once we were out of earshot, mischievously declared, 'Well, that was a load of bollocks.' In Peter's head, I think we were already established in the south of France, waking up every morning to the glorious blue skies and relaxed pace of life. As I was wavering and trying to carefully evaluate our options, Peter was phoning with news of the bargain prices he'd secured on rosé and an update on his new pet project – finding a 'mate' or a 'mate of a mate' with a large empty villa near Aix. 'Help is only ever three phone calls away. Question is, who do you phone?' he said, laughing loudly.

Although my head told me to pause and be cautious, Peter, Tanya and my heart counselled recklessness. 'Edith Piaf used to have a glass of red wine with breakfast,' advised Tanya, 'and a nation doesn't change its drinking habits overnight.' By Friday lunchtime the decision was taken – on Monday we'd accept the offer on our flat.

For the rest of the day I was loose-limbed and light-headed. It was as if the air had suddenly become thinner – we were about to sell our home and with it our sense of security. That night Tanya dreamt that we were both balancing on one leg on the pinnacle of the Eiffel Tower. There was a long way to fall and the wind was gusting.

On Saturday morning I made the mistake of calling my parents and telling them we'd decided to sell. They'd just about tolerated our first trip around France, putting it down to an early career crisis. On our return they were happy to see us get new jobs and they swept over all references to our ultimate intention to live in France. I think they'd assumed that life would present too many obstacles for this to ever become a reality. And so, just two minutes after hearing we were selling up, and despite the fact that I was thirty-three and therefore theoretically capable of making my own decisions, they scrambled like jet pilots on an emergency mission.

The conversation went worse than expected. On the table

in the sitting room, I'd laid out all my research – tables of data showing how our debt repayments would be affected by fluctuating interest rates and figures stretching back a decade illustrating the stability of the French property market. It was all designed to demonstrate that our plans, although a little unusual, had been soundly thought through.

But the figures merited only a cursory glance. Instead we talked about all the values in life that I'd been brought up to respect. About hard work, about sticking at a job, about my responsibility to my wife, about the fact that my two brothers had both just started families and were happier than they'd ever been. And I agreed with nearly everything they said. In fact it could have been me in twenty years' time lecturing my own wayward son.

When they left, I spent a long time trying to rationalise their lack of support. They probably didn't blame me, because parents so rarely blame their children; instead they must have thought that Tanya was leading me astray and that somehow, someday I would return to my senses. If anything, this realisation made everything harder, particularly because it was something I couldn't agree with.

But there was no time to dwell on these issues. On Friday we'd emailed details of our plans to our friends – a disparate bunch of bored but rich bankers, overworked lawyers and media chameleons, who changed jobs and hair colour with the seasons. Despite failing to really connect with them on our return, in my head they were still the same foolish, carefree people I'd known at university. And yet when we switched on our home computer, some of their responses surprised me.

One in particular stood out. It was from a good friend. I still thought of him as the feckless student whom over ten years ago I'd taken to the casualty department of the local hospital. The medical problem – he'd spilt a takeaway vindaloo in his eye. At the time his impromptu solution to the curry-in-the-eye situation had been a puddle of rainwater rather than Optrex. 'A bit of grit won't do any harm,' he'd memorably assured me, as he gathered his long hair into a ponytail and bent down to scoop up the water. Two hours later he could barely see and I'd shepherded him to hospital.

Later the same week we'd sat – against medical advice – in a bar, smoke from a Marlboro Red drifting past my friend's irritated eye and up to the ceiling. I remember him pointing at me, with his cigarette clasped between his knuckles, and earnestly telling me that the people that history remembered had short lives. 'They burn brightly –' he clicked his finger '– and then there's nothing. That's how I want to live.' I refrained from pointing out that I didn't know many famous people who'd died from a vindaloo-induced eye infection.

Now, years later, the same person in bare, well-intentioned language was advising me to take a more cautious approach to life. Having warned me of the considerable risk I was taking, his email finished with the following question: 'And finally have you considered the effect on your pension fund?' Then there was some boilerplate language: 'This email was sent by Darlington Investments. It is not meant to constitute investment advice as defined by the Financial Services Act. The contents of this email are confidential. If you received this email in error, please delete.' And because I didn't quite know how to respond, that's exactly what I did.

Tanya's friends preferred the phone to the keyboard. Over the course of the weekend various voices urged caution. In England she had a job she enjoyed and a husband who could provide security, what else could she want? France was fine for long holidays in the sun, but she'd quickly learn that living there was different.

On Sunday night the phone finally stopped ringing and Tanya called to update her parents. Their attitude had always been a little more laissez-faire than my side of the family and in all their conversations with Tanya they were positive about our plans. But the more committed we became to starting a new life in France, the more responsible I felt to them about the ultimate outcome. Throughout his life Tanya's father had supported his family by working as a partner in a law firm, and although nothing was ever said, I wondered what he thought of me for being unprepared to make the same sacrifice.

When Tanya had finished on the phone, she began to raise doubts about La Vie en Rosé. Had her parents talked her out of the idea? Was she worried about not seeing them so often? Or was it just the cumulative result of peer pressure from our friends?

In any event, instead of soothing words I responded with anger. I felt betrayed – in my head Tanya had always been the driving force behind creating a new life in France, and I'd been trying as hard as I could to make it a reality. Now that she was retreating from the idea I didn't know how to react. By midnight we'd drunk a little too much and teetered to the brink of one of the biggest arguments of our married life. I scattered the graphs and spreadsheets I'd laid out for my parents on to the floor, before picking each sheet up, one by one, and slowly ripping it to pieces. At the time I thought it showed the futility of having dreams; in reality it was a spiteful and hollow gesture. Only when there was nothing left to shred and the paper was scattered across the floor did I stop.

We sat in silence for a while, contemplating the carnage of the evening. Gradually I realised that we were both suffering from last-minute nerves. 'It's harder than you think, changing your life,' I muttered, trying to bridge the distance between us.

The next day we accepted the offer on our flat and I walked into Horatio Hanson's office to resign from work. He was lounging back in his chair wearing his interviewing shorts. He waved me to a seat and offered me a suspect-looking sandwich. Smartly I refused and took a deep breath before starting to make my resignation speech, but Horatio simply held up his hand.

'I know what you are about to say. You see, you picked the square card last, which always meant your intentions were short term. Now, before we see how your prospective replacement reacts to pickled-herring sandwiches, tell me all about your plans.'

Two weeks later my last pay cheque arrived with a small bonus and a quote scrawled across it:

> *Two roads diverged in a wood, and I,*
> *I took the one less travelled by,*
> *And that has made all the difference.*
> Robert Frost

The very best of luck,
Horatio Hanson

3

The Baby Boomers

It was a wet, windy day in late April when we set sail from Dover. An assortment of English society was crammed inside the bars and duty-free shops. Teenage girls swarmed through the decks with their skirts hitched up to their crotches and mobile phones swinging from chains round their necks. At the bar, five obese men competed to break the cross-Channel drinking record, lining up a row of twenty pints and laughing as the boat pitched and the lager sloshed across the floor. They all wore black T-shirts emblazoned with the slogan 'The fatties tour of Europe 2005. Paris, Madrid, Barcelona. If it's liquid we'll drink it. If it's dead we'll eat it, and if it moves we'll f★★★ it.' Not far away a coach tour of pinched-faced tourists sat drinking tea, luxuriating in the solidarity granted by their utter disapproval of everything they saw. It didn't seem like a bad time to be leaving the country.

Just twenty-four hours ago we'd handed the keys of our flat to the estate agent. Our home since we'd been married was now a memory, and leaving had been a surprisingly difficult experience. Standing in the empty rooms had been the hardest part. I'd still been able to see the furniture in my mind – the chest of drawers that prevented the door from opening properly in the sitting room and the wonky table with the missing screws that somehow I'd never replaced. I could picture friends on the sofa on a Sunday afternoon with glasses of red wine clasped comfortingly in the crook of their arm, and as we closed the door for the final time, I'd remembered how Tanya and I had first entered with nothing but a large beanbag to start our married life.

We'd left a bottle of rosé to welcome the new owner, but other than that all our belongings, including all the photo albums and frames in which Tanya hoarded our memories, had been put into storage while we tried to rent a flat in Aix.

The idea was to drive south in Peter's car, an old BMW convertible, which he affectionately called Betty. The boot was to be kept free for the wine we were picking up on our way south – champagne, Sancerre and Bordeaux – and our luggage and Peter's was piled on the spare rear passenger seat. Once we'd loaded up with wine, we would head to Aix, where we were due at the beginning of May. The idea was to open our half of the bar at about eleven o'clock each morning and do shifts through to nine o'clock at night. As yet we weren't sure who our customers were going to be and just how long we were going to stay in Aix, but we hoped that after four or five months spent selling rosé in Hervé's café we'd have enough experience to buy our own bar and renovate it during the winter.

Thankfully we'd also be able to enjoy Peter's sense of humour for most of the summer. He'd shared many family holidays with us in the past, accompanied us on our quest the previous year and was free to help us again. His wife, Jenny, despite being nearly sixty, was climbing Mount Kilimanjaro and then spending a month in an Indian ashram. 'All firm plans need a little latitude,' he bellowed from the driver's seat, 'so why not have a loose one in the first place?'

We came off the motorway just outside Calais and began meandering through the French countryside. It was cold and wet, and the landscape was particularly uninspiring. The flat arable land was crisscrossed by electricity pylons, but somehow it didn't matter. We were back in France and luckily we'd rolled off the ferry at precisely the right time – lunchtime.

It was an important meal for all of us for differing reasons. For Tanya, it was her first meal in France as a non-smoker. She'd quit two months ago and since then we'd managed to sell our flat and she'd said a tearful farewell to her drama pupils, all without resorting to a single puff, but now she faced her ultimate test – France.

According to Tanya, there was no greater luxury in life than sitting in a French café with a glass of wine and a cigarette. In England smokers were treated as pariahs, she explained, but in France the habit was ingrained in the national psyche. Everybody indulged – from teenagers hurtling past on mopeds trailing a pungent mixture of petrol, tobacco and noise to the *chasseur* returning in the still morning air with the steaming barrels of his gun crooked over one arm and a cigarette clamped to his lips. Smoking heightened experiences, raising the beautiful to the sublime, and although she'd managed to kick nicotine in England, she was far from sure she'd survive her first meal in France.

For me, the meal represented the start of gastronomic temptation. When I'd returned to England at the end of last summer, my friends and family had pretended not to recognise me. However much I hoped that it was down to my tan and sun-bleached hair, the reality was I'd put on nearly a stone. My cheeks were puffy, I had two chins instead of one, and I didn't dare look at my belly. Throughout our last trip I'd been seduced by the French *menu* system, under which three courses were often only a couple of euros more expensive than one, and I'd taken full advantage of this ludicrous pricing. But I was determined this year would be different. We were coming to live in France and I had to curb my appetite.

And as for Peter, well, every meal in France was an important occasion for Peter.

★

We stopped in a small, ugly town that didn't even merit a bypass, but it was nearly two o'clock, it was raining hard, and we were anxious to find somewhere. There was one large central car park filled with lorries and caravans, and two drab-looking hotels. In England we'd have been lucky to find a Little Chef, but this being France there were two good restaurants. We chose the less expensive and sat down for what I hoped would be a quick lunch. We were seated in the brasserie section, where the tables were bare and the knives and forks were wrapped in paper napkins and left in a large glass in the centre of the table. The main restaurant, which filled the other side of the room, appeared much more formal, with white tablecloths pleated and creased like smart skirts, and rows of balloon-shaped wine glasses full of water, wine and reflections of the waiters.

Ignoring the well-priced *menus*, I opted for a simple *steak frites*, as did Tanya. The waitress, wearing a white apron over smart black clothes, arrived with the bottle of wine we'd selected, which was placed on a trolley together with four large, round glasses. She poured a small amount into the first glass, swirling it round so that the liquid coated the sides, and then transferred the contents into the second glass and offered it to Peter to taste. He nodded and we were all handed a glass of deep, rich Burgundy.

In retrospect, this was a warning sign for my waistline – if the service was this formal, then the food might mirror the main restaurant as well. But it was a case of so far so good: Tanya had resisted any temptation to have a cigarette, I'd resisted the *menu*, and Peter had managed to limit himself to ordering a three-course lunch, including a rather dubious carpaccio as a starter – *carpaccio de tête de veau*.

Then France fought back. The chef, distraught that Peter would have to eat his raw marinated slices of veal's head alone, decided that he ought to prepare a little *amuse-bouche* for us. And as Peter relaxed into his first French meal for over six months, scarcely able to keep a smile from his face as the finely sliced meat arrived dressed with olive oil and pesto, we were presented with small wine glasses full of a frothy, creamy mix.

The waitress explained that the chef had poached some crevettes in a champagne and butter sauce and was offering them to us with his compliments. Tanya hasn't eaten shellfish since catching salmonella from a Corsican king prawn, and since I presumed it would be unwise to offend the chef, I ate them both. Then Peter scraped the glasses clean.

The main course should have been a simple steak, but then our overzealous chef stepped in again. The chips were replaced by a creamy potato dauphinois, and to add to the flavour, a generous portion of fried foie gras was served melting into the chargrilled beef.

Peter tucked his napkin into his shirt and, with a satisfied sideways glance, began to eat his plate of veal's kidneys, which had been flash-fried in a mustard sauce. 'Marvellous,' he said, as he scooped a taste from Tanya's plate.

By the time the cheese board arrived, my will was all but broken. There were small round cheeses snugly wrapped in dried leaves, boxed dripping-soft cheeses, edifices of hard mountain cheese, smooth slices of Vignotte and a local Brie de Meaux, which was so ripe that tears ran down its rind. Peter restrained himself to a whole goat's cheese, a wedge of crumbly Chaource and a spoonful of Brie. As I politely declined the board, the waitress turned away sharply. She couldn't have been ruder had I just jilted her at the altar, but she needn't have felt slighted – back at the table, I was facing an even bigger problem. Peter was looking at me with imploring eyes. 'Come on, it's the best Brie in France,' he said, handing me a cracker laden with pungent, gooey cheese. I took a sip of my wine, accepted the offering and resigned myself to the gastronomic tour that inevitably ensued when Peter was in France.

By the end of the meal Peter was sufficiently confident to ask to see the chef. The menu had two carpaccios on it – *carpaccio de foie gras* and *carpaccio de tête de veau* – and at the start of the meal he had pondered which to have like a child choosing between vanilla and strawberry ice cream. He'd opted for the veal's head rather than the duck liver, but as he signed the bill, he asked the chef to let him have a small taste of the latter. A pale raw-fish-coloured slither of meat arrived with a basil leaf poking from its centre, and Peter dispatched it with delight. At least there was one benefit – the sight and smell of the uncooked liver was enough to drive any thought of a relaxing post-meal cigarette from Tanya's mind.

For the next week we drove south, enjoying the regional food wherever we stopped, picking up wine and becoming accustomed once more to the French roads. By the second night Peter – like all the locals – was folding back the wing mirrors on his car every time he parked, but thankfully he drew the line at other, more curious automotive habits, such as using the car door as an impromptu roadside urinal shield.

After spending six months in France last summer, we were also better equipped to analyse French driving habits. Rather than cling on in white-knuckled disbelief as other drivers completed potentially lethal overtaking manoeuvres, we now understood their motivation, and learnt never to drive at two times during the day. Firstly at midday, when the whole of the workforce decamped, grabbed a fresh baguette and whipped home. A Frenchman on an empty stomach, we realised, made light of such obstacles as undulating roads, blind bends and other cars. Secondly on the stroke of two – when the entire nation was already late, wine glasses were finally drained and tables reluctantly left – there was a daily fifteen-minute Grand Prix, a bumper-bashing dash back to work. We might have reasoned that everyone should leave a little earlier, but, in our new culturally savvy mode, we knew such a suggestion was heresy – it would interrupt proper digestion.

Unfortunately our knowledge of viticulture wasn't as sophisticated as our understanding of French roads. When we arrived at Vilmart & Cie in the Champenois village of Rilly-la-Montagne, there were horrified looks on the faces of the staff. Yes, they knew that they'd agreed to give us some rosé at a special price, but the new vintage wouldn't be ready for another couple of months – could we come back then? Eventually the vigneron solved the problem by rooting around in his cellar and providing us with several cases of his 1998 Grand Cellier Rubis Saignée.

Unlike other rosés, pink bubbly was traditionally made by mixing small amounts of red wine with champagne. The vignerons carefully controlled the resulting colour by mixing a small sample in a test tube to get the proportion of red to white correct. But a champagne *saignée* was made by bleeding the juices from the grapes and allowing the wine to take on the colour of the skin. Very few champagne houses made rosé in this manner, and they only attempted it in years when the weather conditions had been favourable. The Grand Cellier Rubis Saignée was a rarer, more refined rosé than we'd wanted to pick up, but the vigneron gave us the same deal.

In the nearby village of Cumières, the baby-booming phase of our journey began. Last year Tanya had walked through the cobbled streets chatting to the vigneron Jean-Baptiste about his burgeoning family of girls. At the time he already had four daughters and his wife was expecting their fifth child, so Tanya, who has three sisters, had been ideally placed to both congratulate and commiserate on the joys and perils of an all-female family.

This year, as we loaded the cases of pink champagne into the car, I tentatively enquired the sex of Jean's new baby. 'I think it's genetically impossible for me to have anything else,' shrugged Jean. 'It's another girl.'

Within two days we were admiring another baby, this time sitting in the living room of Nicolas Reverdy's house in the village of Maimbray near Sancerre. Outside the windows, the vines rose at such a vertical gradient that they blocked out the sky. Inside, the room was traditionally French, with flagstone floors and thick terracotta-coloured walls. It was here that we'd discovered possibly the palest bottle of rosé in France, only to be informed that it was the last of its kind and not for sale. We sat on low leather sofas, reminisced and watched as Nicolas opened a bottle of rosé next to the cradle where his new daughter, Garonce, lay sleeping. 'She'll have to get used to the noise,' he laughed, as the cork popped next to her earlobe. 'She'll be hearing it a lot around here.'

Nicolas extravagantly swilled the wine around his mouth, sucked it between his teeth and then spat it into the spittoon, but still Garonce didn't stir. He followed the same routine with a red and two whites from the *domaine*. Each time the cork popped right next to the sleeping baby, and each time her breathing remained peaceful as we spat jets of wine into the spittoon by her cradle.

Finally it was time for the *vieille vigne* white. In the fields last year Nicolas had proudly pulled back the leaves and shown us the knotted sixty-year-old vines that made this wine. And at that moment we'd finally understood the meaning of '*tipicité*'. All the French vignerons we'd met had used this word to describe the wine they wanted to create, but for the first half of the trip we'd been unable to translate it properly. We'd looked in our dictionary to no avail and had falsely assumed it meant something like 'acidity'. But finally when Nicolas had shown us the *vieilles vignes*, which were so deeply rooted in the soil they'd become an extension of it, we'd comprehended. Vignerons wanted their wine to demonstrate characteristics that were typical of the region. To them, the best wines – ones with good *tipicité* – spoke of the land, and to the experienced taster, the accent should be as easily distinguishable as a Provençal twang in Paris.

When it came to their favourite wine, vignerons didn't spit, they drank, and now rather than offer us a taste, Nicolas poured four enormous glasses. I am still not sure how it's possible to comply with France's draconian drink-driving rules without upsetting a host vigneron. In any event I enjoyed a sip of the white – it was crisp and dry with a wonderfully rich undercurrent of taste that lingered in the mouth – before reluctantly slipping my glass, hopefully unnoticed, to Peter.

Half an hour later I was trying not to offend another vigneron. The *vieille vigne* white had been replaced by a large glass of red, my blood alcohol count was rising rapidly, and we were on to baby number three. We were in the neighbouring village of Bué, meeting Nicolas's best friend, the vigneron François Crochet. François's mother had noted our arrival while she was out shopping with her grandson, baby Roman, and had immediately turned on her heels. Roman was wrapped in a blanket and taken down to the cool, smelly *cave* for one purpose. The visitors had to admire the baby, not just for a couple of minutes, but for a full half an hour. Tanya was a natural, asking all the appropriate questions – how much did he weigh when born? Did they know the sex in advance? How did they choose the name? – but Peter proved far from adept, paying more attention to the barrels of wine than the newborn.

To me, one baby looks just like another – wrinkled and slightly anaemic, with their eyes scrunched up like a mole's and their fists tightly clenched. But in an attempt to compensate for Peter's lack of interest, I took drastic action. For baby Roman I did everything but dance – I cooed, I performed what I considered to be a more than convincing mime to illustrate that he looked like his father, and I even gently held him in my arms as we tasted the wine. Finally Madame Crochet gave a nod – I'd passed the test, due deference had been shown, and Roman could now resume his afternoon outing, even if he was sniffling a little from the damp, alcohol-filled air of the *cave*. 'He'll probably end up marrying Nicolas's daughter Garonce,' joked François as his mother left. 'At least we won't have any problems with the in-laws.'

From Sancerre we drove south-west to Bordeaux to pick up some of the region's rosé. A little misleadingly it was called clairet. The previous summer we'd believed that the term 'clairet' referred to a particularly clear rosé but had discovered that the opposite was true. Rosés take their colour from the skin of the grapes either through a direct pressing or by allowing the skin and juice to stay in contact with each other – or macerate – over a short period of time. The maceration for pale rosés typically lasts a couple of hours, but a clairet is made by allowing the juice of the grapes to sit on the skins for up to two days. The liquid was then bled off, and if the resulting wine reached a certain depth of colour, it was classified a clairet. Although the Bordeaux AOC – the Appellation Origine Contrôlée, which is the French body responsible for categorising wines – insisted that clairet was a unique type of wine, plenty of vignerons had confirmed to us that it was a rosé in all but name.

Approximately 75 per cent of the production of clairet was drunk on the Atlantic coastline near Bordeaux, and it was relatively unknown throughout the rest of France. We were therefore keen to introduce this unfamiliar wine to our customers in Aix.

Having picked up several cases, we returned to the small house built on a golf course we'd stayed in the previous year. It wasn't long until our favourite swimming-pool builder, Nibby Paul, appeared. Shading his round, rosy face under a baseball cap, he clutched an empty beer bottle in one hand and yet another new baby in the other. 'All the staff working in the château are celebrating,' he told us, 'because the swans that live on the lake have just had cygnets.'

Nature, it appeared, was trying to tell us something. Our contemporaries in England, the vignerons, even the swans were busy creating a conducive environment to raise their offspring and yet we just seemed to slip further and further from a position where we felt we could start a family. I still believed that what we were doing was right, that we had to pursue our dreams while we were young, but every time we came into contact with a stable, secure family unit, it made me question the path we'd chosen. We both wanted to have children, but just not quite yet.

I felt particularly sorry for Tanya. In England there is a degree of sensitivity about a childless couple. Outsiders are diffident and don't question too much – there might be a medical problem or problems within the relationship, and such matters are best not discussed. But in France once we'd revealed we'd been married for five years, women were brutally direct. They might have only known Tanya for five minutes but that didn't stop them asking where her babies were and making us both feel guilty. Should we selflessly be starting a family instead of selfishly set-ting up our own rosé bar?

Two weeks after leaving Calais we finally reached Provence. On the way we'd met four babies, two cygnets and collected over two hundred bottles of wine. I'd also come to the realisation that all of our suppliers were crazy. Although we didn't count, they probably gave us as much wine as we bought. While this was excellent for our business prospects, it was also rather worrying. They seemed to see us as ambassadors for the vineyard, people who would take their wine across France and introduce it to potential customers. It was a task for which we felt hopelessly underprepared. We had a loose plan, one bar and a half-baked knowledge of wine, yet despite these all-too-obvious handicaps, free cases of wine were continually slipped into our sagging boot. Perhaps they thought we needed all the help we could get.

To preserve the car's suspension, rather than collect more wine ourselves we'd asked a number of Provençal vineyards to deliver to our bar, but there was one final vigneron I wanted to visit personally – Bauduin Parmentier at Château la Dorgonne.

Tanya had fallen in love with this vineyard last year – the rows of lavender curling with the drive up towards the house, the olive trees dotted across the landscape and the sweeping views across the expanse of the Luberon.

But this time our trip was for business rather than pleasure. Bauduin, a former investment banker, was among the shrewdest vignerons we'd met. Rather than rely on other people to sell his wines, he'd built up a network of his own shops. Each stocked a range of products made at the château, including olive oils, tapenades, jams and of course the wine. He also had several property projects, renovating underperforming vineyards and selling them on, which helped fund the development of Château la Dorgonne. But crucially he was an entrepreneur with a heart. There are plenty of wealthy ex-bankers who've bought vine-yards, but Bauduin came close to entering another industry, an industry that would presumably have seen him laughed out of his retirement party – lavender farming.

It seemed to me that Bauduin and Tanya were kindred spirits, romantics who were both in love with the sensuous south – the smells and the dappled light. If there was a vigneron who was going to truly embrace our idea, I felt it would be Bauduin. And deep, deep down I hoped he might get excited enough to offer to help us find our own bar, and even put some funding into it.

As we arrived at Château la Dorgonne, Bauduin came out to greet us, closely tailed by Mong, the stray dog he'd found on his doorstep and taken in. He was dressed smartly in a pair of beige chinos and a pressed shirt. A small smile twitched across his face as he recognised us from the previous year and invited us to lunch with him in a small courtyard shaded by trees. A bottle of pale-pink Château la Dorgonne rosé was placed on the table in a pottery wine-cooler. Around us, the lavender was just coming into bloom, not the deep luscious colour of later months, but a fragile light purple. Beads of moisture ran down the side of the bottle of wine, and in the distance I could hear the gentle song of the cicadas. It was the perfect environment to discuss our idea.

Bauduin listened patiently, encouraging us to speak with softly spoken prompts. He sipped slowly on his wine and clipped some darkened lenses over the front of his round glasses. We ate a *salade niçoise* loaded with eggs and anchovies, and accompanied by a light dressing served from a silver boat. When we'd finished and the plates had been cleared, Bauduin began to talk about the economy we were trying to start our business in.

'There's nowhere more beautiful to live than the south of France. It is why I run a vineyard here, but this is also the problem – the locals become lazy and the tourists go elsewhere. A twenty-euro pizza is not unheard of, the roads are a mess, and everyone wonders why business is bad.'

As Bauduin spoke I began to recognise the complacent France he was describing. In the space of two weeks journeying south, we'd enjoyed fabulous hospitality, but on a couple of occasions we'd been treated with contempt verging on disdain. The worst experience had been the previous evening in a nearby village in the Luberon, where we'd eaten in a restaurant supposedly famed for its regional food.

It was a warm night and we'd dined under pine trees. On each table there was a candle and a small blackboard advertising local wines. We were seated in the lee of an old stone wall on the outskirts of the village and we'd watched as the shadows grew over the valley. It was a peaceful setting, but things started badly and got worse. We all asked for *kirs* as aperitifs and they arrived in glasses barely half full. The waiter then refused to top us up despite serving the identical drink in full glasses to the adjoining table.

At least the menu sounded great – a lamb cassoulet, a *filet de taureau* or a roasted-vegetable lasagne. Peter had nodded sagely and advised that small menus were always the freshest. We each chose a separate main course, but when the dishes arrived they were all dry and overcooked. Even the accompanying bread was stale, and so, desperate for some moisture, Peter had requested some butter only to be informed there was none available.

And then it had dawned on us – there was no chef in the kitchen. All the food was pre-prepared or just needed slapping under the grill, and since the French use butter to make sauces rather than spread on bread, there was no need to keep any in the kitchen. In spite of the food and the service, we still managed to spend an enjoyable few hours watching the light dip below the hills. But then the bill had arrived. We'd chosen wine from the little blackboard on our table and yet the price was nearly twice that advertised. Instead of apologising the waiter simply removed the blackboard, wiped it clean and rewrote the price. We'd protested and he'd argued noisily with us and eventually we'd lost all energy and paid.

Bauduin was also right about the roads. Getting to Château la Dorgonne had proved difficult. It was at the far eastern end of the Luberon valley, and the French government had chosen to begin a major programme of roadworks coinciding, of course, with the start of the tourist season. Traffic jams wrapped themselves round the narrow hills, and cars crawled in the wake of the inappropriately named *convoi exceptionel* – these enormous yellow lorries with their flashing lights and trailers laden with digging equipment were in our experience far from exceptional.

'And as for the wine industry, it's even worse,' continued Bauduin. 'The vineyard up the road has so much excess wine it gives it away for a euro a bottle. How can I compete with that? How can you compete with that? You say you want to serve good wine, but that's not how bars make a profit. They play the vineyards off against each other, demanding every year a lower price for the wine.

'It's not uncommon for waiters to phone before their birthday and ask if they can be sent some wine to help them celebrate.

Vignerons then provide several cases as a bribe to ensure their wine is still sold in the restaurant.

'And we're even lucky to get the money for the wine customers drink. I know that if I haven't been paid by a restaurant or bar for my wine by the end of the summer, I am not going to get paid at all. By then all the money has gone, and the owner can always get wine from another supplier the following year.

'If I were you, I'd set up my bar in London. There's money in London, and there's certainly no money in France at the moment.'

We shared a coffee and discovered that Bauduin was at least optimistic for the future. The French tourist industry was cyclical, he explained. It would take a few years for the locals to understand the problem and then prices would fall, service would improve, and eventually holidaymakers would return.

For us, though, the revival might come too late. We collected our wine and drove disconsolately away from Château la Dorgonne. The boot of the car was heavy with rosé, but it seemed nobody rated our chances of making a successful living out of it. Were we cut-throat enough to play the vignerons off against each other, or to simply refuse to pay suppliers? And if not, were there enough people with enough money to pay for our good but expensive wines?

I was surprised by how dejected I felt so soon into our trip. Until now I'd been able to forget about the comments of Guy de Saint-Victor at the London Wine Fair. But his advice had been identical to Bauduin's – we should try and run our wine bar in England not France. Guy might be eccentric but he'd made a good living in the wine industry, and Bauduin was one of the most rational and successful men I'd met in my life. It was hard to ignore the creeping feeling that we might have made a mistake.

Peter, though, was still upbeat, insisting we stop off to stock up on the €1 rosé Bauduin had mentioned. 'No one believed the world was round,' he said with a childish grin, as he piled yet more wine into the car. 'People just don't like new concepts, but it's going to work because it has to work – and think of the profit we are going to make on this wine.'

4

The Grand Opening

We'd been planning it for months and now it was just hours away – the grand opening of La Vie en Rosé. Worryingly we'd been unable to speak to Hervé. We'd phoned on a number of occasions but each time he'd been absent. And so on our arrival in Aix the previous evening we'd called in at the bar. I'd drawn up a list of questions I wanted to discuss, practical points like how much wine could we store at the bar? How much space was there in the fridges to get it cold? When could our deliveries arrive? And how should we account for our takings? But once again Hervé was unavailable and we were told we'd have to wait until the opening. I reassured myself that since last October we'd written him a letter outlining our plans and had subsequently confirmed on the phone that everything was agreed.

It was early May, but leaving the air-conditioned lobby of the hotel was like stepping out of a plane into the rippling haze of a foreign holiday. The sky was a deep azure blue more reminiscent of mid-August, and although it was still early morning, we could feel the strength of the sun on our skin.

All around people prepared for the day ahead. Shopkeepers wheeled stands full of postcards, perfumed soaps and bunches of dried lavender on to the street. A hawker spread his colourful sheet on the ground and began to lay out rows of metallic replica cicadas, which sang when stroked on the back. And we began the laborious process of transferring our wine and equipment to the bar.

The streets were shut to traffic, so we had no choice but to lug our belongings for the ten minutes or so to Hervé's café. Thankfully the concierge had kindly lent us a trolley on which to transport the wine. It had a couple of wheels and a small ledge on which we stacked the irregular-shaped boxes. We had no firm idea what people were going to drink and so we'd decided to take as many different wines as possible. For this reason we'd selected eight crates – there were six on the trolley and Peter was clutching the other two against his belly. Fortunately our wine buckets had handles so we were able to hook them to the side of the trolley and fill them with our pink tablecloths. The previous evening Tanya had painstakingly written details of all our wines on to a blackboard in a flowery script, and she now held the board proudly in front of her.

We must have looked ridiculous as we set off with all this paraphernalia, dressed as we were in different shades of pink, and in my case proudly sporting a pair of ankle-length shorts-cum-trousers, which Tanya had somehow persuaded me to buy at the local market. The concierge's trolley was designed for carrying suitcases not wine, and the wheels were not built for cobbled streets. My progress was slow and jarring, causing the buckets to clatter against the trolley. I had to stop every 10 metres to readjust the wine, and it took just one irregularly shaped cobble to send the trolley hurtling off in the wrong direction. Gradually I discovered the tricks of the trade. If the street was slightly downhill, I had to walk backwards and tip the trolley towards me, and vice versa on an incline. The biggest hazards were the rainwater gulleys that ran either side of the narrow streets. Twice the trolley pitched into them and I had to madly grasp at the wine as it lurched forward.

A sympathetic lady who was pulling her groceries behind her in a wheeled canvas shopping trolley stopped and offered to help by taking some of our wine. By this stage I could feels trails of sweat feeding down my back and I gratefully accepted. But as Peter and I unloaded a couple of bottles into her trolley, I snatched back my hand. Something had just nipped me. Pulling the bottles of rosé out, I saw that I'd just deposited them on the head of a small white poodle, which was wedged between some broccoli florets and a melon, and was now viciously snarling away at me from the depths of the bag.

It was while I was walking backwards fighting a steep slope that I realised we were attracting quite a crowd. Small children on bicycles were riding in loops around us calling out encouragement, and shoppers simply stopped and stared, without even trying to hide their curiosity and amusement at what they saw. We passed a busker on a monocycle, who, noticing the interest we were arousing, started to follow us through the streets of Aix, past fountains and squares, until the road broadened out and we could make out our bar through the corridors of plane trees.

The area had been transformed since we saw it last October. In place of the mushroom and vegetable stalls there was now a whole market. Brightly coloured awnings stretched away under the trees like a tented village, and shoppers with baskets under their arms meandered among the stalls, pressing the fruit with their fingers to check for ripeness. The whole area was given over to fresh produce, and exotic stalls laden with yellow courgettes competed with vendors offering everyday broad beans.

People pressed forward examining prices, swapping recipes and then falling silent as a strange pink column forced its way through the narrow natural aisles created by the trees. Our man on the monocycle led the way, juggling as he cycled. Tanya followed, holding the blackboard above her head like a placard at a freedom march. Snapping at her heels was the small white poodle, which now had a pink ribbon tied round its neck. I was next, walking gingerly backwards and lurching in all directions as I tried to keep the wine upright. The front and back of my pink T-shirt was covered in long, white stains, where the salt from my sweat had soaked into the material. Bringing up the rear, Peter and the poodle-owning Good Samaritan were deep in conversation about the best way to fix Peter's enormous sunglasses, which were continually slipping from the bridge of his nose on to the top of the boxes he was carrying.

A corridor opened up as onlookers made way for the mono-cycle. There was even the odd clap from people who'd presumably mistaken us for a circus troupe. La Vie en Rosé was ready to open, and given the stir we'd caused, soon the whole of Aix would know about us.

As I bumped the wine up the steps towards the interior of the bar, I noticed that both sides of the terrace were pleasingly full of clients. Despite the early hour there were plenty of people drinking. Pastis and beer were the most popular tipples, but there were also a couple of potential clients sipping rosé and they appeared to be taking more than a passing interest in our arrival. I assumed that we'd just have to wait until each customer on our side of the terrace finished their drink before spreading our pink cloths over the tables and starting to serve.

Inside, Hervé was standing behind the bar. A copy of *Le Provençal* was open on the counter and he was reading an article about the declining flamingo population of the Camargue. Since we'd last seen him he'd had all his hair shaved off, revealing an ugly knife-length scar on his scalp. He looked up from the paper, noticed our arrival and then slowly began to pour a line of beers. None of us were quite sure whether to speak or not, so we stood waiting, closely observing the man who was to be our new business partner. He was wearing jeans and a faded shirt, open at the neck to reveal a gold chain. His eyes moved quickly across the bar, never quite resting on us, and his movements conveyed a restless, twitchy energy, snapping the beertap firmly up as he took a drag on his smouldering cigarette.

When he'd poured six beers, he put his fingers into his mouth and let out a piercing whistle. Two waiters and a crowd of people who I presumed were regulars gathered around the bar. Not quite knowing what to say, Tanya asked where we should store the rosé.

Hervé reached across to a basket of bread that was resting on the bar and bit a large chunk out of a piece of baguette. '*Quoi?*' he said, looking amused.

Peter took over in his more halting French, explaining that we wanted to know where we could put the wine. Hervé pitched another piece of bread into his mouth, and his lip curled upwards as he began to speak rapidly to everyone gathered around the bar. Even if he hadn't had half a baguette stuffed into his mouth, the language he used was so colloquial that none of us stood a chance of understanding. So we just waited, Peter and I in our pink T-shirts and Tanya in a pink sundress, smiling nervously and hoping that everything was going to be OK.

The people around us helped themselves to the line of beers on the counter, and Tanya tried one more time to ask Hervé where to store the wine. Again he responded dismissively, pretending not to comprehend while cramming more bread into his mouth to ensure we couldn't understand him. Finally he finished his mouthful, looked around at the assembled crowd and decided that the time was right for his punchline.

'The terrace is full,' he said, 'but you can have those two tables over there.' He jabbed his finger towards the corner of the bar and started to laugh. The waiters and regulars also began to laugh. Looking across the bar, I saw two small, rickety tables with a bottle of rosé placed on each of them. It might have been a sweet gesture except that next to the bottles were ashtrays heaped with cigarette ends and the tables in question were located directly outside the toilet. The door was wide open and we could see straight into a dirty hole-in-the-floor loo. Even standing by the bar there was a pervading smell of urine.

It's possible I would have stayed for more humiliation and even tried to negotiate moving the two tables outside, but Tanya knew what to do. She walked out without another word. Hervé started pouring more beers and chatting with his regulars. It was back to business and he was making a point of ignoring me. Seconds later Peter took me by the arm and helped me guide the wine back down the stairs.

Outside, there was no sign of Tanya, and because of the wine we couldn't go far, so Peter and I stood and waited. A couple of prospective customers approached the bar. 'The health inspectors have already tried to close it down twice this week,' Peter announced loudly. He chuckled as they scuttled appreciatively away. Winking at me, Peter then approached another couple, who were studying the menu. 'Food's much better next door,' he advised.

I was too furious with myself to enjoy such impromptu revenge. As a lawyer, I'd been trained to write everything down no matter how friendly the client – it all had to go down on paper and be signed and countersigned. But the excitement of starting a new life in France had made me override all my principles. I'd persuaded myself that the Provençal French were just casual people, too relaxed to worry about legal agreements. Clearly I should have become suspicious when Hervé refused to reply to our letters and limited himself to gruff yes and no answers over the phone. No doubt he'd been planning his joke all winter. And how well it had worked.

Next to me, Peter sat down on the boxes of wine and lit one of his cigars. As the mellow smoke wafted in front of my face, I suddenly realised where Tanya had gone. I left Peter with the wine and asked for directions to the nearest *tabac*. Tanya had been nearly three months without nicotine. At times I'd had to block the door to prevent her running out to get cigarettes, but finally the cravings had receded and she'd freed herself from the drug. Eventually she could joke about it, mooting the idea of writing a guidebook to the *tabacs* of France – those that opened on a Sunday, ones which sold foreign brands or had a bar attached. Ruefully she claimed to be able to remember the location of every *tabac* she'd visited, but I hoped her knowledge wasn't as encyclopaedic as she professed it to be – I was sure we could find another bar, but I wasn't sure Tanya could give up smoking again.

Two streets away, I found her standing outside a *tabac* underneath the familiar yellow and red sign. In her hand was a packet of Philip Morris Blue. The plastic wrapping had been removed and the cardboard lid was crumpled. She shook her head as I approached, and handed me the packet.

'He's a f★★★ing arsehole,' said Tanya, as we walked back to the square and I threw the full packet into the nearest bin.

When our initial anger had faded and the wine had been re-stacked in the hotel room, we sat down to talk. We'd been naïve and trusting in an unscrupulous trade, but we still felt bitterly betrayed. We'd put so much effort into the idea and had been left looking like fools. In numbed shock we discussed how we'd somehow become the victims of the cruellest practical joke.

Eventually Peter changed the subject. 'There is a positive side: we've got a boot full of rosé and we can go anywhere we want to sell it.'

'But not Aix,' argued Tanya. 'I've had enough of this place.'

'Not Aix,' I agreed, recalling just how difficult it had been to find a bar in the first place.

5

The *Varicelle*

After our disastrous experience in Aix we headed for Montpellier. Tanya's sister Claire lived with her husband, Neil, and their two children in an old apartment block just off the central square – Place de la Comédie. For us, it was the logical place to go for shelter – we could plan what to do next without the constant expense of paying for a hotel, and just maybe we'd find a new home for La Vie en Rosé.

I am not sure we could have picked a worse time to arrive. As Claire opened the door, Tristan, her one-year-old son, hurtled past at ankle level, crawling like a charging bull towards the stairwell. By contrast her daughter, Rosie, now nearly three, hid shyly behind her. When we finally coaxed Rosie to say hello, her entire face and arms were covered in ugly scabs. The *varicelle*, or chickenpox, had struck. Rosie was recovering, but Claire was waiting to see whether Tristan – who'd lost interest in falling down the stairs and was about to put his finger in an electrical socket – would catch it.

Claire and Tanya hugged, and I scooped up Tristan. It was good to have a home for a while, but Peter felt differently. He tentatively sidestepped his way around Rosie, left his bag in the flat and announced he was off to find a bar to host La Vie en Rosé. Disease clearly wasn't his thing.

Montpellier is potentially a perfect place to run a rosé bar. The Mediterranean is only a ten-minute drive away; lemon trees grow on terraces and vines on roundabouts. The city has more students than Aix, a vibrant street culture and plenty of café-filled squares. There are wide tree-lined colonnades which run from the Comédie down to the crumbling, ancient walls. The palm trees are tall enough to cast shadows over the roofs of houses, and below on the promenades people tarry by the fountains or stop at market stalls.

Yet after just three days of searching for a partner bar – largely led by Peter, who was seemingly anxious to spend as little time as possible in the flat – we were totally dispirited. We'd quickly accumulated a long list of reasons why La Vie en Rosé couldn't work: 'Your wine is too expensive'; 'Our terrace is full already'; and 'Our clients only drink *vrac*.' *Vrac* was the cheapest type of wine available. Typically it was made by cooperatives, and it often had large amounts of sulphur added to preserve it. Rather than bottle *vrac*, the coops sold it from the pump, like petrol, and for the overindulgent drinker the result the next morning was a horrible hangover. The saying '*Je suis vrac*' had even become slang for 'I'm knackered', but people were still prepared to pay €2 a glass in a bar for something that cost €1 a litre at source. We couldn't compete against this type of economics and so, as in Aix last October, we were politely sent on our way with a shake of the head and a dismissive '*Allez*'.

We even drove out to the east of Montpellier and approached the line of trendy beach clubs that stretched along the coast towards the Camargue. The clientele was young, pillows were decadently scattered just metres from the sea, and everyone was drinking pink wine. But not our pink wine – deals had been agreed with vignerons that couldn't possibly be broken, unless we could 'provide wine for free'.

Meanwhile Claire's problems grew. Tristan contracted chickenpox and as a result sleeping at night became impossible. Within minutes of being put to bed he would begin to howl, only stopping when he was held, and Tanya and Claire spent the early hours of each morning gently rocking him. Even this didn't make him sleep, but at least his eyes became heavy and he appeared, for a few blessed moments, too tired to cry.

The next morning Peter began muttering about checking into a hotel, arguing that the flat was too small for all of us and that he felt bad imposing for any longer. Claire insisted that she enjoyed having us to stay and so Peter resorted to plan B and phoned his doctor back in England to confirm whether he'd had chickenpox as a child. 'Marvellous,' he grunted, as he was assured that he'd already had the disease and wasn't at risk, 'absolutely marvellous.'

Continuing with the search for a new venue for La Vie en Rosé, I decided to aim high, so I called Nikki Beach – the beach club we'd fallen in love with the previous summer in Saint-Tropez. I felt I was being cheeky just phoning. Nikki was the *über*-cool haunt of A-listers such as Bono, a coterie of models with endless legs spent their summers lounging by the pool, and champagne came by the jeroboam not by the bottle. But surprisingly I was put through to their Miami office and told that the idea of a rosé bar interested them and that Eric Omores would call me. I assumed he was Nikki's events manager, and I spent the next couple of days waiting for the phone to ring.

Peter meanwhile was following the opposite strategy and aiming low. He'd developed a plan called 'Guerrilla Rosé'. Rather than target bars, the idea was to drive outside Montpellier and find a busy *route nationale*. Then, on an appropriate corner, we would park up, open the boot of the car and try to sell takeaway wine by the bottle. We'd move on every couple of hours before the police had a chance to find us and ask for a licence.

In all probability it was just another excuse to avoid *varicelle-ridden* children, but nevertheless later that day, twenty minutes north of Montpellier, we stopped in a lay-by next to a flat, open road. Visibility was good and we calculated we could be seen from over 100 metres. Next to us was another vendor selling cherries. He sheltered under a beach umbrella and advertised his presence with a small piece of cardboard leaning against a nearby tree reading '*Cerises*'. I estimated that he must have been nearing ninety, he was hairless and toothless and impossible to understand, but he didn't seem to mind us being there, particularly since Peter's car was an old BMW. He pointed excitedly at it and then at his own BMW parked in the shade of a tree, showing us with his fingers that it was twenty-one years old, as opposed to Peter's, which he'd calculated was only fifteen. He clenched his fist and patted his balled fingers against his heart to show that these old cars were good honest workhorses.

To the casual observer, our display must have looked far more impressive than the cherry seller's. Our blackboard dwarfed his piece of cardboard, and Tanya's immaculate flowing script could be read from much further away – '*Vente de vin rosé*'. We'd borrowed a foldaway table from Claire and Neil's house and spread a pink tablecloth over it. Our wines were neatly arranged on top of the table in a triangular shape, and we'd stacked the boxes of wine to the side of the car to show that we were a serious, well-stocked operation.

We sat and waited as the traffic streamed past, the sun crossed the sky, and I reflected what our contemporaries back in London would think if they saw us idling days away spitting cherry stones into the dusty ground. I had to admit that so far our friends who had counselled against us quitting our jobs had been right.

There should have been no competition between us and the toothless old man snoring away in the sun next to us, but after three hours the combined sales figures in our lay-by read fifteen cartons of cherries and not a single bottle of rosé.

Still, there was always Nikki Beach. 'Eric will call soon,' reassured Tanya, as we drove back to Montpellier to face another sleepless night.

The next day, despite Peter's protestations, we promised to baby-sit Claire's children from mid-afternoon onwards, while she went for a doctor's appointment. In the meantime we headed out in search of a bar. This time our target was Nîmes, about forty minutes north of Montpellier. Our first impression as we drove into the city was one of quiet prosperity. Whereas Montpellier at times can seem to be overrun by travellers and buskers, Nîmes was smart and businesslike. Tanya said that it felt like a southern Paris. The shops were full of unnecessary luxuries – over-designed, brightly coloured wooden brooms intended as much as decoration as for practical use, chairs fashioned into curious shapes from wire meshing and of course rail after rail of designer clothes. On every corner there was an olive tree in its own heavy bucket, and teams of workmen in orange overalls continuously hosed the streets. Mingling with the locals, there were coach parties of tourists drawn to the crumbling amphitheatre – *Les Arènes* – where the Romans once slaughtered Christians and where, in between Elton John and Pavarotti concerts, Christians now slaughtered bulls.

But despite the apparent contrast with Montpellier, we discovered that the bar owners of Nîmes knew the word '*allez*' just as well. We tried the Petite Bourse, a bar sheltering in the arches of the Roman Arena, with a view so spectacular that it had made the front cover of our guidebook. We asked in unlikely places hidden in backstreets that in the evening looked like they would have bouncers in black bomber jackets guarding the entrance. We even mistakenly wandered into a couple of teashops. It was all to no avail. We were like a football team on a losing streak unable to shake a pervading sense of failure and underperformance. Privately I began to worry that we would never find anywhere to take us, but the thought of returning to England and admitting failure kept me from voicing these fears.

At least we had one lead. As they '*allez*-ed' us, a couple of barmen had advised, 'Find the *Irlandais*, he might have you.' When we'd left England, the concept of selling rosé in an Irish bar couldn't have been further from our minds. And even now, in our desperate state, the idea was far from appealing. I visualised farm instruments stuck to the wall, dim replica gas lights, plastic leprechauns propping open the loo doors, pints of Guinness served on trays shaped like four-leaf clovers and, hell of all hells, a *Riverdance* tape playing in the background. But where else did we have to go?

When we eventually found Murphy's Bar, it didn't look too promising. Halfway down a narrow cobbled street, there was a small black Guinness sign projecting from the wall. Underneath it was a collection of rickety yellow tables and chairs that looked as if they'd been designed to be uncomfortable. At the far end of the street was an estate agent and at the opposite end a restaurant, but other than that there were only garages and entrances to flats. We could just about glimpse the sky through the lines of washing strung above our heads.

We pushed open the glass door to the bar and entered. John Murphy had long, dark hair tied back in a ponytail, stubble that was threatening to become a beard, and a Marlboro Red smouldering between his fingers. There were big bags under his eyes, and his cheeks appeared bloated. Although he was a couple of inches smaller than me, he had the feel of a bigger man. His movements were slow and heavy, but at least his deep, gentle Irish accent was welcoming, even if his words were not. 'We're closed,' he said, taking a drag on his cigarette.

'It's about a business proposition,' I replied, relieved to be able to speak in my own language.

'Take a seat,' said John, indicating a bar stool with his hand.

'Would you like a drink?' Without waiting for an answer, he poured us all a glass of wine.

The inside of his bar was like a comfortable lounge, with low lighting, scuffed leather armchairs, elbow-height tables and ledges on which to deposit drinks. There was a Guinness tap, but thankfully there was also a tall blackboard with a list of wines from across France.

'The problem with the French,' John explained, 'is that they make the best wine in the world but they never get to drink it because all anyone will sell is the local rubbish. That's why I set up my own wine bar.'

As we showed John the list of wines we hoped to sell, he became more and more animated. He picked up his phone and began to dial some numbers, smiling as he got positive response after positive response. 'That was the local brewery representative and before that a couple of wine journalists. Guess what?'

'What?' we said in unison.

'You're going to run a rosé bar.'

But for the fact that John had stubble that could grate cheese and lived in a carcinogenic bubble, I would have kissed him. Instead I shook his hand. At last we were up and running.

'You'll have to give me a couple of weeks to get the press coverage. How about starting at the beginning of June?' asked John, extinguishing his cigarette.

After successfully agreeing the new location of La Vie en Rosé, we should have headed straight back to Montpellier. It was early afternoon and nearly time for our babysitting shift. But in the two weeks before the beginning of June we wanted to find a temporary home for our bar and John had suggested the medieval town of Uzès, just twenty minutes up the road. He'd also given us an exciting insight into how to improve our pitch.

On the phone to the brewery representative, John had described our idea as a rosé festival and from now on, rather than call ourselves a bar, we'd use the same terminology. France was a country in love with festivals – each town received money from central government to hold an annual fête, and it was impossible to drive around the countryside without encountering a festival of some description. On our travels last summer we'd seen *fêtes de miel, de chien, de melon, de citron*, so why not a *fête de vin rosé*? It sounded like a concept the French would understand, and as far as we could calculate, a detour to Uzès would still leave us plenty of time to get back for our babysitting duties.

It took us all of five minutes to fall in love with the town. On the long, broad avenue that circled Uzès, plane trees steepled skyward. Their green leaves, lit golden by the sun, cast a gentle shadow on everything below. All along the pavement, cafés spilled out on to the streets with their chairs arranged like cinema seats. Any of them would have been perfect to sell our wine, but Uzès held a surprise. At its heart, amid the tight medieval streets, was a green oasis. In a square big enough to simultaneously host a pétanque tournament, a painting exhibition and a market, a copse of plane trees rose into the blue sky. The square was encircled by cloisters sheltering small shops and cafés, and in the centre, in the shade of the trees, a small fountain trickled. People passed through staggering under the weight of their shopping or casually chatting under the arches and yet the square remained at all times sleepily peaceful.

This urban oasis was called Place aux Herbes, and the very sight of it prompted a spontaneous 'Marvellous, absolutely marvellous' from Peter. In the far corner of the square, wedged between the arches, was Café de la Renaissance. Two columns of tables and chairs, divided by a central walkway, projected out towards the central fountain. On one side people finished late lunches, on the other customers sipped drinks as cool droplets of water were sprayed over them by a line of fans.

Inside La Renaissance, the owner, Annie Cellot, sat adding up the takings from lunch. Her clothes were covered by a cook's overall, and she had dyed red hair that appeared to be laced with more colorant than a curry. As we pushed open the door, she regarded us with a world-weary look. I estimated that she was in her late forties, with a wiry frame and a face wrinkled with worry. Her fingers flicked rapidly through a bundle of notes, and she shifted a piece of gum from side to side in her mouth. She listened attentively to our plans for a rosé festival, stacked the cash in neat piles and then regarded us like a mother considering taking in a couple of stray children. Spitting her gum into the ashtray, Annie held out her hand. 'Sure, why not.'

Since Aix we'd approached over thirty bars, and now we'd managed to secure two locations in succession. Our summer had turned round in a day.

Annie was happy for us to start as soon as possible, and as we began to run through the logistics of picking up our stock of wine from Montpellier, Tanya glanced at her watch. It was nearly 3.30 p.m. 'Oh my God, Claire!'

On our return Claire didn't have time to be cross. 'Tristan's medicine is on the table. Anything you don't understand – ask Rosie,' she said as she rushed out, quickly followed by Peter, who was still in full disease-avoidance mode.

As the door closed, Rosie turned round to face us both. 'It's time for Tistin's milk,' she said, taking me by the hand and leading me towards the kitchen. Tristan didn't look to me like he needed any milk, in fact he needed catching, and Tanya just managed to scoop him up before he could damage the television. But who were we to deny Rosie when she had decided it was Tristan's milk time? We put the formula in the microwave and gave it a quick whiz round, before handing it to Rosie to check.

She looked puzzled for a second and then shook her head. 'It's too cold for Tistin,' she said, handing it back.

Dutifully I heated it up some more, before passing it once again to Rosie. 'Too 'ot,' was her verdict this time. Rosie had clearly been watching her *Oliver Twist* DVD, either that or she was socialising with a gang of cockney toddlers at the Montpellier crèche. In any event, with her curly hair and whimsical nature she reminded me of a Shakespearean fairy. The only problem was, Tanya and I were the players she was directing around.

Before I had time to prepare some more milk, we heard Tristan crying from the other room. According to Tanya, he'd managed to wriggle from her grasp and head-butt a table leg, but taking one look at her brother, Rosie decided it was time for 'Tistin's medicine'. She walked over to the table and handed us a tube of cream and a silver-foil sachet that appeared to contain a large pill. With Rosie's help we carefully rubbed the cream into all of Tristan's chickenpox, numbering the spots as we went along. 'Last time Mummy counted a thousand,' said Rosie helpfully.

Next it was time for the tablet. I opened the foil container and went to get the milk to dissolve it in. 'No,' said Rosie stubbornly, 'not right.' I looked at the tablet and I looked at Tristan. How else were we going to get it into him? And then it dawned on me – it was a suppository.

After a brief discussion I agreed to hold down Tristan while Tanya administered the medicine. Even though Tristan was weakened by the chickenpox, he was a brutally strong one-year-old. He wiggled this way and that and I struggled to keep him still for Tanya. Just as we had him pinned down the phone rang. Rosie collected it from the table and handed it to me.

'Go on,' said Tanya. 'It could be Claire.'

So with one hand across Tristan's backside, I answered it, and was put through to Eric Omores from Nikki Beach.

'I hear you want to talk about the global pale-rosé phenomenon,' said Eric in a wonderful American/Euro-trash accent. In the background I could hear some effortlessly cool music and I visualised Eric sitting on a white sofa in a trendy Miami office. Outside his window, girls in bikinis would be rollerblading and the sun would be blazing down on the sea. I didn't have the heart to tell him that now wasn't a good time – he probably had Madonna on hold, so why should he wait for me to administer a suppository?

Thankfully Tanya granted Tristan a reprieve and allowed me to talk to Eric. It became clear that Nikki Beach were as excited about rosé as we were. Eric and I swapped stories about the growing popularity of pink wine, and how it perfectly fitted the mood in the south of France. And although he didn't say we could open La Vie en Rosé at Nikki, he invited us there later in the summer to see if our ideas fitted with the rhythm of a Nikki day.

When I put the phone down, I was momentarily delighted, even if we only opened for a day at Nikki, it would be worth a special trip from Murphy's Bar in Nîmes. But then I remembered Tristan. He'd scrambled away and was trying to shut his head in a cupboard door. Tanya yanked on one of his legs, and I prised his fingers loose. 'I guess we have to try again,' I said.

'We could always wait for Peter,' replied Tanya, heaving Tristan on to the table.

6

La Vie en Rosé

Two days later Tanya, Peter and I sat waiting as patiently as we could on the terrace of La Renaissance in Uzès. The front quarter of the outside area had been set aside for us. It was framed by one of the medieval arches that looped in a cloister round the square, and our tables nestled underneath a cream awning. Two fans blew cold droplets of water into the air around us, and a steady number of people ambled past, entranced like us by the contrast between the leafy copse of plane trees in the centre of the square and the bright sunshine that lit the encircling ancient stone buildings.

Inside the café, our wine was stacked in two large fridges at the rear of the bar. We'd carried it through the streets the previous evening and it was now chilled and ready to serve. But first we had to price it and to do so we needed to speak to the owner, Annie Cellot. It was a still and gloriously hot day and we wanted to start as soon as possible. Instead we endured a nervous few minutes as we awaited Annie.

Eventually she took a seat in the shade opposite us. She was dressed in functional tracksuit bottoms and a loose sleeveless top as red as her hair. Her gold hoop earrings jangled as she nodded a friendly greeting. Two chains hung from her neck – one held a crucifix, the other her glasses, which she lifted to her eyes as she inspected our suggested price list.

'The mark-up is three and a half times the purchase price. If you bought a bottle for six euros, then you should be charging four euros per glass and twenty-one for the bottle.' Annie spoke rapidly and kept glancing towards the kitchen. It was ten thirty in the morning and clearly time to be preparing lunch rather than helping us with multiplication. 'Come on, I need to introduce you to everyone,' she said, as she wrapped a kitchen apron round her waist and led us inside.

The interior was dominated by a deep-purple bench that ran the length of one wall, lending the room the feel of a boudoir. Above it, there was a long mirror with a reflection of the bar – the glasses hanging from a metal rack by their thin stems, the multicoloured contents of the spirit bottles luminous under the spotlights, and a row of black stools with purple upholstery, pulled tightly against the counter. On one of these stools sat Julien. 'This is my elder son. If you need anything, you're to ask him.' Julien was wearing a tight T-shirt and faded jeans. His hair was cropped short, and he raised his hand and gave a little wave as Annie whirled by.

'And this is my husband, Michel, and my other son, Alexandre,' she continued, 'and behind the bar that's Laurent, who's married to my daughter, Natalie. She's the real chef, I'm just the helper.'

I hoped that Tanya and Peter were remembering all the names and the relationships, because I was already floundering.

'So you're all set,' said Annie, giving me an encouraging pat on the back before heading for the kitchen.

None of us knew where to start. Thankfully Annie's husband, Michel, took over. He was a slight man with a full head of grey hair and an angular face. His shirt was open at the neck, revealing his wedding ring dangling from a chain. He called Alexandre over – who was darker and shorter than his brother, Julien – and asked him to help with moving the tables on the terrace. He then led me to the back of the bar and opened a door. 'The ice machine is in the basement,' he said, flicking on the light and pointing down a set of stairs.

I descended on my own while Tanya and Peter went to start setting up. In front of me there were crates of soft drinks stacked on top of each other, boxes full of empty wine bottles, mops, buckets, a discarded old bicycle and a clunking fan that stirred the warm air. My immediate problem was that I had no idea what an ice machine looked like, but I didn't want to ask for help performing such an inconsequential task. There was lots of heavy electrical equipment with flashing lights, but nothing looked like it would make ice. I was so keen to get outside into the sunshine that I rashly started pressing buttons. But rather than making ice, I plunged the cellar into darkness.

On the terrace, Tanya and Peter were having similar teething problems. We'd brought an easel with us to support our blackboard, but the legs refused to remain at a constant height. Each time Peter adjusted one of them, the other leg collapsed and the blackboard went clattering to the floor. And Tanya had already managed to offend one regular by carrying the wine glasses in the wrong way. To avoid multiple trips to the bar, she'd put her fingers inside the glasses and clasped them together, enabling her to carry three in each hand. But the regular had whispered a complaint. Connoisseurs believe that a wine glass can pick up the odour of the cupboard where it is stored and that this can affect the flavour of the wine, and in this context Tanya putting her fingers in the glass was unacceptable.

Meanwhile, in the cellar, I'd managed to turn the lights back on, find the ice machine and successfully fill up one of our buckets. I emerged into the sunshine to my first ever view of La Vie en Rosé. One corner of the terrace was now pink. Our checked

cloths had been spread out, and the blackboard was finally sta-
bilised. Ribbons were draped from its corners – no prizes for
guessing the colour – and our prices had been chalked up. Tanya
and Peter stood behind a central table on which they'd proudly
displayed a bottle of each of our wines. Peter wore chinos and
one of his new polo shirts, and Tanya a white dress with tiny silk
roses sewn all over it. They were crying out like veteran market
traders to anyone who passed, alternating between French and
English, 'Would you like to taste some rosé?'

I couldn't help but smile. Somehow we'd landed on our feet
and found what was surely one of the best locations in France.
It was a Monday and back in England I would have crammed
myself on to the Tube before spending the rest of the day in a
dry, air-conditioned vacuum of an office gazing through the
window towards the glass of another building. Instead the sun
was going to warm my skin and I was going to stand with my
wife and Peter and try to sell rosé.

It didn't take me long to spot our first potential customer.
Sitting at a table in the main part – and by this I mean the
non-pink part – of the Renaissance was a middle-aged woman
drinking tea with milk. As she released her permed hair from her
sunhat, it sprang back into shape like a sponge. In front of her
was a copy of a guidebook to French bed and breakfasts, which
she picked up and glanced through. Freckles were multiplying
by the second on her forearms, and on her wrist was a dainty
bejewelled watch. I crossed to her and enquired if she'd like to
taste some rosé. There was no need to ask where she was from.

'It's only twelve o'clock, so I'd best not,' she answered.
'You're English?'

I nodded, and since our bar was empty and all too apparently
overstaffed by Peter and Tanya, I started to explain about our
travelling rosé festival.

She looked nonplussed. 'So you're a student?'

[66]

'No, we hope to make a living from it.'

A sceptical eyebrow was raised and the subject quickly changed. 'My husband and I love France. We've got a villa just up the road. We bought it a couple of years ago and it's already doubled in value.'

In the next couple of minutes I learnt how Ryanair flights to nearby Nîmes had created a mini property boom and a thriving expat community.

'We're having people over this evening so I'll buy some wine. Can you recommend anything?' she asked.

And that was it. The first sale of La Vie en Rosé was made to a middle-class lady from Finchley with a second home in the hills outside Uzès. We hadn't even considered offering a different takeaway price and so, as Annie had instructed, I dutifully multiplied the original cost by three and a half and handed over two bottles of our Bordeaux clairet – Château Parenchère.

'Everything in France is such good value,' gushed my customer, as her husband appeared on the far side of the square. 'Good luck with your festivals.'

Back in the pink heart of our bar, Tanya and Peter were attempting to sell some wine to a Frenchman. He was short and round, and wore a rugby shirt, which was stretched tightly across his belly. A thick moustache framed his lips and dark stubble covered the rest of his face. I could see from the row of discarded tasting glasses that he'd insisted on a new glass for each different wine and that he'd already tried the majority of our rosés. Peter poured a little of the next wine for him, and with a swirl of the base of the glass, our rugby-loving Frenchman awoke the flavours as professionally as any vigneron. He tipped the glass to the side and watched fingers of the liquid coat its interior before holding it up to the sun and examining the colour. Finally he took a sip, his lips and eyes prescribed an exaggerated circle as he swished the wine round his mouth from his gums to the roof of his mouth and then finally swallowed.

'*C'est assez fruité, mais pour moi un peu sucré. Qu'est-ce que le cépage?*'

Tanya and Peter looked at each other. They'd been asked what grape variety the wine was made from and each of them was clearly praying that the other could remember.

'It's Grenache,' said Tanya in French, taking a chance and holding her nerve as the Frenchman took another sip.

'*Oui, c'est vrai.*'

The final wine we had available for tasting was Bauduin Parmentier's Château la Dorgonne. It lay on top of the ice bucket with tributaries of cold water feeding down the neck of the bottle. The grapes were harvested unusually late because of the high altitude of the vineyard, and the prolonged growing season allowed the rosé to demonstrate excellent *tipicité* and an unusual depth of flavour for such a beautiful translucent pink wine.

As the sun reflected through the liquid, it cast a colourful shadow over the ice behind it. The Frenchman signalled he'd like to try some and so once more Peter poured and the tasting shenanigans of swilling, sucking and swallowing ensued. Five seconds later we received the verdict.

'*C'est comme une soupe,*' he declared, and with a snort of disgust headed off into the interior of the bar. For some reason although the outside of the bottle was well chilled and resting on a pile of ice, the contents were lukewarm.

Peter took a taste from the remnants of the glass and laughed. 'He's right, and it's more cream of tomato than gazpacho.'

During the next hour we sold a couple of glasses and a further takeaway bottle. But then people began to sit down to lunch and the resplendent pink tables of La Vie en Rosé emptied. Next to us, the rest of the Renaissance was nearly full. Salads of feta and sweet pepper, aubergine caviar and basil, Roquefort and apple, and goat's cheese and tapenade flowed from the kitchen, quickly followed by bottles of the house rosé. We munched on takeaway sandwiches from the *pâtisserie* across the square and watched as Julien and Alexandre delivered plates of the steaming dish of the day – *cuisse de canard en confit.*

With no potential customers, Peter excused himself and took a walk around the town. Tanya tidied our bar – smoothing the tablecloths, refilling and moving our ice buckets so that the wine continued to gleam appealingly in the sun and replacing the corks tightly in the bottles. When everything was pristine, she started writing a postcard.

There was little for me to do except sit back and enjoy the view of the Place aux Herbes. The Renaissance was one of six or seven different restaurants sheltering in the shady square. Each was full of customers finishing their lunches and enjoying the early-summer sunshine. Underneath the trees near the central fountain, there was a sculpture exhibition. Pieces of wood had been polished and sinuously shaped. The works were set on podiums, and from my vantage point it looked as if each had been deliberately displayed so that the wood arched and curved in sympathy with the colonnade in the background.

The square's appeal was its sheer size and irregularity. Over the years some of the surrounding houses had collapsed and narrow streets had been allowed to form that led away from the *place* like crooked fingers. Of the buildings that still stood, some had been fully renovated, their heavy grey stones cleaned and re-pointed and the lintels above the windows reinforced, but others were in a state of disrepair, with flaking shutters and crumbling cornerstones. Everywhere the new mixed with the old, and above the height of the uppermost branches of the plane trees, there were several circular turrets that appeared to be medieval in origin. Each was mounted with a weathervane or pennant, hanging still in the warm, windless air.

People began to drift away from the restaurants, crossing the square in ones and twos like extras from a film set, neither hurrying nor dallying. Next to me, Tanya had finished her postcard and in the continued absence of customers began to recite facts from a guidebook. 'Apparently the square was first used in the fourteenth century as a place to expose bandits, prostitutes and debtors to public ridicule. Most of what you see now is eighteenth century—'

The abrupt return of Peter interrupted the architecture lecture. 'Try some of this,' he said, thrusting the remains of what must have once been an enormous tart into my hands. 'It's fried onions, anchovies and black-olive paste. They call it a *pissaladière*, and it's totally delicious.'

Since our first lunch in France, where Peter had almost force-fed me drippingly ripe Brie, he'd insisted that I taste at least a delicacy a day. Clearly he was worried that I might fade away, but already there were signs of my healthy French stomach returning.

The rest of the afternoon passed gently. Plenty of people stopped and stared at the bright-pink bar that had suddenly materialised in the centre of town. My favourite customers were three Japanese girls. Cameras swung loosely round their necks as they stood and pointed at us from the other side of the square. They all wore striped knee-length socks, miniskirts and shirts with their ends knotted in a bow just above their midriffs. Their hair was tied in ponytails by multicoloured ribbons, and as they edged closer I saw that they'd applied outlandish amounts of blue eye shadow to their eyelids. The giggling started when they were about 5 metres away. It was clear that they wanted to come and taste some wine, but no one was prepared to make the first move, so they shuffled towards us, nudging each other closer with their shoulders, while chattering away excitedly.

Peter offered them a small glass each but only one of them accepted, glancing nervously at her friends as she took a sip. Almost before the wine touched her lips, the girls all began to laugh. It was as if they'd dared to cross some forbidden cultural

Rubicon. They were clearly old enough to drink, so quite what it was was beyond me.

'Do you like it?' asked Peter.

The girl who'd tasted looked at her companions. Her lips pursed, her eyes flashed with mirth, and she descended once more into giggles. 'No,' she said, 'not at all.'

The three of them edged tentatively away as if prompted to retreat by some collective brain. When they judged they were at a safe distance, they took several photos of us, chattering excitedly as they did so.

At around six o'clock we sold our first glass of wine to a French customer, a middle-aged woman who worked in the postcard shop next to the Renaissance. She'd been watching our progress all day, and after closing up she came and asked for a glass of pink Sancerre. There was none of the posturing and asking about grape varieties that we'd endured from several locals earlier in the day. She simply took her glass and sat quietly watching as the shadows lengthened.

At dusk, strings of silver lights that were looped amid the branches of the trees blinked into life and the Place aux Herbes was transformed into a twinkling parade square for families and friends. They walked and talked in groups until they felt their appetites stir and the Renaissance began to fill up once more. Julien and Alexandre were soon ferrying bowls of *soupe de poisson* and plates of carpaccio (thankfully beef this time and not the raw duck liver or calf's head Peter was so fond of) between the tables, occasionally glancing over to see how we were getting on.

The answer was, quite well. We'd managed to attract the attention of an accordion player, who was serenading our customers with a version of the Edith Piaf classic 'La Vie en Rose'. The busker had dark, almost black skin and deep-brown eyes set under bushy eyebrows. His fingers appeared far too large for the keys but his rendition was effortless. The romantic spirit of the song and its lilting cadences perfectly recreated the slow life of the south. Thankfully it also seemed to encapsulate our bar, and enjoying the all-too-obvious play on words, our customers applauded loudly and tipped heavily.

Later in the evening the uplifting notes of the same song drifted past the silver lights of the plane trees, lulling our final customers into one further glass before sleep. As a small thank-you, Tanya crossed the square and handed the busker a glass of chilled rosé. The music faded and we collapsed the easel and stowed the blackboard and wine away, contentedly humming the tune that unsurprisingly was to become the theme song of our summer.

We were determined to live only on what we'd sold, but after a day of hard work and what had seemed like plenty of custom, we only had a handful of crumpled notes in our pockets, half of which belonged to Annie. Peter refused to take a euro, insisting he was along purely for the fun of it, and once we'd deducted the cost of the cheap apartment we'd rented, Tanya and I barely had enough to pay for food. At least it was a start.

Our flat was in the eaves of an old house on the outskirts of Uzès. It had two small bedrooms and one large living room. Inside the latter, the landlord had managed to cram a sofa, a kitchen hidden behind a curtain, and a toilet and shower surrounded by a square of temporary boards. But most importantly there was a small outside area.

This roof terrace opened out on to a view of one of the major landmarks of the town – the Tour Fenestrelle, an eleventh-century bell tower built on to the side of the cathedral. Although the cathedral had been destroyed on several occasions, the Tour Fenestrelle retained its original structure, and apart from the fact it stood soldier straight, it resembled the Tower of Pisa, rising in successive arched levels towards the stars. At night we quickly forgot the rickety interior of the apartment as we bathed in the golden spotlights that lit these ancient buildings.

[72]

It was nearly midnight by the time we returned from the Renaissance and the three of us sat down on this terrace, watching as shutters were closed and blinds drawn across the surrounding town. On the table in front of us were two baguettes, already broken into crumbling chunks, and a couple of goat's cheeses, one wrapped in vine leaves, the other marinated in olive oil and herbs. The air was still warm and the cheese heavily scented with thyme, basil and rosemary. We lit a candle, opened a bottle of red wine and began to eat. Above our heads, pink tablecloths and polo shirts hung on an improvised washing line.

I was elated, exhausted and a little worried. Elated because after all the preparation and the false starts we'd finally managed to start selling rosé, and exhausted because I hadn't realised how demanding running a bar could be. We'd been on show all day, talking to people and trying to persuade them to buy our wine. I'd told and retold the story behind La Vie en Rosé and on numerous occasions described the grape varieties used to make the wines and given directions to the vineyards.

This was hard enough to do in English, but the majority of people who'd tasted − but not of course bought − had been French. Mentally it had been a real challenge to mould my limited vocabulary to the message I wanted to convey, and I'd spent much of the day clawing for words. Now, as I chewed on the bread and cheese, I realised that my jaw was aching from forming the unfamiliar shapes demanded by the language and that part of me was dreading the challenge of having to do it all again tomorrow.

And finally I was worried because my reaction to our takings from the first day of trading was so different to Tanya's. She saw the pile of euros on the table as evidence that a rosé bar was a viable concept, but if we did buy our own bar, we'd need to make enough money not just to support ourselves but also pay all the overheads, the mortgage or the rent and for the upkeep of the buildings and equipment. To me, the summer was a test-run to see whether we could succeed in the rosé business, but it was becoming apparent that Tanya was several steps ahead of me – in her mind she'd already kitted out the interior of our own bar and was now vacillating between pink or white umbrellas for the outside area. Was she prepared to let the reality of our meagre takings disrupt this dream?

'*Voulez-vous goûter un petit peu de vin?*' said Peter, proffering the bottle of red, pulling me from my thoughts and making me laugh with the familiarity of the phrase – 'Would you like to taste a little bit of wine?'

The words were so ingrained in my head I heard them in my sleep that night.

7

The Jewel

After just a few days in Uzès we felt at home at the Renaissance. To hasten our acceptance with the mole-like drinkers, who sheltered from sun-up to sundown in the shadowy interior, we'd conducted an all-too-extensive tasting. And from then on we were greeted with a friendly '*Bonjour*' each time we entered. But more important than this developing camaraderie was the kindness shown to us by Annie and her family.

On our second day Annie spotted us buying sandwiches and immediately called Julien over. At Annie's behest, he served us each the dish of the day, and from then on we freely roamed over the Renaissance menu. Little did Annie realise that this was an exceptionally dangerous thing to offer a man with Peter's appetite. Each morning he excitedly scanned the blackboard to see what the *plat du jour* was, before returning to the pink quarter of the bar to tell us his findings. We enjoyed *gambas à la persillade*, *filet de dorade à la Provençale* and an *omelette aux cèpes*, but I don't think I have ever seen Peter quite so delighted as the morning he realised that tripe was on the menu.

We learnt gradually about the history of Annie's family – the Cellots. Her grandmother was originally from Normandy, which explained the red hair and the creamy skin. Until recently Annie and Michel had owned a bar in Nîmes, and their daughter,

Natalie, together with her husband, Laurent, had run a nearby *tabac*. Then, two years ago, they'd pooled their resources and opened the Renaissance.

Julien, it became clear, was the comic of the family. Discovering that Tanya and I had squeamishly turned down the tripe, he began to tease us about the menu the following day, telling us that his mother had found an excellent deal on *pieds-paquets*. Just the mention of the name made Tanya and me queasy, as literally translated it meant 'feet parcels'. In French, the words sounded gentler, but this didn't change the fact we expected to be served sheep's trotters rolled up in the lining of a sheep's stomach. The following day Annie served *entrecôte au poivre* and Julien enjoyed his day off and his joke.

Alexandre, Julien's younger brother, was a little quieter but just as kind and helpful. He helped move the tables every morning, ferried clean glasses out to us and crucially taught me how to fill an ice bucket. However naïve this might sound, I'd assumed that the way to prepare an ice bucket was simply to pile it high with ice, and on the first day we'd laid the bottles on top of the ice, as you would a dozen oysters. But after Alexandre's intervention I filled the buckets with a mixture of ice and water, totally immersing the wine and ensuring that the south of France's first and last soup station was shut for the summer.

Our only difficulty was trying to win over Laurent. He stood behind the bar, cleaned glasses and smoked so many cigarettes during the course of each day that his lips had turned black. His conversations with us barely exceeded the monosyllabic, and his range of facial expressions was limited to frowns and grimaces. But ever so gradually he became accustomed to our presence and started splitting notes and filling our ice buckets without the deep sigh that had accompanied these activities earlier in the week.

As well as getting to know the Cellot family, we relaxed into life in Uzès. Every morning Peter and I rose early and visited the local grocery. Outside the shop, punnets of wild strawberries and raspberries and peaches soft to the touch were lined up in wooden boxes. The presentation was as pretty as any market stall, and we tasted everything on offer before making our selection and breakfasting high on our roof terrace, watching as the swallows darted between the arches of the Tour Fenestrelle.

It became customary for us to get lost on our way to work. Uzès is a small town, and the Place aux Herbes is a big, dominant square right in its centre, but somehow we always seemed to take a wrong turn on the way. The tiny cobbled streets twisted and turned in a disorientating fashion and it was easy to pick a narrow alley seemingly heading in the right direction only to emerge minutes later less than 50 metres from where we'd started.

Whichever way we set off, we eventually found our way to a grand old building known as the Duchy. It was constructed much like a fort, with a four-turreted tower at its heart, and an additional smaller tower, the roof of which had been tiled red and then encrusted with a mosaic crest of the duke. Cast-iron bells were mounted on many of the surrounding buildings, and with a lethargic swing against the blue sky, they rang out eleven thirty as we finally reached our bar. It never mattered that our morning walk to work took twice as long as it should and that as a consequence we were permanently late. Uzès was a city to be enjoyed, one that invited meandering and which, despite the plethora of bell towers, frowned on punctuality.

One of the delights of working together was that at any stage two of us could slip away to explore. At sunset Tanya and I took to walking around the outskirts of the town. The circular road was almost as impressive as the Place aux Herbes. Two rows of giant plane trees curved with the street, so only a small crescent of early-evening sky was visible between their leaves. Beneath the trees, cafés lined the pavements and people hurried amid the pharmacies and banks, shading their eyes as they entered one of the shafts of dying golden light that penetrated the canopy above.

The circular road led us back towards our flat and the nearby cathedral, behind which was a series of benches that looked out over the surrounding countryside. Most evenings, as the sun fell from the sky, Tanya and I made our way to these benches. And before getting lost on the way back to the bar, we sat with a row of cane-wielding locals, watching as the shadows enveloped the plum and olive orchards below and waiting for the warm, vibrant smells of the south to fade from the day.

At work we each naturally assumed different roles. Peter was the marketing director and publicity guru. He visited a local design shop and had posters and flyers designed bearing an image of ripe grapes, a red rose, barrels of wine, a bottle of rosé, the Luberon hills and a burning sun suspended in a blue sky. Across the whole poster was a splash of pink, as if a glass of rosé had been thrown over it at the last minute. Peter proudly described it as 'Monty Python meets Impressionism'.

For a couple of hours each day he picked a different street corner and handed the flyers to whoever was passing. We couldn't fault his intentions, but all too often he reappeared from his forays still clutching a fistful of flyers. The problem appeared to be an almost forensic level of interest in the lives of passers-by. On one occasion a former melon farmer waylaid him and taught him how to choose the perfect melon by touch and smell. The directions were so precise that Peter can now tell how many hours any given melon is from optimum ripeness. On another he met a chef who'd just started a restaurant in the area. Apparently the chef had trained under Raymond Blanc, worked in a number of Terence Conran's establishments in London, and his best dish was seared scallops with black pudding. Manoeuvring a conversation from flyers to signature dishes is something only Peter could manage.

Back at the bar, Tanya was proving to be a natural, covering for my woefully inadequate French and frequently charming customers into ordering another drink. With tourists her trick was to act as a kind of surrogate travel agent, and after last summer she had plenty of advice to pass on. Her repertoire included the best beach in France for babies – the endless stretch of golden sand and gently lapping water just outside Calvi in Corsica; the best sundowner on the Côte d'Azur – the terrace of the Chèvre d'Or in Eze, where you are so high the yachts on the Mediterranean appear like white pinpricks on a blue canvas; and the best place to celebrity-spot – Le Café in Saint-Tropez. Hidden at the back of Place des Lices, it was one of the few restaurants likely to lure the stars away from their Ramatuelle hang-outs.

She spoke with authority on places she hadn't visited, such as the best place to see the lavender before it was cut in mid-July – Valensole. I even overheard her explaining to one customer that many of the lavender fields had been replanted with a hybrid called lavandin, which was easier to grow but resulted in a less refined end product. Rather than using the plant to make essential oils, lavandin was used in the large-scale manufacturing of soaps and detergents. The problem was that as the demands of industrial consumers fluctuated, so did the fortunes of the lavandin growers. One year it was boom, the next bust. Tanya was so animated as she discussed the blazing purple fields and the sweeping view up to Mont Ventoux that nobody could have guessed all the information was gleaned from that morning's newspaper.

And me? I had the difficult job of ensuring everyone paid. In England there is an easy and logical way of doing this – you take the money as you serve the drinks, but on the Continent things are far more relaxed, at least for the customers. On our second day we'd lost the profit from a bottle of wine to an absent-minded man who'd departed without settling the bill. And so although

I tried to be a smiling, charming host, I couldn't help but nervously look over shoulders to see who was ready to leave. I also developed the skill of carrying on conversations while constantly adding up bills in my head. Translating numbers into French might seem easy, but a number like '*vingt euros quatre-vingt-dix-huit*' was quite something to get my head and tongue around.

Thankfully our takings were rising on a daily basis. Julien and Alexandre began to promote our wines in the restaurant at the Renaissance, and this doubled sales. We were also lucky enough to make some lucrative on-off deals, the best of which was to a couple from New Zealand who were touring Europe. They wanted a bottle of champagne to drink with each of the three upcoming All Black rugby Test matches and a further three to take home. But despite our success we were still struggling with our biggest set of potential customers – the French.

To our surprise, plenty of the locals claimed to be non-drinkers. It wasn't clear whether this was the new government health campaign kicking in or not, but a significant percentage of the population seemed to think a single glass of wine might damage their liver. So they walked past and said, '*Je bois pas*,' before rubbing their stomachs as if they were in great pain. Then there were the individuals who admitted to drinking but steadfastly stated, '*Je bois pas le rosé.*' When pressed they explained that rosé would give them both a headache and stomach-ache and that they hadn't touched it for years.

More interesting were the French who tasted but didn't buy. It didn't seem to matter whether it was a businessman or the person who emptied the bins, everyone was keen to prove they knew more about wine than we did. Without fail they smelt the wine, inspected its colour and finally all too formally tasted it. They then interrogated us about grape variety, vinification and storage. One potential customer enquired which model of pneumatic press was used and then waited for an answer as if he'd just asked what car I drove.

Young men accompanied by their girlfriends were among the trickiest customers. Displaying an extensive knowledge of wine appeared to be some sort of macho badge of honour, an accessory to be prized as much as the latest mobile phone. And with the chance to outwit an Englishman in the process, our little bar became the trendy place to be seen. Conversations turned into verbal jousting matches, with each piece of information quickly trumped by something more impressive.

I informed one customer how our Bordeaux clairet had first been shipped to England centuries ago, hence the English name 'claret' for wines from Bordeaux. But clearly this was the type of basic fact a Frenchman learnt at primary school, and I spent the next twenty minutes listening with interest as my customer-cum-tutor explained that the trade in wine between Bordeaux and London had in fact given rise to the world's first insurance market.

Apparently it was common for ships to lose a certain amount of wine overboard on the passage to England. Typically the crates lost were those loaded last on to the boat. To prevent disputes over which wine was stored where, vignerons agreed to give a certain percentage of the profits from the wine that was safely delivered to any vignerons who'd lost their wine, creating a simple form of insurance.

But despite their all-too-apparent expertise, and willingness to taste every wine we had on offer, very few Frenchmen actually ordered a drink from us. The biggest culprits turned out to be vignerons. These were the people who'd spent the whole of last summer teaching us only to buy wine from *récoltants* – vignerons who made and bottled their own wine. They'd explained that the *vrac* from the local cooperative had all sorts of chemicals added to prolong its life and that as a result it gave you awful hangovers. But the moment a vigneron arrived in our bar all this seemed to be forgotten. Rather than show any solidarity for his colleagues, he would taste all our wines, pull a faded cap over his sun-weathered face and then order a *pichet* of *vrac* from Annie.

Fortunately French women turned out to be rather more open-minded than their male counterparts. The woman from the newsagent next door became a regular customer, sampling a different rosé each day and even bringing friends along. We also managed to attract a couple of Uzès's *grandes dames*. Never seen without a full face of make-up, heavy pearls swinging from their necks and enough combined gold round their wrists to fill a treasure trove, the two old women developed a strange attraction to our bar. Thankfully it seemed that their day wasn't complete without a glass of pink champagne at sundown, and we were their location of choice.

After a week running La Vie en Rosé we allowed ourselves an afternoon off. Our plan was to visit a place Peter had discovered while handing out a flyer to a local artist. Its nickname was the Jewel. To the south of Uzès towards Nîmes, the road curled through a valley cut by the river Gard and it was common practice for people to park and climb down to the river and swim. It was easy to tell the popular spots because rows of cars were pulled tightly into the cliff side. But the artist had told Peter about an unknown path by which we could gain access to the river and swim in two sparkling plunge pools.

We headed out of town under yet another sumptuous blue sky, crossing a high bridge over the Gard and then following the road as it wrapped round the cliffs. The instructions from the artist – if Peter had understood them correctly – were a little peculiar. Apparently we should wait until the road turned back on itself like the meander of a river and then look for a flame-red rock by the roadside before taking the dirt track that led away from it. A further kilometre up this track, there was a tree that had been struck by lightning and from here we could descend to the Jewel.

Surprisingly the directions proved easy to follow and within half an hour we were stumbling down a small path towards the river. We kicked dust into the air and clung to trees and large boulders as the gradient became steeper. As we neared the river, we ducked into the welcome shade of trees and Peter took great delight in pointing out marks on the trunks that he claimed were caused by rutting wild boar. As the path levelled out, we caught glimpses of the Gard flowing past in the bright sunlight. Finally we emerged on the crest of a large rock. Above us we could see steepling cliffs, blue sky and hawks riding on thermals. There was no sign of the road or even the path we'd just climbed down. We were alone with the sound of running water. Peering tentatively over the edge of the rock, I looked for the river.

Set amid the rocks were two deep pools. They'd been carved by the Gard in angrier times when it had gushed down the valley, but they now lay isolated in a meander fed only by a stray tributary. It was obvious how they had earned the name the Jewel. The surface of the water mirrored the azure blue of the sky, and the gentle ripples caught every glint of the sun. Through the clear water I could pick out the mottled colouring of the rounded rocks on the bed. A path fed down to the lower of the two pools, but there was no obvious way into the deeper, higher one.

'I guess we just have to jump,' said Peter, stripping off. 'Do you think it will be cold?' We found out seconds later as he plummeted in and then rose back to the surface, shaking water from his mane of hair. 'Come on in, it's marvellous, absolutely marvellous.' For once I didn't believe him.

Tanya and I were eventually coaxed into the icy waters, and we spent the next few hours dipping in and out, enjoying the contrast between the baking sun and the chill of the river. At times we lay on the rocks without speaking, simply looking upwards, somehow mesmerised into matching the stillness of the valley, but then someone would break the silence and we'd leap into the water. We'd brought a simple picnic – a *poulet rôti*, a fresh baguette and a pot of mayonnaise, which we'd kept cold by wedging it underwater between stones next to a bottle of rosé. We made sandwiches in the late-afternoon sun and munched contentedly away, trying to forget that sometime soon we'd have to leave the Jewel and clamber back up the hill.

In five days we were due to leave the Renaissance and head to Murphy's Bar in Nîmes. Annie had been such a helpful host and we didn't want to put pressure on her to let us stay longer. We also didn't want to let John down at the last minute. But at the same time none of us could imagine a better home for La Vie en Rosé than the Place aux Herbes. As our takings had increased even I had begun to think our business could be viable in such a location, and there was always the chance we might be able to return on a more permanent basis in the future.

So on Tuesday evening I left Peter and Tanya and went in search of advice. On the opposite corner of the square was a small delicatessen and café. It was run by a Scandinavian called Tom, and like most Scandinavians he was irritatingly fluent in any number of different languages. Although I could have asked Annie about running a business in Uzès, I wanted to understand the basics in my own tongue.

Tom was a small, energetic man with short, curly, red-tinged hair. Within minutes I was feeling totally inferior. I learnt that he'd headed up Pizza Express's expansion into France and had over a decade of experience in the retail trade. The inside of his shop was immaculately laid out with neatly stacked displays of various olive oils, tapenades and vinegars. There was a shelf full of expensive wine and a small kitchen at the rear that served simple dishes to the customers crowded on to his small terrace. Tom offered me an espresso and began to talk about doing business in France. The first rule was not to even bother if you didn't speak French.

'You do speak fluently, don't you?'

'Nearly,' I bluffed, 'my wife's the real expert.'

Before we could continue Tom disappeared into his shop to serve a customer. A Frenchman wanted to buy a single bottle of red wine, but before he parted with his money he asked to be talked through the entire range of reds. I watched as Tom removed each of the bottles he had on offer from the shelf and explained their provenance. As far as I could understand, Tom was able to name the soil and grape type for each of his wines, describe the different regional characteristics and whether the producer he'd chosen matched or differed from those character-istics in any way. It was a humbling lesson in how to sell.

After the Frenchman had paid, Tom returned to talk to me. 'So, as I was saying, the only way to operate in France is to set up your own business. Never, ever think about buying an existing French business, because you'll have to pay a minimum of three times the turnover and you'll end up with employees. The last thing you want is employees.'

I was confused. It seemed to me that having a few employees wasn't such a bad idea.

'It's cheaper to adopt a new family than employ someone in France,' clarified Tom, in a flat, no-nonsense tone that made it impossible to tell whether he was joking. 'You pay nearly their salary again in social security contributions, and then there are the rules – each employee must have a locker a minimum of fifty centimetres by seventy centimetres, you must have separate male and female staff toilets and cold and hot water in the staff changing room. At the beginning of every week you must put a roster on the wall detailing the precise hours everyone is work-ing, and to make sure you are complying with these and any number of other regulations, you can expect frequent visits from the *inspecteur de travail.*'

Tom paused for a sip of coffee. 'Of course, if you are foolish enough to buy a business that already has employees, then you'll be sued for some long-forgotten minor infringement of all these regulations.'

This wasn't exactly the positive, heart-warming news I wanted to hear about doing business in France. We wanted to sell rosé, not get locked in jail for providing a locker that was a centimetre too small. But the bad news kept on coming, and as it did, my reservations grew.

The risk of losing a lot of money seemed high and yet I was also sure that Tanya would see the difficulties as little more than minor hurdles. Whereas I was becoming increasingly nervous about our plans, Tanya was ever more excited, and this realisation made me feel guilty about hiding my doubts from her. Still, I reasoned that they were my problems to deal with and that given time I would overcome my worries, and so I kept trying to suppress negative thoughts and remind myself how liberating it had been to give up my career and pursue a life in France.

'You'll need a *licence quatre* to sell alcohol, and these are available on the open market for about €25,000 to €50,000. The French government aren't issuing any more of them, which means the price is kept artificially high, and of course there are all sorts of associated rules – you can't have licensed premises near a school or a metro station or within fifty metres of another licensed premises.'

This didn't seem to make sense. Across the square from me, there were any number of licensed premises within 50 metres of each other.

'Ah, those cafés have old licences. The government changed the law after the Second World War and so it's now impossible to start a new bar within fifty metres of another bar,' clarified Tom. 'So if you want your bar in a popular area, it means you are going to have to buy an existing bar, which means buying a business, the exact thing I've advised you not to do.'

We finished our coffees and talked some more about terrifying things such as the type of business plan a French bank would need to see before lending money. And my introductory lesson to doing business in France ended with a final warning from my Scandinavian business guru: 'The saying is the same here as it is England, it's all about *emplacement, emplacement, emplacement,* and unfortunately for you there's nothing for sale in the Place aux Herbes.'

8

Uzès *en fête*

We knew the French were fond of their festivals, but Uzès appeared to have an obsession with them. Our final three days in the town were to be filled with three of the biggest fêtes of the year. On the morning of the first festival – the Fête de la Musique – we watched as the Place aux Herbes was gradually transformed. Stages were erected in various corners of the square, and for a couple of hours the usual steady flow of pedestrians was interrupted by vans delivering loudspeakers, scaffolding and microphones. Even more silver lights were draped between the trees until their branches sagged with the weight of the illuminations.

All across town the pattern was the same. Wherever there was open space and the possibility of gathering some people together, stages were erected. By late afternoon Uzès was humming to the sound of pianos being tuned, guitars being gently strummed, and just occasionally a blast of woodwind echoing down the narrow alleys like a ship leaving port. In every town across France the scene would be the same, anyone with a dusty instrument under the bed would pull it out, tune it up and once more live the dream of being a musician. For one night they were guaranteed a more than receptive audience.

By eight o'clock the Place aux Herbes resembled a Christmas

high street. Two steady streams of people passed elbow to elbow in opposite directions under the twinkling lights that were draped between the trees. Rather than the usual crowd of tourists, many appeared to be local labourers straight from the fields. Their clothes were often soiled, and heavy mud-clogged boots replaced the loafers and deck shoes that had crossed the square all week. The restaurant at the Renaissance gradually filled, and plenty of people stopped for a glass of rosé to enjoy the balmy evening. They were entertained by our friendly accordion player, who now based his entire repertoire on variations of 'La Vie en Rose'. After three almost identical renditions we tipped him with a glass of wine, and with a nod and a grin he headed off into the music-filled night.

Almost immediately he was replaced by another busker – an old man wearing a panama hat with a grey ponytail peeking out the back. In front of him he pushed a box-like contraption similar in size to a child's pram. It had a bell mounted on the handlebars and on one side a painting of a pastoral scene. Stacked underneath the box were what appeared to be a series of leather-bound books. Doffing his cap to all the drinkers in the bar, the busker selected a book, removed the binding and revealed a thick card punched with holes like a sheet of Braille. He placed it in a slot in the box and began to wind a handle. The resulting music was worse than a bad gramophone recording, but nobody seemed to mind. Generous as ever, Tanya offered our new-found friend some wine and we were treated – if that is the word – to another tune, the somewhat inappropriate 'Un Petit Verre de Vin Blanc'. At least we could watch a display of immense skill as the busker placed his rosé on top of the box and managed to play the vigorous tune without spilling a drop.

As people finished their meals the temporary stages that had been erected across town began to fill up. There were pop groups singing English songs in woeful accents and bands playing country and western desperately trying to capture the twang of the American Midwest. Next to us, a group as ancient as the Rolling Stones creaked on to the stage complete with electric guitars and a synthesiser. Thankfully they played in French and their dancing was limited to gentle foot-tapping. By the end of their set, which only lasted a few songs, the lead singer was gasping for breath and the guitarist was cracking his knuckles to prevent his fingers from stiffening.

Bringing down the average age of the performers considerably, a choir of schoolchildren filed neatly on to the stage. They were organised in strict height order like the ascending notes of a piece of music and sang unaccompanied in Latin. Somehow it was the right music for the setting and conversations stopped and people listened in awe as the unfamiliar language reverberated through the colonnade of arches.

Throughout most of the evening La Vie en Rosé had looked pleasingly full. But after an hour I began to realise that we had a problem. The customers were not moving on. The glasses on nearly all the tables were empty, and Peter had toured the bar asking people if they wanted a top-up. The universal answer was no, but there was no impetus for anyone to leave. Instead our customers relaxed in the warm evening air and watched as a succession of acts took to the stage. By midnight, with nobody to serve, the only people drinking in the bar were us.

Trade in the rest of the Renaissance was similarly slow. Annie sat at a table at the back of the terrace sharing an enormous ice cream with her daughter, Natalie. They dipped long spoons into a fast-melting cocktail of cream, chocolate and colourful ices. She gave me a rueful smile as I took a seat next to her. 'It's always the same with the Fête de la Musique. People come from the countryside and they buy one drink for the whole evening.'

As we began to pack away and the lorries returned to collect the musical paraphernalia, we heard the sound of a clarinet drift towards us from near the central fountain. An old man with receding wispy grey hair sat with his back against the stone and his eyes closed as he played. In the middle of this small market town, in a square filled with cafés and plane trees and redolent of all things French, the tune made us all stop. Peter put down the glasses he'd been collecting, Tanya rested the blackboard against a table, and I stood with an ice bucket clasped to my chest. None of us moved as the first bars took hold of the square, curling round the arches and floating up to the slowly fluttering pennants. Each note dallied in the late-evening air, and the plaintive call of the clarinet even captured the men taking down the stages, who momentarily ceased their work.

The musician turned out to be a retired bus driver from Birmingham, and the tune he'd chosen to close the Fête de la Musique with was 'I Vow to Thee My Country'.

As I listened to the last bars I thought of friends and family back in England and the familiar routine of life in London. Surprisingly and unnervingly, the comfort of a regular salary now seemed an attractive proposition. With one final, fading call the clarinet was quiet, and I resolved that for now these were feelings I had to try and suppress.

Rosé sales had been unexpectedly slow the previous evening, but when I awoke the next day I was full of excitement – the Fête d'Ail was upon us. I'd seen pictures of a town called Menton during its Fête de Citron and the town square had been deluged with lemons. They were piled on top of lorries, scattered over pavements and sculpted into yellow figurines. There was even a dolphin made from lemons. Taking this as my guide, I expected to encounter a mountain of garlic piled as high as the branches of the plane trees in Place aux Herbes.

On the way to work, my nose began twitching with anticipation. The smell of the overripe, flaking purple bulbs was overwhelming. It was as if several thousand new restaurants had opened overnight and simultaneously started cooking snails in garlic butter. But as we neared La Vie en Rosé, the odour faded. I assumed we were either becoming accustomed to the aroma or a stray gust of wind had driven the heavy reek in the other direction.

I was wrong. Instead of a square festooned with strings of garlic, we found an enormous market. La Vie en Rosé was totally obscured by a series of stalls that had set up directly in front of the Renaissance. All sorts of odds and ends were on sale – there was a table full of hundreds of different types of door handles, there were multicoloured hammocks strung between the arches and displays of luminous-yellow jackets and red warn-ing triangles for the road. I could have bought Tristan a super-soaker water pistol, and Rosie some beautiful pink flowers, but from our position behind the long white rear of a bread van, I couldn't see a single bulb of garlic. Once again a steady crowd of people had gathered in the square and they mingled between the stalls, but our custom was distinctly down for the simple reason that people couldn't see us, hidden as we were behind the bread van.

We sent Peter off into the square with his flyers to drum up trade, but two hours later our bar was still quiet and so I headed off after him. It didn't take me long to work out why we'd lost him for so long – all the way round the square a ring of local producers were offering free *dégustations*. There were small plastic spoons to dip into lavender honey, a chopping board and a serrated knife to serve yourself *saucisson de sanglier*, bread to dip into lusciously green virgin olive oil, and pieces of crumbling goat's cheese encrusted with peppers. I envisaged Peter trapped in his own version of Groundhog Day, continually circling the square oblivious to the fact he was in a self-repeating loop.

I eventually found him, still loaded down with flyers, by a large herb and spice stall. The stall was set out in a U shape in front of a particularly warped arch that was supported by an iron cross nailed to the wall. In a square full of attractions the spice seller was the most noticeable. Large wicker baskets had been lined with floral cloths, and within each basket was a neat cone-shaped pile of herbs and a silver serving trowel. There were rows and rows of various mixes – barbecue spices, fish spices, soup spices – but the real stars of the show were the individual spices: the saffron, the turmeric and the paprika, which resonated with a colour as intense as the ochre rocks of Roussillon. Despite the fact that we'd given up hope of working the oven in our tiny kitchenette and that Annie was feeding us, Peter was busy buying pretty pouches of various spices, attracted like a magpie to the vibrant colours.

Once I'd lured him back to La Vie en Rosé with the promise of an ice-cold glass of wine, Tanya and I headed off in search of the garlic. We left the Place aux Herbes and followed a narrow alley under the arches, moving alternately from bright sunshine to shade. We passed stalls laden with tablecloths and ducked under multicoloured curtains that projected in racks on to the street. On one table there were rings and necklaces with amber and aquamarine stones, which glinted in the light, on another pestles and mortars and pepper grinders made from polished olive wood. There seemed to be no logical order to the market, and a van offering *gésiers de volaille* and *foie de volaille* could easily be located next to a stand selling bath oils.

Finally, in a large *place* located just off the circular road, we found the garlic. Wisps of white skin drifted in the air, hanging in front of our eyes like a snow storm. Stretching for at least 100 metres away from us was table after table spread with garlic. It was trained to the legs of the table, hung from the wing mirrors of cars and gathered together in the type of bright-orange net I usually associated with fishermen. The bulbs made the garlic available in UK supermarkets appear positively anaemic – each clove was robust and round and splitting from its mottled white and purple skin.

The vendors all looked alike with faded colourless caps pulled low over their dark eyes. The skin on their faces was creased from the sun, and their noses pockmarked. Their quick, dextrous hands moved quickly, separating bulbs from the woven stems and smashing the cloves with the flat of a small knife. One of them took a piece of fresh bread, rubbed it with garlic and half an overripe tomato and handed it to me. It was delicious, strong and fresh, and prevented from being overpowering by the juice of the tomato. I bought a small bunch of bulbs and resolved to collect some bread and tomato on our way back. It was time that I made Peter a culinary treat.

But I should have known that this was the last thing that he needed. Left alone with hardly any customers, he'd started talking to the girl on the nearest market stall. Her name was Audrey and she sold what can only be described as an eclectic mixture of individually made handbags and African masks carved on the streets of Marseille. She was an attractive girl with dark hair, a wide, easy smile and an affable manner that had made her a favourite with all the other traders. At her suggestion, she had started ferrying small glasses of rosé around the market, returning to Peter with a delicacy from each of the stalls in exchange. And so, on our return, we found Peter sitting with two customers and enjoying a plate of spit-roasted chicken wings, slices of pizza and a handful of bright-pink crevettes. 'I've turned us into a tapas bar,' he grinned.

As the market packed up and the smell of garlic drifted away, our trade improved. The lights flicked on and we prepared to enjoy our last evening in the embrace of the ancient square. Our plan was to leave once the Fête Médiévale finished the following day, and as we worked for the next few hours we tried to take in our surroundings, tracing the arches, memorising the irregularity of the stones and recording the gentle play of the fountain. And above all marvelling at each other – dressed from head to toe in pink, standing proudly in front of our blackboard and serving our ice-cold wines. For two weeks La Vie en Rosé had been a successful reality – we'd sold enough wine to cover our living expenses, we'd attracted repeat customers including the French, and we'd proved that the concept of a rosé bar might work – but we'd also been very fortunate to find the perfect location in Place aux Herbes. How could Murphy's Bar and a side alley in Nîmes ever match up?

After two successive days of festivals, arriving in the Place aux Herbes each morning reminded me of a children's story – wondering which magical land the characters, or in this case us, were going to enter next. But nothing had prepared me for the madness that was the Fête Médiévale. The scale of this latest festival only became clear to us gradually. On the way to the Renaissance, we passed a man wearing rags with a blackened face, and as we entered the square we heard the sound of metal ringing on metal. We stepped round some fresh horse manure and nearly bumped into a maiden wearing a flowing blue dress.

In addition to the market stalls that had populated the Place aux Herbes the previous day, there were blacksmiths hammering shoes on to horses, and forges sending sparks flying into the air as swords were bent into shape. It was quite possible to purchase a luminous roadside warning triangle at one moment and then from the adjoining stall an implement of medieval torture. Above the heads of onlookers, noblemen sat astride horses, dressed in full regalia. They were seemingly experts in method acting because they'd perfected an air of arrogant disdain. In the corner of the square, Tanya noticed a sign that read, '*Location des costumes*'. Laid out underneath an arch on clothes rails were hundreds of outfits.

We'd thought we'd looked fun in pink all week, but nothing compared to the sight of Peter and me in breeches that billowed out around our thighs and shirts with ruffled necks that appeared to invite a casual passing noble to chop off our heads. Luckily we had swords to protect ourselves. Tanya looked far more demure, shaded by a veil and wearing a dress that transformed her from barwoman to princess. The staff of the Renaissance were similarly attired, the men in gilded tunics emblazoned with coats of arms, and the women in intricately woven skirts. We set up our part of the bar and waited for what we were sure would be a good final day's trading.

As we popped the first cork, a drumbeat began on the other side of the square. The rhythm was slow and the sound was heavy and foreboding and completely incongruous against the deep-blue sky. People were drawn from all corners to the noise and a press developed. '*Voulez-vous goûter un peu de vin rosé?*' shouted Peter, but nobody listened, because for now, at least, there was another show in town.

Slowly the heavy beat of the drum edged closer. Taking my acting cue from the noblemen on horses, I put my hand on the hilt of my sword and ushered Tanya behind me. Whatever was coming this way wasn't going to take my princess from me. The surrounding crowd peeled apart. People jeered and screamed, and children clutched their parents. The monster that was pro-voking such a reaction slowly came into view. It was at least the size of Peter and me put together, there was blood dripping from its fangs, and wedged in the back of its mouth was what appeared to be half a human leg, severed at the knee.

'I didn't know they made wolves this big,' said Peter, as he drew his sword and prepared to tackle our papier-mâché enemy.

'It's frighteningly realistic,' said Tanya, pointing out the toothmarks in the boot that hung limply from the end of the prosthetic leg. 'Apart from the wheels of course.'

Seeing that he'd met his match, the wolf moved slowly on, but what followed was even worse. 'They've unleashed the dogs of hell,' I cried in a pathetic attempt to mimic the hero of an action movie.

Misshapen, hobbling excuses for human beings stumbled by in

rags. Their faces, including some of their teeth, were blackened out and their hair smeared with dirt. Talons had been attached to the ends of their nails, and warts and boils sprouted from their faces.

'Glass of rosé?' asked Peter cheerily, but the only response he received was a malignant hand raking the air. 'Perhaps a bar of lavender soap – it will help get the dirt out.'

Thankfully the procession soon became cheerier. Acrobats rode bareback on white stallions, performing handstands on the rear quarters of their mounts and then forming a human triangle between horses. Following them was a fire-eater, tossing flaming batons into the air, before extinguishing them in his throat. Next came a tumbler vaulting skywards and somersaulting back down to the earth and finally a jester, who cheerily accepted a glass of wine. The drumbeat by now was only just audible in the distance, and the remaining crowd in Place aux Herbes joined the end of the procession and followed it out of the square.

It was lunchtime and the perfect time for a sun-soaked aperitif, but the drummer appeared to have led the people away as successfully as the Pied Piper. And so our final afternoon in Uzès was a relaxing one, chatting with our sparse custom, doing the accounts for the week and, in Tanya's case, buying a small present for Annie – some rose oil to remember us by. At five o'clock we served our last glass and then posed for a photo with the Cellot family. We still hadn't taken off our costumes and so our memento of the Renaissance is a shot of us all standing under the cream awning, swords at the ready, looking for all the world as if we are about to battle a marauding army rather than potter down the road to an Irish bar in Nîmes.

9

Unlikely Ailments

During our two sunlit weeks in Uzès a major concern had been my worsening relationship with John Murphy. He'd phoned on a number of occasions to speak about getting the press involved in our rosé bar in Nîmes. And in his deep Irish brogue he'd told me to expect calls from journalists at the *Midi Libre*, the *Gazette* and various English-language publications. As time passed and nobody made the short trip to Uzès to interview us, John became increasingly tense. He kept promising that the journalists would eventually call, and if and when they did, he made it clear he expected us to drop everything.

This created a problem. Between finishing in Uzès and starting in Nîmes we had two spare days, and we wanted to use this time to develop our ability to effectively sell wine to the French. After two weeks of intensively speaking the language, I still found it difficult to describe our wines properly. Peter was in the same situation, and even Tanya, who spoke very good French, struggled with some of the vocabulary of viticulture.

My temporary solution had been to let the French customers do the talking. Last summer we'd discovered what I believed to be the most useful word in the French language – *donc*. It was wonderfully colloquial and could be deployed at any point in a sentence and operated rather like an English 'um' or a 'well'.

But responding to a customer with a string of *doncs* became rather repetitive, and it hardly moved the conversation on. So thanks to a quick lesson from Tanya, I began to litter my speech with even more words that meant next to nothing but which hopefully made it sound like I could speak French.

When asked if I recommended a particular wine, I responded, '*Donc* ...' followed by a slight pause '... *en fait, franchement je crois que* ...' I would then punctuate the sentence with another dramatic silence, before continuing, '*sans doute, oui.*' Literally translated into English this meant 'Well, in fact, to be frank, I think without doubt, yes.'

If we were going to be successful, we had to do a lot better. Which is where our two days off came in. We'd decided to learn precisely how to describe each of our wines in French from the most qualified man in France. His name was Gilles Masson, and he was the director of the Centre de Recherche et d'Expérimentation sur le Vin Rosé in Vidauban, about 50 kilometres from Saint-Tropez. We'd met him during our quest for France's palest rosé, and it was time to look him up again. But John Murphy was far from pleased about us going to Vidauban and forfeiting the possibility of a press interview. After a short argument he concluded our conversation with a sigh, 'Well, if that's what you feel you have to do, Jamie.' Then the phone went ominously dead.

The receptionist at the Centre de Recherche sat behind a modern desk in a utilitarian reception area. The lighting was uncomfortably bright, there was a noticeboard advertising the latest advances in rosé research, and the floor smelt of antiseptic. As we'd learnt on our previous visit, the place rarely had visitors, so we were prepared for a few initial difficulties.

'We're here to see Gilles Masson,' said Tanya confidently.

The receptionist regarded us coldly, and her hand moved towards the phone and hovered above it. Even without the haughty look on her face I could guess what was running through her head – was this motley group of English tourists worth disturbing Gilles for? We stood waiting for a response and eventually she picked up the receiver and motioned for us to take a seat.

It was just under a year since our last visit. On that occasion we'd turned up out of the blue with an unlikely story about hunting for France's palest rosé, and I could still remember the cold, penetrating stare with which Gilles had greeted us. It had taken half an hour to persuade him that we were serious and then minute by minute he'd begun to loosen up. He'd shown us his collection of over 500 rosés which he'd judged at the Concours Mondial in Cannes and had treated us to a tour of the laboratory.

We'd parted on friendly terms, but now we were back with an equally dubious story. A nervous ten-minute wait later Gilles entered the reception area. He was wearing a pair of heavy boots, faded jeans and a slightly eccentric multicoloured shirt. His complexion was lighter than I remembered, but the blue eyes staring out from under his dishevelled brown hair were still intimidating enough, and his body language – crossed arms with one foot set aggressively forward – hardly screamed out, 'Welcome.' In fact he resembled a man who'd been interrupted in the middle of something important and was struggling to hide his irritation. Then slowly a smile spread across his face, laughter lines fanned out from around his eyes, and he shook his head in disbelief. '*Les fous de rosé,*' he said warmly, shaking our hands. There were two ways of interpreting this phrase – we were either the rosé fools or the people who were crazy about rosé. Out of the two I thought the latter had nicer connotations.

Tanya explained why we'd returned, and after a few moments' thought Gilles decided that the best way to help us was to conduct a blind tasting of our wines.

'After all, we are in the same business – I try and help the vignerons make the best rosé possible and you promote it, so we have a mutual interest,' he explained, as he opened the door on to a room adjoining the reception. 'If you'll just excuse me, I'll see what I can organise.'

The room we were shown into resembled a school classroom. There was a central seating area consisting of roughly ten desks, which had been pushed together to form a rectangle, a white-board and an overhead projector. We didn't know whether to stand or sit. If we chose to sit, then the moment Gilles returned – which could be any second – we would have to bolt to our feet; on the other hand he could easily be gone for some time and standing behind the chairs was far from relaxing. So instead we perched on the edge of the tables or leant against the wall in a self-conscious attempt to look nonchalant. Secretly we were all worried. What would happen if Gilles tasted our wines and declared them to be awful?

'Can I introduce you to Laura and Theo? Laura will be doing the tasting with us, and Theo is our *oenologue* and will be serving the wine,' said Gilles, as he sat down at the head of the table.

Theo was a small young man scarcely taller than Tanya, with short dark hair and matching dark eyes. He began to arrange the room for the tasting. First he flicked a catch under each of the desks and slid wooden partitions upwards, so that we were each enclosed in a separate cubicle. Next he removed the false tops from the desks to reveal spittoons set in the centre of each of them. Two tulip-shaped glasses were placed in front of us, one blackened, the other clear.

Laura, who was about the same age as Tanya and me, organ-ised the wine. We'd given her a bottle of each of our rosés, and she zipped them into tight blue jackets so that the label and even the shape of the bottle were totally obscured.

'Before we start, let me caution you,' advised Gilles. 'Don't be surprised if we are not too complimentary about the wines. We taste thousands of wines a year and it takes a very special wine to earn praise from us.'

We were each handed a pen and paper, and then Theo poured the first wine into a blackened glass. I decided to copy Gilles as closely as I could. First he gave the blackened glass two clockwise swishes, then he stuck his nose so deep into the glass I was afraid it might get stuck. Keeping his nose rammed beneath the rim, he began to write.

This was where I struggled. I knew that there was no right or wrong answer, and that I should just write down the smells I detected, but I always felt hopelessly inadequate when it came to describing a wine. I'd been to enough tastings and had enough opportunities to learn the skill, but I was still in awe of people whose noses were sensitive enough to discern an aroma such as freshly sawn wood. And so, unable to detect a hint of anything remotely impressive, I wrote down 'lemons' on my piece of paper. Looking over at Gilles, who was still sniffing and writing at the same time, I decided that I had to do better and so I added 'mown summer grass' to my list in an attempt to avoid embarrassment. After all, French and English summer grass probably smelt differently so how could our host contradict me?

Gilles then took a sip of the liquid from the blackened glass and transferred it around the various tasting glands in his mouth, from the gums up to the roof of his mouth and then to the back of the throat. I found this part of tasting easier than identifying smells; it also seemed more subjective. It was a matter of individual taste whether a wine was too acidic or too sugary or was sufficiently round in the mouth, whereas with smell, as far I was concerned a wine either had the aroma of newly laid tarmac or it didn't.

We then transferred the wine from the blackened to the clear glasses. 'It was important that we did a blind tasting first,' explained Gilles. 'Colour is one of the most important factors in determining a person's reaction to a wine. If you take two glasses of the same wine and add a little food colouring to one of them, eighty-five per cent of people will identify different flavours in the two glasses.'

Holding the wine up to the light, Gilles tilted his glass to study the colour. Ever the willing student, I did likewise, wishing that I could come up with something to write other than 'pale pink'.

Gilles spent just as long examining the colour from different angles as he had smelling and tasting. 'This is how people will drink the wine and so it is important that we analyse what the colour brings to the tasting experience,' he explained, before calling on Laura to describe the first wine.

Laura looked up from her notes, presumably trying to find an impressive opening comment. 'For me, it offers little on the nose and is lacking in fruits, but the colour is very agreeable – pale salmon or perhaps even eggshell – it's typical of Provence.'

Gilles sat watching Laura intently as she spoke. The palms of his hands were pressed tightly together, and his facial expressions oscillated between nodding assent and a bewildered frown. Suddenly I felt quite sorry for Laura. There she'd been minding her own business on another quiet day at work, when suddenly Gilles had appeared at her door and press-ganged her into this tasting. Now she was effectively being examined – it was like having an annual appraisal thrust on you without being given any opportunity to prepare.

'Peter, which wine do you think it is?' asked Gilles.

'*Donc, en fait,* Château de Roquefort, *franchement,*' replied Peter tentatively.

Laura stood up and removed the covering from the bottle, revealing the Château la Dorgonne label.

'It's a very similar wine from a similar area,' explained Peter, flushing red.

I was just glad that Gilles hadn't asked me and that I still had what I considered my killer phrase in hand for the rest of the tasting – 'mown summer grass'. There was one small glitch,

though: I had no idea how to say it in French, and even by resorting to charades I doubted whether I could convey the idea.

And so the tasting proceeded. The English language is renowned as one of the most descriptive in the world, but when
it comes to wine, French has the edge. We'd brought along
over twelve different wines, but I don't think Laura or Gilles repeated themselves once. As they spoke I busily wrote down their
thoughts on each of the wines – '*fruits exotiques élégants*', '*structure
tannique légère*', '*pur, léger et coulant*' and '*fruits rouges intenses*' – so
that they would be ready for use next week in Nîmes.

Thankfully Gilles and Laura praised most of our wines.
Apparently they displayed good *tipicité*, and despite being unaware what wines formed part of our collection, they successfully identified the Sancerre, Bordeaux and Languedoc rosés and
could place each of our Provençal rosés to within a couple of
miles of the village that made them. Before removing the cover
from each wine, Gilles asked us to identify it. Tanya and I did
reasonably well, succeeding with the first nine wines, but Peter
failed to get a single one correct.

Towards the end of the tasting I heard sniffling from behind
Peter's partition. His ailment developed quicker than we could
taste. Soon he had a rather dramatic hacking cough comple-
mented with periodic bouts of sneezing. And so after Peter had
failed to identify the final wine correctly, completing a clean
sweep of incorrect answers, we took him outside for a quick
health check. His skin was a dark golden brown, his eyes bright
and alert, and his breath clear and regular. In short he looked a
picture of health.

'It's this wretched cold,' said Peter as he stood in the bright
Provençal sunshine. 'How was I supposed to identify the wines
if I couldn't smell a thing?'

'How indeed?' said Tanya, raising an eyebrow.

The further we travelled from the Centre de Recherche, the

better Peter felt. Within half an hour he'd recovered sufficiently to suggest a detour to the coast. For years Tanya had wanted to visit Saint-Jean-Cap-Ferrat. Nestling between Nice and Monaco, its very name conjured images of opulent villas and decadent levels of wealth. Heaving with palm trees, bougainvillea and sticky pines, the *petit* promontory was a microcosm of all that was legendary about the south of France. It was also a six-hour round trip, but faced with Tanya's pleading eyes and a fully revived Peter, I was outnumbered and so we headed east towards the *cap*. It was a decision that was to leave one of us, quite literally, scarred for life.

It was mid-afternoon by the time we arrived and started to try and find a room for the night. Peter drove his dirty and dusty fifteen-year-old car up the tree-lined drives of various hotels. We parked next to Maseratis and Ferraris, but within minutes were heading back down the same drives, appalled at the prices. Several Lamborghini-littered hotels later we realised we were out of our financial depth. Trapped in blue friezes amid the branches of the umbrella pines, we could see super-yachts basking at anchor, and luxury villas built down to the water's edge. The *cap* was too beautiful for our budget and so we resolved to head back inland to look for somewhere to stay. But first we wanted to have a quick swim.

Just the other side of Saint-Jean-Cap-Ferrat was a rocky beach set at the base of a steep cliff. It was enclosed by pine trees, and on the far corner of the bay was an old villa complete with perfectly manicured gardens full of verdant vegetation, shady colonnades and overflowing fountains. Underneath it was a shabbily chic beach club. The once-white umbrellas had had the colour drained from them by the sun, the paint on the wooden restaurant and bar area was flaking away, and the sun loungers were faded from years of washing. 'It's the type of place you'd bring your wife, not your mistress,' concluded Peter with approval, as we made our way down the rickety steps.

Peter and I took a quick dip and then dozed on our towels, but Tanya stayed out at sea. I closed my eyes and waited as the burning imprint of the sun slowly faded from my retinas. The hushing play of the sea on the rocks was only interrupted by the odd snore from a contented Peter. I buried my feet under the wet stones and made a pillow out of a pile of small rocks. Opening my eyes one more time to take in the view before falling asleep – snoring Peter permitting – I saw Tanya swimming frantically towards the shore. She was doing more strokes per second than an Olympic swimmer. Emerging from the water, she stood shivering in the sunshine clutching her forearm. 'I don't know what happened. Something wrapped itself round my arm and now, now it hurts more than anything.'

The commotion woke Peter and also attracted the lifeguard from the beach club – a teenage girl with short blonde hair tied back in a ribbon and long golden legs. She ambled leisurely across, as interested in the admiring glances she attracted as the developing emergency.

An ugly welt had materialised between Tanya's wrist and elbow. The skin was popped and blistered, and from the central red smudge, tentacles of affected skin wrapped round her arm.

'*C'est une grande méduse,*' said the lifeguard as she examined it. The word '*méduse*' carried magically through the air back to the beach club and soon Tanya was standing shaking amid a crowd of onlookers.

'She's going into anaphylactic shock,' said one wrinkled old woman.

'Ammonia is the only thing for *méduses,*' added another.

'You need to suck out the poison,' commented a third.

'Rub sand on it,' 'Keep it out of the sun,' 'Put vinegar on it,' 'Give her some Armagnac' – each new onlooker had their own piece of advice. I noticed that the sea had emptied and that people were huddling together in groups. Floating by in the air from all directions came one distinctive word: '*méduse*'. My only consolation at this point was that I knew the French were a nation of hypochondriacs so I presumed it couldn't be that bad. Tanya seemed to be shivering less and she confirmed the pain had subsided.

As the lifeguard dabbed some antihistamine cream on her arm, the surrounding people filtered back to their sun loungers. Most grabbed one last look at the wound, feeding their excited chattering with this final glance and using phrases that I thought had been confined to the dustbin of linguistic history and/or French textbooks. '*Oh là là,*' they said, waving their hands in front of their mouths in horror. '*Quel dommage.*'

'*Q'est-ce que c'est une méduse?*' I asked the lifeguard.

'Jellyfish,' she said, wrapping her arm consolingly round Tanya. '*Mais ça, c'était une grande méduse.*'

For the following few hours the jellyfish sting seemed to worry the French far more than it did Tanya. We followed the lifeguard's advice and went straight to a pharmacy to buy some cream. As we queued amid shelves full of slimming body scrubs, rejuvenating face creams and heat treatments for cellulite, people began to crowd around Tanya. Once again the word '*méduse*' was whispered in awed tones. The name was far more evocative than the English 'jellyfish', conjuring up visions of the snake-filled hair of the mythical gorgon Medusa.

Another series of unlikely treatments was recommended by the ten or so amateur physicians queuing with us, including bathing the sting in walnut oil and putting it under ultraviolet light. Once we'd run through all the possible cures, it was time to establish the cause of Tanya's unfortunate encounter. And on this subject there was universal, if surprising, agreement.

It was all the fault of the Americans. According to a pharmacy full of wealthy Cap–Ferrat residents, it was without doubt down to George W. Bush. How they'd managed to connect the president of the United States with a jellyfish sting bemused me. It seemed like an appropriate question for a TV show or a Christmas parlour game – what links George Bush and Mediterranean *méduses*?

As we shuffled slowly forwards we were enlightened. If George Dubya had signed the Kyoto Protocol on climate change, then global warming might have been halted. But instead, every year the Americans – and this word was said with a distinct hiss – pumped more and more carbon into the atmosphere. The earth warmed and so did the seas. And there was nothing that *méduses* liked more than warm seas. The Mediterranean was suffering from an epidemic of them. Every morning lifeguards plucked them from the water with a net, but at least one bather was stung a day. It was beginning to threaten the French way of life. After all, if you couldn't swim safely, what was the point in going to the beach, and if people didn't go to the beach, what would happen to the beach clubs? Dining with your toes curled in the warm sand next to the glistening Med would soon be a thing of the past. Yes, everyone agreed, as they ushered Tanya to the front of the queue, George Bush had a lot to answer for, starting with my wife's swollen arm.

Despite the fact that Tanya insisted the sting wasn't hurting that much, I was quite prepared for the encounter with the jellyfish to cost us a lot of money. I'd been to French pharmacies before and I knew that since the French state paid for every available medicine, French people insisted on them all. Of course this was only problematic if like us you were foreign and had to pay upfront for everything, even if we could claim some of it back. The pharmacist tentatively took hold of Tanya's arm, turning it in all directions to examine the sting. Interestingly the wound had now turned a rather putrid green, and large blisters were weeping in a line where the tentacles had wrapped themselves round her wrist.

'*C'était une grande méduse,*' the pharmacist said, and then began to pile products on to the counter. There was a suction-pump contraption to remove any of the remaining poison, then a cream for burns, then an antihistamine cream, then some cortisone tablets, a disinfectant spray, some dressing for the wound and a pile of bandages. 'If it gets any worse, you must go and see a doctor,' the pharmacist advised.

As we left the shop, struggling to hold all the medicine, I could hear people still discussing *méduses* and clicking their tongues at the mention of George Bush's name.

That evening we were just settling down to eat supper in a small restaurant when the waitress spotted Tanya's arm. She gasped, let loose a couple of '*Oh là là*'s and then said we must go and see a doctor at once. Tanya explained that we'd been to the pharmacy and already had a bag full of medicine, and what she really needed was a large glass of wine. The waitress nodded but took a long time to return with our drinks.

'I've phoned the hospital,' she said, as she placed our wine on the table with a concerned look, 'and they want you to go and see them at once. It's only a twenty-minute drive.' Tanya politely declined and began to look at the menu. 'If you're not going to go, the nurse gave me some advice,' she persisted. 'You must get somebody to pee on it.'

It was as if she'd just made a perfectly reasonable request like asking us to change table. She put her pen and notepad away, making it clear that we couldn't order unless I complied. To eat, I had to do the unthinkable. For about a quarter of an hour a stand-off developed. The waitress refused to serve us and I refused to pee on the sting.

'It's clearly an old wives' tale,' I argued.

'But it was a nurse who advised you to do it,' countered Peter, clearly thinking of his stomach.

'It isn't even hurting that much,' said Tanya.

As we sat sipping our wine, I caught the waitress looking dismissively at me. She was talking with a couple of regulars at the bar and it became apparent that they all thought my behaviour was reprehensible. What was the world coming to if a husband wouldn't help to relieve his wife's pain? We'd reached stalemate – either we found another restaurant or I acceded to the waitress's demand. Taking one final gulp of wine, I took Tanya's good arm and paraded her past the regulars to the toilets.

Five minutes later we resumed our seats. 'It's much better,' Tanya thanked the waitress as we finally ordered.

The wet bandage round the sting began to drip on to the table and Peter looked enquiringly at us.

'It's only water,' I whispered.

10

Murphy's Bar

On Sunday 10 June I picked up the phone to discuss what time we should arrive at Murphy's Bar the following day. The conversation didn't last long. I agreed with John that we would meet him at three o'clock in his bar. But there was something brittle about his voice, the normal broad Irish lilt had disappeared and instead he spoke in a clipped, flat tone. 'Do you know what day it is, Jamie? It's a Sunday, Jamie, and it's my only f★★★ing day off. We'll talk about your plans tomorrow.'

Then the phone went dead. It was the second time that John had hung up on me.

The following day Peter and I dropped Tanya outside Murphy's Bar before parking five minutes away next to the new library – a Norman Foster-designed glass box with a jacket of bright-white metal. In the square opposite, crowds of people circled the Roman version of architectural modernism, the completely symmetrical Maison Carrée – a temple built in AD 5 and dedicated to the sons of the Emperor Augustus. Pleasingly my second impression of Nîmes was as promising as the first. There was something wonderfully progressive about erecting such a stark modern building opposite an ancient wonder. And there was a sense of quiet forward-looking affluence all around, a pleasant bustle about the place, which I didn't usually associate with the sleepy south.

We sweated down the street looking for shade from the attritional heat and stumbling under the weight of the wine. It was mid-afternoon and the terraces of the cafés were reassuringly full with a mixture of camera-clutching tourists and businessmen in light cotton jackets. Murphy's Bar was located just off the main road that ran between the Maison Carrée and the Roman Arena. After a couple of wrong turns we found the narrow alley. It was deserted and distinguishable only by the black Guinness sign jutting out above our heads. Piling our wine on the pavement outside the bar, we entered.

The lighting was low and the air heavy with smoke. Tanya and John were sitting at the bar and the cramped space between them was filled by an ashtray smouldering with cigarette stubs and an unpleasant atmosphere. Tanya's swollen arm hung loosely by her side. Her other elbow was planted on the bar, and her index finger was pointing straight into John's face. He sat opposite with his hands curled into fists. More smoke trailed across the room from a cigarette concealed between his fingers. In the half-light his skin looked sallow and the only colour visible in his face was the yellow of his teeth. His eyes were hidden under heavy, hooded brows, giving him the appearance of a pugilist who'd taken too many blows.

'As I was just telling Tanya,' said John, addressing the rest of the room, but still staring angrily at my wife, 'you're a f★★★ing disgrace, the lot of you.' The Irish accent was once again absent, as apparently was the happy-go-lucky barman we'd met just two weeks ago. Then, a rosé bar had seemed like a fantastic crack, but now things had changed.

Tanya slid off her stool and slipped by me, whispering as she went, 'I think it's best we leave this one to you. Peter and I will just lose our tempers.'

I took a seat opposite John and as calmly as I could explained that I didn't know what he was talking about. I then listened as the complaints came tripping from his mouth, swearword tumbling over swearword. For ten minutes he talked and I said nothing. Sanitising the language, John argued that we'd made it impossible for La Vie en Rosé to be a success. We'd disappeared to Vidauban, we hadn't been available for the press to interview us, we'd not been in touch, we were totally disorganised, and we'd – and this appeared to be his major gripe – called him on a Sunday.

Apart from the last item on the list none of this was true. I'd spoken to John continually during our time in Uzès and we'd responded to his various requests. We'd written a small press release for him to send to newspapers together with a description of all the wines we would be selling. He'd asked for more posters claiming that he would pin them up all over Nîmes, but the extra ones we'd had printed were now sitting redundant behind the bar. And as for the press, I'd kept my mobile on for the last two days in case we needed to dash back for an interview. It hadn't rung.

'Well, what do you want to do?' I asked, when John finally fell silent.

He placed his cigarette between his chapped lips and blew smoke through his nostrils, letting it curl towards the ceiling.

Filling the silence, I continued, 'I don't agree with what you've said, but I can only say sorry for the trouble we appear to have caused you.'

He shifted his heavy limbs from the bar stool and stubbed his cigarette in the growing mound. Once out of the low spotlights, John's face disappeared into shadow, his thick stubble blending with the darkness. He ducked under the counter so that he stood behind the bar. Pouring himself a beer, he took a long slug and then turned to look at me.

'Don't mind me, Jamie.' The Irish accent had crept back into his voice. 'As my mother will tell you, I've always been a grumpy old bird.' This sentence, and the way it was delivered with its soft inflexion and hint of self-deprecation, changed the mood. The anger and the recrimination drifted away with the smoke. 'We open at six. Have a drink and then I'll help you stack your wine upstairs.'

To say our first night wasn't a success would be an understatement. The idea was to set up a temporary bar in the street and to serve the six or so tables that were lined up against the wall outside Murphy's. Rather than the Place aux Herbes, our backdrop was now a metal garage door sprayed with lurid graffiti, but to show willing I'd put on what I considered to be my killer rosé outfit – the ankle-length white shorts I'd been talked into buying in Aix and a bright-pink shirt. The moment we started to trade I realised I looked quite ridiculous. Standing in a narrow alley in sailorboy shorts, I had more chance of being propositioned than selling any rosé.

Although it had been a hot day, a shroud of grey slipped over the evening sky and a light drizzle began to fall. Tanya's jellyfish sting started to throb and she wrapped some ice from the wine bucket in a serviette and used it as an impromptu compress. Peter wandered off with our leaflets to try and attract some customers, and we stood and waited as people hurried by, glancing over their shoulders at Nîmes's new novelty.

'*Voulez-vous goûtez un petit peu de vin rosé?*' we cried after them, but if they bothered to turn round, the residents of Nîmes – or the Nîmois as they were known – wanted to make it very clear that they didn't drink. They rubbed their stomachs and shook their heads before scuttling away in their smartly tailored clothes. One man whom we did manage to attract taught me a new trick. Like the rest of his countrymen, once tempted to try some wine he took the process incredibly seriously. We stood and waited as he performed the familiar rigmarole of smelling, swilling and examining the colour. By this stage it was like the rerun of a favourite comedy – despite knowing all the jokes and the punchlines, watching retained an intrinsic charm. I was ready for our customer to start quizzing me about grape variety and soil type, but instead he suddenly just spewed the entire contents of his mouth into the gutter.

Had we left the wine in the sun too long, or was it just an allergic reaction? Tanya put her arm round his shoulders and patted him gently on the back in an attempt to reassure him. But the man looked at her strangely and simply proffered his now empty glass and asked to try another wine. Once again he sipped, swilled and then spewed the wine into the gutter.

'Is there anything wrong with our wine?' I asked.

'*Vous êtes anglais*?' he replied. I nodded and he nodded too, as if that was excuse enough for my ignorance.

As he tried the rest of the wine, he explained that the best way of ensuring all the tasting glands in the mouth were coated with liquid was to spit the wine out forcefully. 'Everybody knows that,' he said, as he left without buying a glass.

As this pantomime had progressed John's bar gradually filled, but nobody else showed the slightest inclination to taste rosé in the drizzle. As well as indifference there was a hint of antagonism, as if we'd invaded a personal space. The worst offender was a middle-aged woman who sat sagging on her bar stool and spent nearly an hour staring at us. Her thin cotton dress was creased in rolls round her midriff, and she had the forearms of a labourer-cum-arm-wrestler. Her hair was a wiry grey, and it rose in all directions from an oversized scalp. She spoke to nobody and sipped her drink transfixed by us. Even if La Vie en Rosé had been full I think she would have put me on edge, but given our complete lack of customers and our earlier run-in with John, an element of unease crept in.

As in Uzès, we decided that the best way to the hearts of the regulars was to give them some free wine. Our grey-haired nemesis gruntingly declined, but the rest of the people inside Murphy's crowded round and proffered their glasses. The majority turned out to be expats – forty-somethings who'd sold their businesses in the UK and moved to France in search of the good life. Others were Brits and Americans working on temporary contracts, repairing planes at the local airport or providing IT support to French companies. I thought they would be fertile ground. They were far from home and would presumably be quite keen to swap a few anecdotes and buy a few glasses in return. But once our free wine had run out, they turned to face the bar, shutting us off from the conversation.

Back outside, there was trouble in the alley. A passing drunk had spotted our table full of unattended rosé and was about to help herself. In Uzès we'd only encountered the darker side of bar life on one occasion. Towards the end of the Fête de la Musique, a tramp had staggered through the Renaissance, aggressively slamming forks into tables, implanting their prongs into the wood and leaving them quivering with the customers in his wake. Laurent had watched from behind the bar and simply waited the tramp out. 'If I had intervened, things would have got worse, and there was no point in calling the police – he'd be gone by the time they turned up.'

Now we had our own incident. The drunk was a middle-aged woman with a mixture of dirt and her own greasy hair matted to her face. She wore a rag for a dress, striped knee-length socks with holes in them and a pair of clogs. Seeing me approach, she poured herself a large glass of wine and finished it in one gulp.

For an experienced barman, it would have been a relatively easy situation. There were no customers to risk offending, so I could have led or if necessary manhandled the woman away. But I simply didn't know what to do. I found myself wondering whether she might have a knife.

Deprived of alcohol, the woman lay down in the middle of the street and began to mutter obscenities to herself. Tanya joined me behind the bar and we followed Laurent's approach of waiting the problem out. In our case it proved to be a disaster. The rain had stopped but any chance that we might attract our first customers had vanished with the arrival of our now resident drunk. Presumably thinking that she hadn't done enough to disrupt our evening, the woman placed two fingers in her mouth and simulated fellatio. Our choices were to drag her away across the cobbles or see who got bored first. We chose the latter option and lost another valuable hour of sales time.

Shortly afterwards John came out of his bar to see how we were getting on. He had the smouldering end of a Marlboro Red in his mouth and accepted a glass of rosé from Tanya. 'As I told Jamie earlier, I am a grumpy old bird sometimes.' He raised his glass. 'Cheers.' Looking at the empty tables and chairs, he gave a wide grin and a shrug. 'It's Monday in Nîmes and it's been raining – it's going to be a very quiet night.' Obviously feeling that we were in need of a little company, he scratched his stubble and lit another cigarette.

A couple of Nîmois scurried by, casting an anxious glance at the pink apparition that was La Vie en Rosé and shouting a warm greeting to John. Without taking the stub from his mouth, John shouted out in return, '*Bonsoir* there,' but the Nîmois had already disappeared. 'Maybe tomorrow will be better for you,' he said, as he ground the Marlboro into the gutter with the heel of his cowboy boot.

Peter returned just before closing still clutching a fistful of flyers. I expected him to be full of tales of exotic restaurants and places to visit, but instead he was despondent. Pouring us all a glass of wine, he took a seat at one of the tables. 'Funny people, these Nîmois. You invite them to a wine tasting and they look at you as if you've just offered them heroin.'

'Cheers,' I said, raising my glass.

[117]

La Vie en Rosé had just experienced its first ever day without selling any wine, and there seemed nothing for it but to have a drink.

That night none of us slept. The principal cause of the problem was the *méduse* sting. All evening the ache in Tanya's arm had been getting worse. It appeared that the poison had stayed dormant for a day and then suddenly awoken. The affected skin had blistered and risen, and it was possible to trace the tiny troughs and furrows of the head of the *méduse* from the indentions round Tanya's wrist. Worse still was the area where the tentacles had wrapped themselves. Here, the skin was singed and pushed upwards so that it looked like an ugly purple rope had been fastened tightly round her forearm.

Despite the small fortune we'd invested in medicines, the only treatment that relieved the pain was an ice pack. This was fine while we were working in the bar, but as in Uzès we'd rented an old apartment with few mod cons. We couldn't find an ice tray, and in any event the freezer was showing little sign of working. So as the night wore on and the pain intensified, Peter and I headed out on to the streets. The handiest receptacles we could find to carry the ice back in were the shower caps we'd appropriated from various hotels. 'If we put ice in that you'll get your hair wet,' I was teased out of the only open bar I could find within twenty minutes of the flat. 'Anyway, what was the *méduse* doing in the bath?' Peter was more successful, discovering a nightclub run by a Corsican just a street away from our apartment. And after discussing the wines of Patrimonio and debating the relative merits of blackbird and starling pâté, the Corsican filled Peter's shower cap and promised him ice whenever he needed it.

Fortunately the nightclub stayed open until the early hours of the morning and Peter and I took it in turns to ferry more ice to Tanya. Unsurprisingly this activity wasn't conducive to sleep.

And so when I wasn't pulling on my clothes and hurrying off, I lay on my back in bed with my eyes wide open, staring at the lethargic fan which barely stirred the warm air. I was trapped in the room with my thoughts. What could we do to help Tanya? Should we take her to a hospital? Why had we ignored the anthology of advice we'd been given about *méduse* stings? Then there were the less immediate worries. We'd been in France for six weeks and apart from our time in Uzès when we'd managed to make a living from rosé, we'd just been running through our savings. Our first night in Murphy's Bar could only be described as a disaster. People passing in the street had looked at us quite contemptuously, as if our little pink bar was somehow sullying their city. And even the regulars had seen us as a source of amusement not refreshment.

We also had to consider our relationship with John, the self-confessed 'grumpy old bird'. At the beginning of the day when I'd sat and listened to his cold, hard rant about our shortcomings, I'd thought that our experience in Aix was about to repeat itself. John had appeared to be a great bully of a man and one that none of us would choose to spend any time with. But throughout our evening in the bar he couldn't have been gentler. I couldn't help but wonder which barman we were going to work with tomorrow.

Light began to creep into the room but it did little to banish my worries.

We'd worked from six until midnight without selling a single glass of wine. We simply couldn't afford to keep doing so badly. The height of the summer was upon us and we needed to be trading somewhere, but when we left England trumpeting our grand plans to spend the summer running a rosé bar, I don't think any of us had contemplated ending up in a dirty alley in Nîmes.

Although we'd only been outside Murphy's Bar for one evening, it was clear that if things didn't improve dramatically we'd have to take an important decision – should we persevere, or should we head off and try and find somewhere else? In the humid half-light one doubt fed another – what would happen if nowhere else would have us? Part of our plan had been to partner with French cafés and restaurants to gain the necessary experience to run our own bar, but what if we couldn't get that experience, and what if the whole concept of a rosé bar was flawed anyway?

Until now I had hidden my doubts from Tanya, but unless our fortunes changed I would have to broach the subject, and I knew that giving up would not be easy to discuss, particularly since we had no contingency plan. We'd all set our hearts on trying to make our future selling rosé and we'd focused on the idea to the exclusion of all others. I'd convinced myself that such single-mindedness often bred success and that if we started exploring other options then our rosé business might somehow suffer.

I tried to grab a couple more hours' sleep, but a relentless flow of thoughts swept into my mind. Pictures of Tanya and me running a small *gîte* or earning a living teaching English teased my consciousness, but neither of these alternative lives in France held any appeal. Perhaps it was because I was still so desperate to make La Vie en Rosé a success, but possibly it was more than that. Running a rosé bar, we were continually learning, visiting new vineyards, discovering more about wine and challenging ourselves to integrate fully into local life. If we couldn't succeed in the wine business, then did we want to stay in France?

11

The Nîmois

I thought finding a doctor to see Tanya might be difficult. In this most bureaucratic of countries, I expected to need all sorts of pieces of paper that we didn't have and to spend a day or even a week completing forms before finally being sent to some faraway surgery. Instead a quick reconnoitre revealed doorways covered in engraved golden plaques advertising the services of legions of doctors. Taking potluck, we picked Dr Nicolas Arsac. Pushing open a large, creaking set of gates, Tanya and I found ourselves in a cool courtyard. There were no signs to indicate where we should go, but one of the numerous nondescript doors that faced us had been left ajar and so I tentatively poked my head into the room beyond.

A group of middle-aged women were sitting on hard upright chairs arranged in a square. They were chattering furiously away. Some had brought their knitting, others simply waited with their handbags clasped on their knees, but each one of them was engaged in an animated conversation with her neighbour. The atmosphere was slightly disconcerting, rather than the staples of a doctor's surgery – a dusty silence punctuated only by the slow tick of a clock and the occasional scream of an ailing child – I could have been at a meeting of the local Women's Institute. There was a low table scattered with dog-eared magazines and a pot plant but no other giveaway signs – not a hacking cough or swollen limb in sight. Everyone seemed far too well and quite happy to be there.

I was about to retreat and try another door when I spotted a rack full of health leaflets. It had to be the right place and so Tanya and I entered and took the only spare seats. As the eyes of the waiting women flicked up and down us, the conversation hushed like a wave dying on a sandy beach. But before long the women's voices were rolling in again and we sat for half an hour trying to tune our ears to the words crashing around the room.

It quickly became clear that we'd been identified as English and therefore genetically incapable of speaking any French, and this made us fair game to have our lives dissected. From the ice pack that Tanya held firmly against her arm, the assembled women deduced that she'd been badly bruised, which led to speculation about the possibility of a fight, and from one corner of the room a whispered debate began about whether I was her husband or her lover. In turn this sparked a conversation about how English men didn't always wear wedding rings, which everyone seemed to agree was '*dégueulasse*'. Ironically this was a word I knew well because wine connoisseurs had used it to describe rosé. It meant 'disgusting'.

There was still no sign of Dr Nicolas, but no one fidgeted or showed the slightest bit of impatience, perhaps because they were all delighting in discussing the marital habits of the English. But much as I was enjoying deciphering the debate, I was beginning to get worried. In a UK surgery patients are turned over quicker than a ticket queue at a station, but if we were experiencing the typical French wait per patient, then we were looking at spending the whole morning, if not the day in this room.

After we'd been in the surgery for forty-five minutes Dr Nicolas emerged. He was quite the trendiest doctor I'd ever set eyes on. He wore a deep-blue shirt tucked into faded but pressed blue jeans. The shirt had a wide collar, and the top two buttons were undone revealing just a smattering of chest hair. His eyes were a dark chocolate brown, and a boyish quiff flopped over his forehead and tickled the bridge of his nose, but most impressive of all was the collective intake of breath he engendered from the waiting room. Ten pairs of breasts heaved upwards in unison as the delectable doctor called for his next patient. Whether it was out of genuine sympathy for Tanya's plight or just simply to prolong the anticipation of a session with Nicolas, the woman at the head of the queue insisted we were seen first.

There followed one of the most thorough examinations imaginable. Sitting behind a high mahogany desk, Nicolas listened patiently as Tanya described in halting French the encounter with the *méduse*. He then took her over to a raised bed in the corner of the room, put on a white knee-length coat – presumably to ensure he looked suitably professional while carrying out the business part of his job – and flicked on a bright-white halogen light. Tenderly taking Tanya's arm, he turned it from all directions to catch the light, making notes on a little pad after each rotation. He then began to apply pressure to different parts of the sting.

'The scarring will last for several months,' warned Nicolas, 'and in some areas where the tentacles touched the skin, it may never go. Being stung by a jellyfish like this is akin to suffering a first-degree burn.' Sweeping his hair away from his face, he began to write a prescription. 'You must also be careful to keep it out of the sun. The poison injected into the skin has an effect similar to severe eczema, and if it is irritated in any way, it will keep recurring.'

Nicolas assured us the prescribed medicine would ease the pain and start the healing process. He ushered us out of the door, and as I turned back to say goodbye I caught him arranging his hair in the mirror. It appeared he kept a comb and some hairgel rather than a stethoscope in his top drawer.

Caught in the middle of his beauty routine, Nicolas suddenly became all professional again. 'Be careful with those cortisone tablets,' he warned, fixing Tanya with a stern look. 'They're so strong they might cause your heart to flutter.'

I couldn't help but think that this was the last thing Tanya or, for that matter, any of Nicolas's female patients needed. Just by walking into the waiting room earlier Dr Nicolas had set off a wave of palpitations.

Back at the bar, sales were improving. In fact Peter delightedly informed us they were up 200 per cent. Unfortunately this was hardly saying much. The responsible couple were young and French and had seen one of our posters and made a special trip to Murphy's Bar as a result. They ordered Sancerre and sat and fingered their glasses for the next hour, barely wetting their lips with the wine. Had they been English tourists we'd have managed to sell them a whole bottle in the time it took these two youngsters to make it halfway down their glasses. Instead they eventually left without finishing the wine.

After just a day in town we'd learnt to use a new adjective to describe this sort of behaviour; it was 'Nîmois'. Other archetypal Nîmois habits included declining a tasting but inspecting the alcohol percentage on each of our bottles. When a local found one over 12 per cent, he or she would shake their head and walk away as if making a 13 per cent wine was one of the great evils of the modern world.

John Murphy was our resident anthropological expert. 'The Nîmois, Jamie, make the Irish Presbyterians seem like a bunch of hard-drinking, drug-popping ravers,' said John, as he inhaled deeply on his cigarette. 'They'll sit for hours with an empty glass in front of them. In the end you just have to tell them, "This is a bar not your living room and in a bar you drink."'

He then launched into a history of why it was a mistake for us to set up in Nîmes. According to John, the reason we weren't managing to sell any rosé was traceable to the Wars of Religion.

Nîmes was a Protestant town that had been invaded and pillaged countless times over the centuries by the Catholics and as a result the inhabitants had taken a dislike to foreigners. Over the years this inward-looking mentality had been augmented by the arrival of mountain people from the Basque region of Spain, drawn by the city's reputation for bull fighting. The Basques, John assured us, 'make Irish Presbyterians seem welcoming'.

'It takes generations to be assimilated into the social life of the city,' continued John, 'and yet you're expecting people to happily approach you in the street after just one day.'

Making matters worse, there were also economic problems. 'Of course, you know why denim is called "denim",' drawled John. 'It's because it was initially from Nîmes – "*de* Nîmes". But now of course the textile industry has gone and you are left with a town with one of the highest unemployment rates in France. Added to which you can't borrow money in this country in the same way you can in England. Credit cards as you understand them don't exist. Everything has to be paid off at the end of the month, and if you fail to do so, you are added to the list of debtors at the Bank of France. And that means it is next to impossible to open another bank account ever again.'

The Nîmois, we quickly learnt, were John's favourite subject. Each evening he would stand in the street smoking and talking to us. Unfortunately he was usually explaining why our bar – and quite frequently his – were empty. Either there was a pop concert going on in the Roman Arena or the crowds had been attracted away by exhibitions or night markets taking place in the central squares.

Even our new-found ability to describe all our wines accurately in French didn't seem to help. The Nîmois we persuaded to taste were determined to prove they knew more about wine than us. And so despite the fact that I was quoting directly from Gilles Masson's tasting notes, they would shake their heads at my description of the wine. If I said a rosé was 'salmon-coloured' they would insist it was 'peach', if I claimed it was 'round' in the mouth they would say it was 'acidic'. It didn't seem to matter that I had the backing of France's foremost rosé scientist – I was English and therefore wrong.

I finally realised that I was fighting a battle I couldn't win when I found myself debating the smell of one of our Bordeaux clairets. Gilles's tasting notes described it as *'fruits florals violets'*, but my customer, a short squat man with two-day-old stubble, insisted on lecturing me about the closed nose and lack of fruit. I wouldn't have minded but as he held the wine to his nose and made a great show of sniffing the aroma, fingers of smoke from the Gaulois that was clasped between his knuckles curled up the outside of his glass into his nostril.

On Wednesday night John suggested we halve our prices; on Thursday night he moved us away from his bar towards the main street in an attempt to help us generate trade; and when we arrived on Friday evening we found that he'd erected signs at either end of the alley to direct people to our bar. It was all to no avail. If we sold a bottle of wine a night we were fortunate. Foolishly we hoped the weekend would be better, but according to John, Friday and Saturday were two of the worst nights because everyone went to the beach during the day and didn't get back to town until late.

And so for hours on end we would stand behind our full wine buckets and absorb the rituals of the street. As inoffensive and empty as our little rosé bar was, our arrival was far from popular with the residents. Partly it was because our presence interfered with daily life. On our first evening a key attached to a piece of string had come clattering out of a fourth-floor window. It smacked against the garage door and narrowly missed Peter's head. We then had to fish it out of a glass of rosé before handing it to the person trying to get into their house.

After a while we became used to being harangued by residents leaning from their windows. I don't think they meant any harm, beyond wanting to pass some time on another sleepy night in the city, but I also don't think we did ourselves any favours. Typical of such exchanges was when a string-vest-wearing man leant out of his window with a can of lager in his hand. '*Il y a beaucoup de vins*,' he shouted down.

Peter looked up at him quizzically, presuming that he was angling for a free drink. 'Yes, but you still have to pay,' he replied politely, as he tried to ignore the fact that the man was repeatedly shouting the same phrase.

Eventually the window was closed in disgust. It wasn't until a gust of wind knocked over a glass that Peter realised what he'd been talking about. We'd assumed he was a drunk with a one-track mind, but instead he'd been attempting to be friendly by talking about the weather. He'd done so in a heavy Provençal accent so that '*vent*' had sounded like '*vins*'. For the next half an hour Peter paced up and down practising a new accent – '*pain*' became '*paingg*', '*boisson*' became '*boissang*'.

Undoubtedly our most serious infringement was preventing a woman from entering her garage. Every night at eight she would pull into the end of the street and raise her fist angrily at John and us. It turned out that she had a parking space in the garage in front of which we were now operating. It had been allocated to her by the prefecture of Nîmes, but unfortunately the prefecture had also granted John the right to have a terrace on the street. The result was that she could never get her car into the garage because John's tables and now La Vie en Rosé were in the way. So every evening she would abandon her car in the middle of the alley, trailing a different selection of expletives.

After a week selling next to no wine and upsetting the locals, we were all dispirited. We'd known that Murphy's Bar was never going to match Aix or Uzès in terms of the prettiness of the location; nevertheless we'd still felt that we could make a go of our rosé bar in Nîmes. However, in seven days we'd been taught a very harsh lesson: location was everything. We could operate outside Murphy's Bar for the rest of the summer but all we'd be left with would be a carload of unsold rosé and a hefty bank debt.

Just as we were beginning to think about moving on, John produced the masterstroke that he was convinced would transform our fortunes. 'A journalist from *Midi Libre* is coming to interview you tomorrow night,' he said, as he lit up a celebratory Marlboro Red, 'and an article in the paper could make you for the summer.'

Three random English people standing behind a table of rosé clearly wouldn't guarantee us the column inches we craved, but a thriving new rosé bar in the heart of Nîmes would hopefully be newsworthy, so Tanya picked up the phone and called Claire and by 7 p.m. on the night the journalist was due to visit a throng of people had gathered. They included friends of Claire and Neil from England, Neil's work colleagues and neighbours from Montpellier, and most importantly Rosie and Tristan had also come. They were both now free from the ravaging effects of the *varicelle* – or chickenpox – and had begun to put on weight.

Rosie was dressed in a pink sundress and had a small bonnet pulled down over her head but nevertheless the odd stray curl still escaped and dangled in front of her demure eyes. With one hand she clasped Claire's leg and with the other she held a pink gerbera large enough to obscure most of her face. We couldn't have wished for a sweeter mascot. Peter popped several bottles of Laurent Champs's champagne, and we toasted the evening we hoped would turn around the fortunes of La Vie en Rosé.

The joy of having a busy bar is that people naturally attract more people. Quite soon, instead of handing out free champagne we were enjoying our most profitable night in Nîmes. And thankfully Marc Caillaud, the journalist from *Midi Libre*, arrived in the middle of the party. All our tables were full, and there were people standing around the serving area tasting the different wines. Tanya and I went inside with Marc, leaving Peter to run the bar. John poured us a drink and we began to conduct our first ever press interview.

Marc was a little older than us, softly spoken and had a tentative personality. It was almost as if he regarded it as offensive to ask a question. He took out his little flip-pad, which was covered in notes made in scrawled handwriting, and turned to a fresh page. Then there was silence. If he'd been a Fleet Street hack, I'd have suspected that Marc was trying to lure us off guard with a pregnant pause; instead I think he just didn't know where to start.

Tanya prodded the conversation along by asking which area his paper covered. And for the next half-hour rather than make his own notes Marc ended up drawing various maps in my accounts book. Next to all the figures showing the wine sold to date in Uzès and Nîmes, Marc sketched the distribution area of *Midi Libre*. It ran from Perpignan on the Spanish border, past Montpellier to Arles and then across to the west of Nîmes.

'But when people speak of the Midi, I thought they were referring to the whole of the south, including Provence,' queried Tanya.

'No, if you are in Nîmes, the Midi is the area I have just described to you. I'll give you another example: people think that places like Vence, Grasse and Draguignan are in Provence. They're not. Provence ends at Saint-Maximin-la-Sainte-Baume. Then you enter the Var and after that, further east, the southern Alps.' Marc drew the regional boundaries as he talked. 'So you see, words like "the Midi" and "Provence" are used generically by people who don't live here, whereas they actually refer to quite specific areas.'

Despite having drawn a detailed map of the whole of the south of France for us, Marc then let it slip that he was from near Nantes. And when Tanya confessed that we knew very little about the wine of the Loire, we were off again. Marc started sketching, marking every inlet and cove of the Atlantic coastline, the major cities and rivers and his favourite wine producers in each area. By the time he finally got around to asking us our first question, John Murphy had topped us up twice.

Then, with the alcohol loosening our tongues, we began to explain how we came to be running a rosé bar in Nîmes. We talked about our quest for the palest rosé, our desire to leave London and make a new life in France, the fall-out with the bar in Aix, our success in Uzès and finally about the difficulties of making people accept rosé as a serious wine. I thought the story had everything – a human-interest angle, a lashing of betrayal and even a ready-made photo opportunity with Rosie clasping a flower in front of our bar. Marc nodded his head. 'I'll get a photographer sent down to get some pictures and we'll try and get it in the paper in the next couple of days.' He closed his notebook and got up to leave. 'I think the editor is going to love this.'

Outside, the bar was still full and Peter was proudly utilising his new Provençal accent: '*Voulez-vous une boissang?*' Whether they understood or not, for one evening at least the Nîmois seemed to have shed their puritan spirit. We'd run out of cold Sancerre, all our champagne bottles were upended in the wine buckets, and people were clamouring for fresh glasses quicker than we could replenish them. John kindly turned the music up in his bar and a mini-fiesta ensued. We even served the famous old matador who ran the restaurant at the end of the street. And by the end of the night we were twirling with our customers amid the empty wine boxes, celebrating the rebirth of La Vie en Rosé.

12

Hold the Front Page

It seemed our fortunes were on the rise. Before Marc had had a chance to return to the offices of *Midi Libre* and get typing, we received an invitation from a local vigneron. Denys Armand owned a vineyard just outside Nîmes, and news of our rosé bar had reached him. He was keen to get his new rosé, which he promised was something quite special, on to our wine list and so the next morning we drove into the hills to the west of Nîmes for a tasting.

It was another hot and dusty day as we wound our way through the slumbering countryside. It appeared we'd arrived in the wake of a number of important local festivals. Stages had been erected in the squares of most of the small villages together with temporary seating. Iron railings ran the length of pavements, and impromptu barriers had been created by upending bins and nailing pieces of misshapen wood together. Local banks and some of the larger vineyards had draped banners from the sides of the buildings. Despite the festive trappings the only things that moved in the slow heat of the day were the shadows that unfurled across the baked tarmac.

We stopped at a garage, and while Tanya and Peter asked for directions, I studied a collage of pictures that had been pinned to the wall. They turned out to be entries into the region's annual photographic competition, and there was one common theme – bulls. There were pictures of groups of local men wearing cowboy hats and frilly white shirts sitting proudly astride their horses. And in between them, at about saddle height, I could make out the heads of baby bulls. Their horns had been decorated with colourful ribbons and streamers, but there was still menace in their dark eyes.

As I switched my attention from photo to photo, I was able to follow the various processions as they'd entered the villages. Gaggles of teenage boys had leapt from the pavements and darted between the legs of the horses. They appeared freeze-framed on the photographic montage pulling at bridles, ducking past hooves and even commando-rolling across the cobbles. For whatever misguided reason, they were determined to get at the bulls. And as my eyes flicked to the final photos, the inevitable happened – the protective cordon of horses broke and the young bulls ran free. One youngster was caught on camera clutching a horn with one hand and waving at his friends with the other. Both his feet were off the ground but such was his nonchalance that it appeared little more than the local equivalent of a skateboarder showing off by clinging to the bumper of a car and hitching a high-octane lift.

'That's the first French festival I've been glad to miss,' I commented as we drove away.

'I'm not sure we've missed it yet,' said Tanya, pointing at a banner that hung from the branches above the road. It read, 'Beware – bulls on the loose.'

We drove deeper into the countryside. The road became ever narrower and more unkempt. Peter slowed the car to a walking pace as we negotiated potholes and bumps, stirring dust into a cloud that enveloped the landscape. Eventually, kilometres from the nearest village – and hopefully the nearest bull – we arrived at Mas d'Espanet. The vineyard was deserted. There were two old barns with crumbling brick walls, a forlorn table-tennis table with holes in the net, and a rambling farmhouse. The noise from the engine stirred a cockerel and then a dog and finally Denys, the vigneron, emerged from the house.

He was a short man, about forty, and wore trainers and dirty, loose-fitting jeans. His hair was tinged red – the colour of the local soil – and he gave a big grin, revealing a glinting silver tooth. We shook his dry, coarse hand, and he led us around the vineyard, showing us the old goat shed that he was converting into a *cave*, explaining how the cool climate mirrored the Hermitage-producing area in the Rhône, and then introduced us to his long-limbed, dark-haired wife, Agnès, who dwarfed him.

At times I think they wondered what we were doing there. We nodded when they explained about tannic reactions and measuring the extractability of the anthocyanin, and even managed to ask the odd semi-knowledgeable question, but it was clear we were not the experienced bar owners they'd expected. Even so, after the tour they invited us in for some food.

I have never found lunching with the French easy. First there's the language barrier, which means that the two hours or so spent around the table resemble an oral exam. Secondly while the manners may be relaxed, the food is treated with great respect. Each course is beautifully presented and then analysed as it is eaten – which wine is the best accompaniment? Which herbs have been used? Does the sauce complement the meat? There is an innate and intense desire to discuss the food, and usually my palate and vocabulary are woefully inadequate for the task.

Agnès had laid out a variety of dishes on the table – a dense-looking pâté, a whole chicken still in its roasting pan, a green salad, what appeared to be a nut tart and three goat's cheeses on the verge of implosion. Confusing matters still further, there was a jug of pale-coloured juice and five different bottles of wine. 'Help yourself,' said Agnès.

In England I would have just heaped a selection of everything on to my plate, but this was France and I knew better. So instead I copied Denys, pouring myself a large glass of the juice and diluting it with a little bit of water. 'It's pasteurised grape juice,' explained Agnès. 'We make some every year at harvest time. It's refreshing and good for cleansing the palate before you eat.' Next I helped myself to some pâté, choosing the same red wine as our host to accompany it. Far from the coarse country fare I was expecting, it turned out to be a terrine of slow-roasted pork. The meat had been cooked until it fell from the bone and then pressed into a mould and covered with a cranberry crust. It was moist and drippingly tender, and after a suitable discussion about the intricacies of its preparation, our plates were changed and the chicken served with the lighter red wine.

The conversation shifted to a debate about the optimum hanging time for various birds after their slaughter. We discussed woodcocks and partridges and the free-range chicken we were eating. It was so fresh I could hear the clucking of the rest of the flock in the courtyard outside. Salad followed and then the cheeses, and so far – unlike Peter, who'd helped himself to an enormous slice of pistachio tart as a starter – I'd managed to eat a flawless French meal.

Unfortunately overconfidence got the better of me. Perhaps I was buoyed by my increasing ability to understand the conversation around the table. We chatted about the recent bull-running festivals, which were apparently a test of manhood for adolescent boys. The objective was to split the protective cordon of horses and pluck the garlands from the horns of the bulls. It was quite safe, Agnès assured us. At this point I helped myself to a large glass of the heavy red wine – thankfully Peter was driving – and cut myself a slice of smoked cheese. Denys smiled a silver-toothed grin and shook his head. 'With the smoked cheese, you have oaked white, and with the goat's cheese,' he said as he prodded his fork into the semi-liquid cheeses, 'the lighter white.'

I was more than bemused. I thought drinking red wine with cheese was one of the central tenets of world gastronomy, but my glass was removed in disgrace and replaced with a fresh one. It took only a sip to confirm who was right – the woody flavours of the white blended perfectly with the smoked cheese – and I contently cut myself another block and replenished my glass.

At 2 p.m. precisely lunch ended and Denys took us downstairs to the tasting area. He explained that at the moment the vineyard's wines were only classified as '*vin de pays*', not '*appellation contrôlée*'. Ten years ago the vignerons from the local cooperative had been given the opportunity to join the Appellation Origine Contrôlée but had chosen to opt out. Now Denys had to apply individually, a process that took years. In the meantime, although he had an excellent *terroir*, he was forced to sell his wines at a much lower price. 'Restaurants don't want to pay much more than a euro for *vin de pays*,' he confessed, as he called out to his son to fetch the rosé.

Moments later a lanky teenage boy loped into the room. His head was held uncomfortably in place by a neck brace and he had to turn his whole body to face us as he poured the wine.

'The rosés of this area are typically much heavier than this, but Agnès likes a much lighter pink wine and so I made her this one. It's the first year we've produced it,' confessed Denys. We all took a sip. Thanks to our recent refresher course at the Centre de Recherche, we were able to evaluate it with at least a hint of professionalism. In colour it was as pale as the coastal rosés, but to taste it was sharper and more acidic. On the nose, it was fresh and full of floral summer fruits. Perhaps the only disappointing thing was a lack of distinct regionality – or *tipicité*. But most importantly for us, since it was a *vin de pays*, we could buy it at a more than reasonable price.

As Denys's stiff-necked son disappeared to box up some wine, I asked what had happened.

'It's a broken collarbone,' said Denys, shaking his head.

'How did he break it?' asked Tanya.

'Playing with bulls,' replied Denys, as if it were a run–of–the–mill mishap, like falling off a bike.

Back at the bar, the revelries of the previous evening were long forgotten. Once again we were without customers and I scanned the *Midi Libre* for our big media break. Three whole pages were devoted to the rescue of a baby owl that belonged to a rare migratory breed – it was lost in the Luberon when it was supposed to be in the Sahara. There was also a double-page spread on how environmental changes were making the sea greener. It seemed unfair – thousands of words on owls and the sea but not a single column inch on La Vie en Rosé.

Each subsequent morning we read the paper cover to cover looking for favourable coverage. There was nothing. The only consolation was that the baby owl had started eating again and was reported to be getting stronger by the hour. And at least we were learning as we read, even if some of the knowledge we were picking up was a little bizarre. One afternoon I was playing boules with Peter and as yet another one of my shots fell hopelessly short of the target, he turned to me and grinned. 'It's fallen on a dead man.' Seeing my perplexed look, he nodded knowingly. 'You know – *tomber sur un mort.*'

I certainly didn't know, and by the end of the game I was beginning to think he'd become strangely obsessed by death. As I prepared for my final shot, he advised, '*La boule pour faire la mort,*' and then slapped me on the back as my boule success-fully sidled up to the *cochonnet*. 'Well done, you've killed off the game,' he said with a wink, still enjoying his own private joke as he tapped me on the head with a copy of *Midi Libre* before wandering off for a *pression*. Only when I examined the paper did I understand – there was a page given over to the most popular boules expressions, and Peter had memorised them all.

In La Vie en Rosé, anxious customer-free day followed

anxious customer-free day. John's regulars seemed to have lost all interest in us. Instead their attention was monopolised by the baby owl, which, as the day approached for its release back into the wild, continued to dominate the press and their conversation. Maps were plotted showing the route it would need to take to resume its natural migratory pattern, and all sorts of ornithological experts offered views on the likelihood of success.

Peter suggested donating €1 a bottle to the Maurice (the owl now had a name!) Release Fund, but even so we were lucky if we sold a glass a night and it was a struggle to keep occupied behind the bar. John was always on hand with a cigarette and a ready excuse for our difficulties, but his reasoning became weaker and weaker. I think I finally lost faith when he blamed another quiet night on the start of the summer sales – all the Nîmois were apparently too busy shopping to stop for a drink.

Making matters worse – although I may be imagining this – the residents of the street seemed to want us out and the key that clattered down on the string from the fourth-floor window flew with increasing velocity and regularity towards our heads. As the empty hours drifted by and the sport of key-dodging lost its appeal, irritable words and impatient shrugs crept into my behaviour. Gradually I realised the problem was worry.

Although it had seemed hard at the time, setting off on the adventure had been a relatively easy thing. The unknown is a supportive crutch and it was possible to believe whatever we wanted. Every time we'd cut a tie with our lives in London – giving up our jobs, selling the house, ignoring the advice of our friends – we'd done so with a sense of daring and with a swagger to our stride. But the longer the adventure continued, the more reality crept into my thinking. Barring our honeymoon period in Uzès, our high concept of running France's first rosé bar had been a failure.

Unless the long-promised press coverage finally materialised – which was unlikely given that all the papers were concentrating on a campaign to ban hunting on the day of Maurice's release – we would have to leave Nîmes, and what then? For how long could we stumble from bar to bar searching for the right formula? Standing in the empty street outside Murphy's Bar, it seemed that the hardest thing about an adventure was not setting off but knowing when to give up. And yet I still clung to the hope that in the end the gods might reward blind faith.

Two days later we sat having lunch with John Murphy. He picked at his *salade niçoise*, taking drags from a smouldering cigarette between mouthfuls. People passed in the street and waved a cheery hello to their favourite *Irlandais*, and John called a greeting back – 'Hello there, *ma chérie*' or '*Bonjour* to you too' – saluting the person concerned with his fork. Over our two weeks in his bar I'd developed a grudging respect for John. Since our initial run-in, he'd been nothing but helpful, always finding time to talk to us and thinking of ways to improve our trade.

I'd also appreciated just how hard he worked. He shut every night when the last customer left and was up early the next day swabbing down the floors, putting out the tables, taking stock and propping open his eyelids with tendrils of smoke. His bar was a one-man show, and he lent his company to loners and hugged regulars as he struggled to eke a living from the feeble Nîmois economy.

'Even the Catholics in Nîmes behave like Protestants,' confessed John, as he forked a boiled egg into his mouth and gave a yellow-toothed grin. Perhaps it was just fear of failure that had led him to shout at us on our first evening.

In any event, in the absence of any press coverage, we'd decided to head south to the sea. Following the collapse of our plans for the summer in Aix, we'd searched in an ever-extending circle from Claire's old house in Montpellier and almost by accident we'd alighted on Uzès and Nîmes. Now, with over a month's experience, we needed to gamble. Our best chance to sell rosé had to be amid the palm trees and the glitz and the glamour of the Côte d'Azur rather than in the Midi, didn't it?

And so we ate with John in the sunshine and grudgingly agreed that Nîmes probably wasn't ready for La Vie en Rosé – after all, it barely tolerated Murphy's Bar. John shrugged his shoulders as if to say there was no accounting for taste and told us the story of the most popular place in town. It was an Irish pub run by a Frenchman. It sold the most beer in Nîmes and had been artificially created in one weekend thanks to a crate full of goodies supplied by Guinness, containing all sorts of Irish bric-a-brac, a mock-traditional Gallic fascia for the bar and a box of folk CDs with instructions on what music to play to maximise drinking revenue. The owner didn't speak a word of English and had paid thousands of euros for the privilege of having his pub 'Irished', and the French, they loved it.

We finished our food and said our goodbyes in the local fashion. For me, this meant kissing a gorilla of an Irishman with nasal-hair issues. Our cheeks met and his stubble grated against my skin. 'À bientôt, Jamie, and good luck,' said John in his deep Irish drawl. He left us finishing the wine in the restaurant, and his cowboy boots clicked away down the street. Later, as we passed Murphy's Bar for a final time, we watched as he put out the tables, opened up the doors and prepared for business. We waved, but John didn't see.

13

Tanya's Coat of Many Colours

As we left Nîmes, passing under the shadow of the crumbling Roman Arena, Tanya and Peter were apparently upbeat, looking forward to the next adventure. It was the end of June, golden fields of sunflowers bloomed at every turn, lavender blazed purple, and the land breathed a heady scent of herbs, but I couldn't shake a feeling of dissatisfaction. We'd spent the whole of last summer racing from hotel to hotel, packing and unpacking suitcases, and by the time we'd returned to London we'd vowed that if we came to France again, we'd avoid such an itinerant lifestyle. But we'd been forced once again to become travellers, and however beautiful our surroundings, it was unsettling.

Since Aix, our lives had been so full of incident that we had barely discussed how Hervé's little joke had affected our lives. We'd simply had to get on with things and salvage something from the summer. I suspected that Tanya and Peter were probably as uneasy as I was about how events had turned out, but to discuss these feelings seemed somehow ungrateful. We were living a life that would make many of our contemporaries back in London envious, and so we all buried our concerns and waited for our fortunes to turn.

We'd agreed that for the rest of the summer our focus would

be to find a permanent base for La Vie en Rosé, and while we searched we would try and hold as many two-week rosé festivals as possible – as we'd learnt in Uzès, persuading bars to host us for a short period was far easier than asking to spend the summer. But even so I couldn't shake a sense of foreboding – what if it all went wrong again? I needn't have worried, because hope was about to arrive from an unusual source – a shopping expedition.

For weeks I'd been promising Tanya a present as a reward for giving up smoking and as a small consolation for the pain of the *méduse* sting, and ever since her clothes antennae had been twitching. She'd pause as we passed shops, appraising the goods inside with a swift glance and then moving on with a shake of the head. Pretty boutiques glinting with bejewelled clothes were rejected out of hand and gradually I came to realise there was a slight discrepancy between my idea of a suitable gift and hers.

But then, two hours' drive to the south-east of Nîmes, as we were on the motorway heading towards the Côte d'Azur, the antennae began to pick up a signal. To our right was the village of La Cadière d'Azur. It sat perched on a rocky outcrop, just kilometres from the sea, in the heart of Bandol wine country, equidistant from Marseille and Toulon. The vineyard of Domaine Ott sheltered in the valley beneath, and it was here the previous summer that we'd discovered the rosé of the stars – according to the slick press pack, Kate Moss and David Beckham were partial to a glass of Ott rosé.

As the road climbed on the approach to the village, the view unfolded below. It was like sitting on a plane just after take-off watching as the earth morphed into a toy town. Low Provençal farmhouses – *mas* – were liberally scattered amid the vines, tractors inched across the land, and in the distance the blue sky merged with the Mediterranean. The road looped in a one-way system below La Cadière, affording a final glimpse of palm and pine before curling into the top of the village, past a pottery and several artists' houses.

A roadside sign advised we were about to enter '*un village Provençal*' but how anybody could fail to realise this for themselves was beyond me. Tiny cobbled alleys fed off the main street, ducking under stone arches and winding towards the summit of the town. Unusually there was not really a square, just a widening of the road, freeing enough space for a row of plane trees, terraces for a couple of bars and a restaurant. There was a small market, not the type of all-singing, all-dancing markets so typical of France, just two or three tables loaded with fresh fish and fruit.

But there was a distinct lack of any clothes shops. Tanya's sixth sense for shopping appeared to have failed her and so I thought La Cadière would just be a convenient stopping-off point, somewhere to rest for an hour before we headed further east. But in just sixty minutes the village captured our hearts. It began when Peter discovered a bakery that he declared must be the best *boulangerie* in France. The entrance was raised up above street level and accessed by a flagstone staircase bordered by an iron railing draped with bougainvillea. Tied amid the lush purple flowers were bunches of dried Provençal herbs, and attached to the wall were several blackboards listing all the artisanal breads. 'Good food is all about the anticipation,' said Peter happily, as he climbed these steps and dipped his hand into the basket full of seeds that was being used as an improvised doorstop.

Inside, the shop didn't disappoint. There was every different type of bread imaginable – baguettes stacked together and leaning at precarious angles as if craning to catch a glimpse of prospective purchasers, round rustic loaves encrusted with hazelnuts or dusted with poppy seeds, dry rye breads and even some Italian ciabatta scattered with green olives – but what excited Peter were the two glass counters full of cakes and pastries. The layered raspberry and strawberry gateaux were so immaculately and intricately made they were almost too beautiful to eat. Next to them was a multi-layered *feuilleté* bursting with cream and a line of mini marzipan pigs hungrily facing a selection of *tartes* – *aux pommes, aux pêches* and, Peter's favourite, *aux abricots.*

Each item was arranged with the utmost care – the pastries and cakes were gently spot-lit, and the supporting cast of warm breads and croissants were positioned prominently under the noses of customers. Together they combined to give an irresistible sensory performance. The smell of the baking dough, the golden glow of the ovens and the rows upon rows of sweet pastries quite overwhelmed Peter and he reached into one of the many baskets that ran the length of the counter and started munching on a miniature cookie quite oblivious to the fact that he hadn't paid for it. It took a promise to return, a slice of *tarte aux abricots* and a miniature *pain au raisin* for us to eventually bribe him outside.

Tanya led us away following a siren song that neither Peter nor I could hear. We passed a dark-fronted building with a couple of battered tables and chairs outside. Written above the door was the following inscription: '*Cercle des travailleurs, cercle privé, carte obligatoire. Fondé 1884.*' 'I think it's the old Communist Party headquarters,' said Peter as we climbed the cobbled street, past the butcher's and the village shop. Just ahead of us was our destination. A headless mannequin stood in the street with a scarf wrapped round its neck, and pinned to the window were excerpts from old magazines showing women with the high permed hair of the 1980s and wearing oversized coats. Peter and I glanced at each other. It didn't look promising, but Tanya was already inside.

The owner, Valérie, sat at a loom twice the size of a grand piano. Threads of different material were stretched across the wood, and they hummed as Valérie's feet played across the pedals, while her hands simultaneously tightened and twisted various handles. There were racks of thick, heavy, dark coats together with miscellaneous sculptures and paintings. Tanya began looking amid the rails, moving from coat to coat with the speed of someone flicking through a magazine.

In the far corner of the room, two old women were trying on woolly hats and looking at themselves in the full-length mirror. They had jewels on every finger, and heavy necklaces of pearls, which clattered together as they twirled on the catwalk in their heads. Their make-up was immaculate, and they'd each brought a separate pair of shoes with them to match with anything they bought. They slipped their high heels on and had a fantastic time debating what to me was an obvious question – was the weather too hot for the hats?

Meanwhile one fabric in particular had caught Tanya's attention. It hung from the wall above a workstation scattered with sketches. The predominant colour was a light sky blue, and threads of gold, silver, orange and pink had been woven into it. Valérie measured Tanya, and for the next half-hour they discussed making a coat from it – apparently the inspiration for the style and cut was Audrey Hepburn in *Breakfast at Tiffany's* – but of course the one thing they didn't discuss was the price. As she draped a tape round Tanya's waist Valérie explained that most of her clients were Parisians shopping for their winter wardrobe, hence the ongoing discussion in the corner about woolly hats.

Measurements complete, the price was handed discreetly to me on a piece of paper. Before I could object, Tanya pointed out that it was nearly the exact equivalent of three months' worth of cigarettes. And so the coat of many colours was commissioned.

As we stepped outside on to the street, my eye was caught by the empty shop opposite. Sheltering under an arch was a large, full-height oval window. The glass was dirty and covered with fly posters and it was difficult to see inside. Through a gap I managed to make out a cave-like interior, the size of an average living room. Peter, Tanya and I stood in a row and looked at the shop and then at each other.

'Interesting,' said Peter, 'very interesting.'

'And it's thanks to my new coat that we found it,' added Tanya.

It's amazing how quickly the brain can work. Within moments, rather than looking at a dusty, run-down shop, a picture of a French nirvana had appeared in my head. Since Uzès I'd been anticipating a disagreement with Tanya. In Place aux Herbes, I'd discussed with Tom, the owner of the delicatessen and coffee shop opposite La Renaissance, the difficulties of purchasing an existing French business and had concluded that the expense of buying a bar rather than setting one up from scratch was too great. However, I knew that if Tanya's eyes had alighted on a pretty property in the shade of some plane trees, she might have easily fallen for the place and disregarded the risks.

But now we appeared to have found another option and a relatively risk-free one. The shop was so small a refit could be carried out reasonably cheaply, and even if La Vie en Rosé didn't succeed, at least the property would hold its value. I glanced around and ascertained that there were no bars within 50 metres. And having satisfied myself that government legislation wouldn't prevent us setting up a new bar here, images from our earlier stroll around La Cadière played across my mind – the village shop full of expensive wines from all over France, the bottles of rosé lined up on the butcher's counter, the delicatessen with half-bottles of Sauternes positioned next to the foie gras. There was a gentle air of affluence; in fact, the only thing missing was the Côte d'Azur staple of a *salon de chien-toilettage*, or dog-grooming salon.

My brain kept working and within seconds I'd stripped away the dirty glass and opened up the cave-like interior to the elements. I had installed a small counter and a couple of fridges and mentally arranged six sets of tables and chairs on the pavement sheltering under pink umbrellas. After another couple of moments of reflection twenty or so satisfied customers materialised in my imagination chatting happily in the sun as they sipped on different shades of rosé.

The village had everything we wanted. It was busy but not overrun by tourists, and small but hopefully still large enough to maintain some life through the winter months. It was about 4 kilometres from the coast and had easy access to major cities like Aix.

'It is very interesting,' repeated Tanya as she returned from her personal reverie.

'Don't get too excited,' I cautioned as I pictured where we would hang the blackboard.

We knew enough about France not to rush to the nearest estate agent and subject ourselves to the horrific level of commission they levied. Instead – at Peter's suggestion – we returned to the *boulangerie* and tried to discover who owned the property. The young girl who had served us earlier had been replaced by a middle-aged woman with dyed blonde hair tied back tightly into a bun. She wore perhaps a little too much make-up, but it had been immaculately applied, as if she were about to go on a date rather than serve bread. Completing the ensemble was a tight black T-shirt with the words 'Lick me' emblazoned across it. If it was an ironic reference to working in such close quarters with so many cakes, I think it went over the heads of most of her customers.

We purchased an enormous cream *feuilleté*, and then by buying an additional assortment of cookies and miniature Danish pastries, we finally elicited the necessary information – the empty shop was owned by Madame Bérard, wife of René Bérard, the owner of the famous Hostellerie Bérard, which was located at the other end of the village.

Peter nodded his head as the information was relayed. 'I knew it was somewhere around here. I've read all about it. René is one of the region's most famous chefs. He's really keen on local seasonal ingredients and traditional Provençal menus. Apparently half of the hotel is housed in an eleventh-century monastery, and there's a main restaurant for the serious foodies and a brasserie. Come on.' He beamed as he bustled off down the street, leaving me in little doubt that he was more excited by the discovery of this culinary Mecca than our chance to buy a property in the village.

Outside the *hostellerie*, the menu of the day was set in a glass case on top of a golden bookstand...*Saint-Jacques en coquille, pigeon crapaudine, Lotte enrubannée au jambon italien, gnocchi de potiron.* Peter savoured the words as if the dishes had just been set before him.

The fascia was painted in fresh red paint, and through a large window we could see a sitting room full of comfortable leather chairs, low wooden tables and heavy glossy books about food and wine. And at the back of the room, at the end of a short corridor, we glimpsed the white tablecloths of the restaurant. Tanya made us all touch the wooden doorframe for good luck and then we entered and asked the receptionist – a young girl – for Madame Bérard.

If all went smoothly, we were moments away from opening negotiations to own our bar. I knew that I had to be hard-headed, forget the emotional lure of the village and treat the whole discussion as a business transaction, but at the same time the property was perfect – it was just the right size and in a wonderful location perched above the vineyards of Bandol.

'Madame is not available at the moment,' smiled the receptionist. 'If you leave me your details, I will get her to call you. May I ask what it is about?'

Explaining our idea succinctly in English was difficult enough, in French it was nearly impossible. The temptation, as always, was to fall back on familiar words and phrases, and so I began to tell the whole story of the hunt for France's palest rosé and our determination to run our own bar. Perhaps I hoped that by displaying such commitment to rosé I'd gain some emotional sympathy and somehow further our cause. Instead all that happened was that a perplexed look spread across the receptionist's face.

I realised I had committed one of my common errors when speaking French – mimicking Tanya and Claire. While both of them speak the language much better than me, they do so in all-too-expressive accents. For the girls, it seemed to work terribly well, but when I attempted to copy them, it sounded like I was singing out of tune. And so the receptionist simultaneously listened and tried to figure out how she would explain to Madame Bérard about the curious Englishman with the unusually high-pitched voice. Finally I got to the point and, slipping into my best gruff monotone, asked whether the shop was available to rent or buy. Waiting for the response reminded me of my A-level results finally arriving after weeks of worry.

'Yes, I think so, but as I say you'll have to wait to speak to Madame Bérard. If you leave your number, I'll get her to call you later today.'

Even my impersonation of a French-speaking eunuch hadn't ruined our prospects. Our tight jaws relaxed and smiles spread across our faces. Tanya and I turned to leave, but Peter wasn't finished. Brandishing a copy of the menu, he asked, '*Qu'est ce que c'est le pigeon crapaudine? Et la millefeuille liquide au chocolat et au safran, vous pouvez m'expliquer un peu plus?*' Peter's French still wasn't great, but when his tummy demanded, it more than rose to the occasion.

'I know we've had lunch,' he argued as we pulled him away, 'but this is more like high tea. We could at least try the *légende caramel.*'

With a car full of pastries from the *boulangerie* and a disconsolate Peter still dreaming of the *légende caramel*, we left La Cadière and headed east. For the rest of the afternoon every time our mobile rang we scrambled to answer before the rings died away. Inevitably it was either buried at the bottom of Tanya's handbag or mislaid under a crate of rosé. For anxious moments we flung maps, books and sunglasses around the car, and then when we finally grasped the mobile, it was either a top-up reminder or a call from England rather than any news from Madame Bérard.

Our destination was Cannes – even if our negotiations with the Bérards were successful, we would still need at least a couple more temporary bases while the refit progressed. And in Cannes we had a contact – the previous year we'd enjoyed a few drinks in a bar called the Saint-Antoine. It was located at the unfashionable end of La Croisette, opposite the bus station, and I could still picture it well – a row of motorbikes had been parked in the street outside, and high above their handlebars the name of the bar had glowed in neon-red lettering. In the shadow cast by this electric haze, rows of multicoloured signs advertised chariot racing, the state lottery and a *tabac*.

As I recalled, the bar was split into two. One side housed the *tabac* and had a conventional terrace with seats arranged around low tables; the other side was chaotic. There was no formal terrace, and the interior and exterior flowed together as drinkers stumbled between the series of shoulder-height round tables on which the regulars rested their elbows. People had stood in great gossipy groups swilling cloudy yellow pastis and small glasses of rosé.

Then there was the owner, Jean-Claude, who in the space of one evening we'd become friendly with. He had a bushy moustache, a prominent nose and a pair of glasses positioned high on his forehead to control his sweeping grey hair. When we first saw him, he was hunched over a game of dice and he'd reminded us all of Omar Sharif. Within moments of our arrival, he'd explained that he was Armenian. He correctly guessed that Tanya had an Eastern European background – her mother is a Lithuanian who was raised in Canada before moving to England when she met Tanya's father – and as a result offered us a drink on the house. We'd spent the rest of the evening standing on the street, drinking and laughing with an eclectic collection of nationalities, learning words in a random selection of languages from Polish to Portuguese. It had been among the best evenings of the previous summer. The only question was, would Jean-Claude remember us?

It was getting dark as we pulled up outside the Saint-Antoine. We parked by the bus station and left Peter's car, Betty, amid a crowd of movie stars – the wall above her had been converted into a huge mural – Fred Astaire and Ginger Rogers shared a clinch, R2-D2 and C-3PO peered out to sea, and Batman and Robin chased Mickey Mouse from window to window. Just as we were walking away from the car towards the bar, we heard the muffled ring of the phone from the back seat. 'Madame Bérard,' I mouthed as I scrambled for the keys.

On the tenth ring I found the phone and my fingers slipped nervously across the numbers for the answer button.

'*Allo. C'est* Valérie,' said a gentle female voice. For a moment I was disappointed, but then I was relieved – at least it wasn't a no.

I passed the handset to Tanya to confirm the pick-up details for her new coat in two weeks' time. By then doubtless we would have heard from Madame Bérard, but in the meantime we had to convince Jean-Claude to let us run a rosé festival. We turned back towards the Saint-Antoine, with Peter and me gently teasing Tanya about her new purchase by whistling the theme from *Joseph and His Amazing Technicolor Dreamcoat*.

14

The Saint-Antoine

It wasn't quite the answer we were expecting. Jean-Claude immediately recognised us from the previous summer and spent ten minutes listening to our idea for a two-week rosé festival. He then stubbed out his cigarette and pushed his glasses back on to his forehead. 'Do you play chess?'

Peter and I nodded and Tanya shook her head.

'We'll have a game,' said Jean-Claude, leading us inside.

He looked older than I remembered, more troubled. His forehead was creased, his cheeks crisscrossed by wrinkles, and his skin a yellowy colour rather than a rich brown. There may have been a gentle flicker of humour in his nut-coloured eyes when he suggested the chess, but when I looked again it was gone.

I assumed that given his experience importing three-dimensional Thai chessboards, Peter would be the better player and so I let him take the seat opposite Jean-Claude. Around us was a curious meeting of cultures. Behind the bar a Budweiser sign proudly proclaimed, 'It Buds for you.' A Stars and Stripes flag was pinned to one of the walls, and hanging over our heads were photos of semi-clad women reclining over the backs of Harley Davidsons. But the American memorabilia was counter-balanced by the heavy smell of French tobacco, the yellow Ricard ashtrays, the Kronenbourg 1664 beertap and the small

TV mounted on a high bracket showing the latest chariot race.

And around us was a collection of faces so typical of France it would have pleased even the most demanding of casting directors. Features were enlarged as if transplanted from giants. People had ears like saucepans, and bulbous noses that years of drinking had left flushed and pockmarked. Alcohol flowed through oversized veins and meandered across faces, trailing ruddy red tributaries across rounded cheeks. Blue eyes as distinctive as those of any contact-wearing model stared out from beneath faded caps, and chest hair was displayed and decorated with chains rather than hidden. One man in particular seemed to believe that he was the reincarnation of Elvis. He had swept-back dyed dark hair, a cream suit, wore aviator sunglasses, and his protruding pelvis swung towards us like a radar.

Peter and Jean-Claude were busy setting up the pieces and the early signs were not good. Peter was struggling to remember whether it was the knight or the bishop that went next to the castle, and once Jean-Claude had corrected him, he turned and whispered to me, 'Is it the queen or the king that goes on its own colour?'

It was all I could do not to shove Peter out of his seat and take over, but it was too late – Jean-Claude had already made his first move and was looking expectantly at Peter. The game was taking place on a raised dais at the back of the bar and from my seat I could see into the stockroom. Wine boxes of rosé were piled to the ceiling and yet when Jean-Claude had offered us a drink he'd poured from a bottle. The mystery was soon solved when a member of staff topped up a serving bottle from one of the boxes. If we were going to sell wine in the Saint-Antoine, our prices were going to have to be very cheap.

I turned my attention back to the game. Peter's last two moves had prodded a couple of pawns forward, but he hadn't noticed that Jean-Claude had freed space for his queen to slide right across the board. It was a basic error, and because I'd spotted it I was sure Jean-Claude had. He could checkmate Peter with his next move, which was worrying, because although nothing had been said, there was a possibility that Peter was playing for our right to sell rosé. Instead of moving his queen, Jean-Claude advanced a pawn and once again I thought I saw wry humour in his dark-brown eyes.

After his early slip Peter's form improved. Both players established solid defensive formations, and as the game progressed Jean-Claude began to talk to us about the Saint-Antoine. The bar was famous in Cannes. It used to be a favourite with US marines and also bikers, who travelled for hundreds of miles to visit. Now it was notorious for selling more pastis than any other bar in town. It was open every day of the year from 6 a.m. to 2 a.m., and its customers consumed 3,000 bottles of the cloudy yellow liquid a year. I did some quick maths – roughly ten bottles a day didn't sound that much, but when I considered that each dash of the spirit was diluted by a glassful of water, my respect for the livers of the regulars returned. Rosé sales were also high, running at about sixty bottles a day.

'How much do you intend to charge for a glass?' said Jean-Claude, as he deprived Peter of another piece.

'About four euros,' I replied.

Jean-Claude almost snorted his drink over the board. 'And how much have you paid per bottle?'

'Between six and ten euros,' I answered.

Jean-Claude pulled his glasses over his eyes and scratched his head in distress. 'We buy our wine at a euro a litre and sell it at a euro fifty a glass. How can I work with you?'

While I searched for an answer Peter pulled off what appeared to be the best move of the match. With his remaining knight he pinned Jean-Claude's king on one square and his queen on the other. 'Check,' said Peter with delight.

Our pricing discussion had distracted Jean-Claude and he

turned quickly back to the board. A few of the customers also began to show an interest – Jean-Claude losing at chess was clearly an event. An old waif of a man nearly fell off his bar stool, clutched his pastis to his chest and then negotiated his way across the room like a disorientated crab, zigzagging in our general direction but never once able to take a forward step.

A peroxide blonde with fishnets that looked like they'd been shredded by a school of piranhas followed. Her rosé sloshed on to the floor as she teetered up the steps balancing precariously on the point of her stilettos. And finally, completing the threesome, was a middle-aged man with the dress sense of a rock-band roadie. He had a narrow, unshaven face, long dark hair that fell in curls beneath his shoulders and wore nothing but a tattered waistcoat on his upper torso. Battered drainpipe jeans and ragged trainers with their ends cut off to expose his big toes completed the unusual fashion statement.

Jean-Claude looked around at his new audience, apparently unperturbed at the trap he'd fallen into on the chessboard. 'This,' said Jean-Claude, shaking hands with the rock-band roadie, 'is our rosé expert. He never drinks anything else.' We all nodded a friendly *bonsoir* but received nothing but a cold stare in return.

Jean-Claude turned back to the game and, as he was obliged to, moved his king and surrendered his queen. 'Marvellous,' whispered Peter, grinning like a child prodigy about to defeat a grand master. I hoped he wasn't jeopardising our chances by playing too well.

'If you can provide cheap wine, say at two euros a bottle, and sell it at two euros a glass, then maybe your idea will work. You might even be able to offer some more expensive wines,' said Jean-Claude, unperturbed by Peter's continuing revival.

It didn't sound a bad suggestion. If sixty bottles of rosé were sold a day in the Saint-Antoine, there was clearly a good market for us to try and build on. I nodded and shook Jean-Claude's hand. He smiled, extinguished his cigarette and then moved his bishop the entire length of the board, crossing the square from which Peter had just moved his knight. 'Checkmate.'

The next day, as the sun peaked above the still sea, Tanya, Peter and I made our way to work. We paused for a coffee and a croissant and watched a lone water-skier cut across the broad sweep of the bay. He lassoed a small trawler in his wake and then as the speedboat cut its engine sank from sight. Behind us, the only traffic was a municipal road-sweeper brushing the kerbs with its mechanical arms, but as we neared the Saint-Antoine the cobbled streets of the old town slowly awoke.

Waiters, shop assistants and beach boys spilled from the train station on to the streets having just enjoyed the best commute in the world – Beaulieu-sur-Mer, Antibes, Juan-les-Pins, Cannes – what price a view of the sea rather than someone else's sweaty armpit? It must have been akin to flicking through the pages of a holiday brochure – second by second a different alluring image would be framed in the train window, a slice of still sea, a crescent of sand, a shady tennis court, palms and pines.

At Jean-Claude's request we were set up and ready to serve by 10 a.m. He'd allocated us a small corner of the terrace at the front of the bar. As well as serving the regulars, we hoped to be able to attract pedestrians from La Croisette – the un-disputed *grande dame* of French promenades, where only the palm trees were longer-limbed than the models strutting below. Admittedly we were at the wrong end and our view of the sea was frequently obscured by buses pulling into the station oppo-site, but we could just about see the Palais des Festivals, where Hollywood's finest paraded every year. And it was only a couple of minutes' walk to the grand old hotels with their resplendent euro-swallowing terraces and pontoons stretching into the sea bedecked with umbrellas and millionaires. 'It certainly beats a dirty alley in Nîmes,' concluded Peter, as he watched a roller-blader overtake a Ferrari.

Our arrival created a carnival atmosphere in the Saint-Antoine. Despite the early hour, people were drinking liberally and joking and laughing at the pink fête that had appeared outside. The moment we uncorked our first bottle of wine, the regulars stumbled over to us. They tasted wine after wine without any of the rigmarole we'd become accustomed to. However large the glass I poured, it was dispatched in a gulp and the empty glass was immediately proffered for more. Sniffing and swilling were foreign nature to the regulars of the Saint-Antoine, and spitting would presumably result in being barred for life. Once the free tasting concluded, many of the regulars bought glasses and for the rest of the morning happily drank our wine. But the man whom Jean-Claude had introduced as the Saint-Antoine's rosé expert sat at the bar, bare-chested apart from his waistcoat, and refused all offers of a *dégustation*.

In a city where poodles wear diamonds and menus are in Russian – oligarchs tend to reach for their wallets rather than smile in amusement at a starter of mixed tomatoes for €100 – it wasn't long until we encountered the high life. Always alert to English voices, I eavesdropped on one of the conversations taking place at a nearby table. Two middle-aged men with tight jeans and bright shirts stretched over potbellies sat talking about rain.

'Of course I wouldn't have minded, but it was the wrong sort,' said one of them as he stretched for his drink, revealing a heavy gold Rolex. 'It's blown in from the Sahara at this time of year, and even a small shower like last night causes problems. It takes the crew hours to clean the sand from the plane.'

The other man shook his head, stretched his arms above his head and showed me his Cartier.

Before I had a chance to pluck some rosé from the ice bucket, Peter had crossed to them with a bottle of Sancerre and some sympathy. 'Dirty rain, it's a real bugger,' he said as he poured them a taste and settled down to discuss the average yearly rosé consumption onboard a Learjet.

By mid-morning the city was full of map-clutching tourists. They strolled the streets with cameras bouncing against their oversized stomachs, studying menu after menu. And as the clock struck twelve the Saint-Antoine began to empty. The zigzagging crab-cum-man who'd watched the chess the previous evening came hurtling from the bar and cannoned off two lamp-posts like a pinball before disappearing sideways down a side street. And men who'd spent the entire morning dispatching glass after glass of pastis clambered on to mopeds waving farewell to white-gloved policemen.

The afternoon passed slowly. Jean-Claude played dice and chess with the few remaining customers, and we tried with limited success to attract people from the street. By early evening the bar started to fill again. The same customers who'd spent the morning in the Saint-Antoine resumed their stations, dressing for the evening session by wetting back their hair and changing their shirts. Soon lively bubbles of conversation floated from the bar. They were all a little drunker than earlier in the day and the humour was bawdier. 'You look so pretty in pink,' slurred a young woman as she wobbled on her bar stool.

Her boyfriend reached out and embraced me in a hug, kissing me on the cheek. 'You know men wear pink for a reason,' he laughed and let me go, patting me on the bottom dismissively.

As the sun faded, super-yachts bigger than naval frigates returned to port, and the old wrapped themselves in Chanel and promenaded along the front. Music blared from bars and open-top cars, and as darkness finally fell, the bay was lit by showers of golden fireworks. Short skirts and high heels clicked past us on La Croisette. The young were interested in discos not La Vie en Rosé and by 10 p.m. Jean-Claude advised us to pack up. We'd sold nearly twenty bottles of rosé in a day, the equivalent of our entire week's takings in Nîmes, but we couldn't really celebrate until we had heard from Madame Bérard.

★

During the following week we left further messages at the Hostellerie Bérard. And while we waited for a response, our rosé sales climbed. Our arrival every morning was greeted by a rowdy round of applause, and as I filled up the ice buckets and carried them through the bar, people patted me on the back, crying, '*Bonjour*, Monsieur Le Rosé.' And soon the saying was taken up by the whole bar: 'Monsieur Le Rosé *est arrivé*.'

It would be nice to think that La Vie en Rosé had finally been truly appreciated, that we'd found our niche among men who appreciated good wine but who'd rather drink than sniff. However, I think the truth was that the regulars hadn't seen anything quite as funny as our travelling rosé festival for quite some time. They were forever wandering over and offering advice, designed as much to amuse them as to assist us.

'You'd sell a lot more wine if you moved up the street to Rue Saint-Antoine – the bars are much better there,' advised an overfriendly customer, clutching me with one hand and a pastis with the other. 'This bar is rubbish.'

'But Jean-Claude said that he sold sixty bottles a day,' I replied.

'Who's Jean-Claude?'

'The owner.'

'No, I am the owner,' insisted my new best friend, grinning wildly.

Seeing my perplexed look, Peter rescued me. 'Never argue with a drunk,' he whispered. 'Like your mother, they are always right.'

Exchanges like this were typical. Every day the bar was thronged full of the same crowd of people, spilling raucously on to the street. Glasses were never empty until the money ran out, and then a curious thing happened. The customers became the staff. Alcohol was such a prized commodity that people were prepared to work for it. One example of this was the piranha-tighted woman we'd met on the first night. She visited the bar perhaps three times a day, and on each occasion changed her clothes, putting on designer belts, garish miniskirts and stilettos like skyscrapers. Given the amount of money she spent on the rest of her wardrobe, I can only assume that the holed tights were a fashion statement.

In any event for our first two days in the Saint-Antoine, all she did was drink glass after glass – rosé, gin, pastis, whatever she could get her hands on. Then, with her purse empty, for the next two days she cleared glasses, took orders and served drinks. Her behaviour was typical – one day a regular would barrack us, the next he would be washing up our glasses and persuading people to buy from us.

It took Jean-Claude's son, Igor, to explain the situation to us: 'Cannes is a crazy place. The people who live here are mad – they see all the glitz and glamour and they spend like millionaires but they have nothing in the fridge.'

For bar novices like us, Igor proved to be a great source of information. He had short dark hair and his father's gentle manner. His girlfriend was American and he was keen to practise his English and so during quiet moments we sat and talked about the difficulties of running a bar like the Saint-Antoine.

When the family first bought the bar, they'd used Igor as a plant for two months prior to the purchase to check the takings matched the claims of the previous owner. Only when any possibility of fraud had been eliminated did they go through with the transaction. Igor told us this story in an unassuming manner, as if this sort of activity was an everyday part of the bar business.

I was still curious about the south of France Mafia, which Guy de Saint-Victor had mentioned at the London Wine Fair, and so I asked whether there was a problem in Cannes.

'No, not really. Whenever you open a bar you have incidents,' Igor replied. 'In our first week two men with knives sheathed to their forearms came in. I sprayed them with a pepper gun and that was that.'

Igor assured us there had been no trouble since and pointed out that rather than a machete-wielding Mafioso, the biggest threat to La Vie en Rosé was an accidental collision with our favourite regular – the zigzagging, sideways-walking crab. This scrawny old man was always sitting at the bar when we arrived in the morning. He looked somehow nicely dishevelled – his shoes were polished but his laces were undone, his shirt ironed but un-tucked, and some days he even wore a jacket, but it was beige and showed the dirt. It was as if someone had made an effort dressing him but then it had all come apart on his way to the bar.

For two and a half hours he moved only to add some extra water to his newly replenished glass of pastis. His smile grew wider and wider, and then when the clock struck twelve, he vacated – or fell from – his stool. We assumed that his wife awaited him at home, and that although she tolerated his drinking, she wouldn't accept him missing lunch. In any event his rubbery legs bowed under the sudden weight and he came careering from the bar as if he needed to reach some sort of critical velocity to stay upright.

And Igor was right – he was a danger. On a couple of occasions he'd shaved the edge of one of our tables, sending glasses crashing to the floor. For a moment he'd wobble on the spot, lurch this way and that like the bottles of wine he'd just disturbed, then gravity would pull him in the opposite direction and he'd typically right himself with the help of a parasol.

And so by the beginning of our second week in the Saint-Antoine, at the stroke of midday, we formed a protective barrier in front of our bar. We liked to think it showed we were getting the hang of the place.

15

La Vie en Jaune

Our walk to work every morning took us via the port and Tanya and I had fallen into the unfortunate habit of gazing at the super-yachts, purring over the polished wooden decks and counting the accoutrements of the rich – the Jacuzzis and the jet-skis. It was the Côte d'Azur version of property porn – dreaming of the freedom of setting sail for Monaco or Saint-Tropez and forgetting the reality of the tiny apartment we'd rented.

As we walked we speculated about smooth-talking our way on to one of these floating palaces. If we could just persuade one yacht owner to let us conduct a rosé tasting, then he might tell his friends. People who burnt cash for show in the casino wouldn't balk at a few crates of our champagne, and if the whole idea worked, it could be a useful sideline to our bar business.

One morning we found ourselves opposite a sleek silver boat that had dominated the harbour all week. It was long and broad and sat low in the water with a prow tapered to a point like the tip of an arrow. Standing on the stern, trying to stay out of the bright morning sun was a young man with flowing dark hair. Everything about him was a mess – his tie was at half mast, his shirt unbuttoned, his belt hung loosely from a single loop, and whereas one of his feet was cosseted in a red suede slipper, the other was bare.

I don't think Tanya could help herself. She was wearing a white sundress with silk pink roses sewn into the material, the sun was shining, and she was feeling pretty. In her hands she held a couple of bottles of Sancerre, which she was bringing to the bar to replenish our stock. And something about the youth and the dishevelled look of this particular boat owner removed the barrier that a million-pound bank balance usually erected between people. Tanya cocked her head and gave a flirtatious smile. Sunglass contact was instantly made, and for the hell of it she shouted across the water, 'Would you like to taste some rosé?'

The man removed his sunglasses, swayed slightly, tried to focus his eyes and then gave up and grabbed for the rail of the boat. He smiled broadly, put his sunglasses back on and said in English with a heavy Russian accent, 'Sure. Come back later with champagne.' He hung his head over the railing as if he was about to be sick. 'My name's Alexis,' he burped. 'As you can see, I had a late night last night.'

We were still inventing an impromptu Green Cross Code of the sea – don't get left alone with a playboy on a super-yacht, do mark up the champagne five times – when we arrived at the Saint-Antoine and found Peter facing a different form of temptation. Sitting outside hunched over a piece of paper with one of the regulars, Peter looked up at us with a beatific grin on his face. 'Guess what Fabrice is cooking today? Bouillabaisse.'

Ever since Peter had first visited the south of France, he'd raved about one dish more than any other – bouillabaisse. He dismissed the *marmite du pêcheur* happily served up to grinning tourists in most restaurants as a mere broth and an inferior imitation. According to Peter, bouillabaisse was no ordinary fish soup – it was the height of culinary perfection. As he pointed out, legend had it that Venus served bouillabaisse to her husband, Vulcan, to lull him to sleep before she consulted with Mars, and French cookery writers hailed it as the *soupe d'or* – golden soup

– a dish that achieved a magical synthesis of ingredients. Just the sight of the word 'bouillabaisse' on a restaurant menu made Peter swoon with desire. Typically it had to be ordered twenty-four hours in advance and to date we'd never been organised enough. And then there was the cost: bouillabaisse had started out its culinary life as the food of the poor, made from the remains of the fish the rich wouldn't eat, but in a restaurant in Cannes, a portion could easily have set Peter back €60, and even his persuasive stomach couldn't justify the cost.

But salvation for the salivating Peter had arrived in the form of a regular at the Saint-Antoine. Fabrice was a barrel of a man with long shaggy hair and a varying amount of facial hair – it ranged from sandpaper stubble to bedraggled beard, depending on the day and his mood. He was always trailed into the bar by his dog – a British bulldog called Howard, which he'd taken from a rescue centre. We'd learnt that he was a seaman who'd captained various commercial boats, but was now making his living skippering his own small fishing boat and selling his catch in the market every morning. 'Never trust big fish stalls,' he'd advised. 'None of it will be fresh. Always go to the sellers with the smallest selection.'

When we'd arrived in the Saint-Antoine, Fabrice had been quite shy, acknowledging our presence with a nod before taking a bar seat and ordering a beer. But as each day had passed we'd come to know him a little better. And now, judging by Peter's arm wrapped round Fabrice's shoulder, we'd reached the status of friends.

Tanya and I took adjoining seats and listened as Fabrice explained the intricacies of making bouillabaisse. 'The secret is all in the base – in French *"bouillir"* means "to boil", and this is what you have to do to the base. Take onions, tomatoes, olive oil, garlic, some little rock fish, a bouquet garni and, most importantly, some saffron. Other people add fennel seeds and orange zest,' cautioned Fabrice, 'but this isn't how the traditional dish is cooked.' He then listed the cooking time for the base — at least an hour of furious boiling — and the main fish that were to be added at the last moment — *saint-pierre* (John Dory), *tranches de congre* (slices of conger eel), *rougets grondins* (gurnet), *grosses rascasses* (large scorpion fish), *chapons* and *seiches*.

At this point Peter looked a little disconsolate — he couldn't translate the last two fish. To begin with, I didn't see the problem. I assumed he was going to take the recipe back to England with him and dream of the Med on a grey winter's day, so we could always check our dictionary later. But then as I watched Peter's continued attempts to understand, I finally clicked: he was intending to cook his own bouillabaisse that evening.

Tanya and I exchanged worried glances — the high price of living on the Côte d'Azur meant our apartment in Cannes was smaller than anything we'd stayed in to date. There was one bedroom, a small sitting room with a couch that Peter had made into his bed, and a tiny galley kitchen. Peter was rubbing his hands together in anticipation as he went through the final details with Fabrice — adding the potatoes, making the mouth-achingly hot *rouille* and toasting the croutons. 'Marvellous,' he repeated, as he ticked off each cooking stage on his list, not giving a moment's consideration to the fact our flat would smell for the rest of the week.

Later that evening, as I opened the door to our apartment block I detected faint traces of an unpleasant aroma, and as I mounted the stairs the smell became stronger and stronger. It pervaded the whole of the fourth floor of the building, seeping under doors, clinging to the fibres of sofas and curtains, infiltrating kitchens and bedrooms. Standing outside our flat, the smell was almost tangible. I sensed it creeping up my body and invading my pores. I entered, held my nose and exposed myself to the full blast of the aroma of boiled fish that was radiating from our kitchen.

Peter was standing before a massive pot with an equally

massive grin on his face. His white hair was projecting out at the most incredible angles as if the oil from the boiling fish had somehow become stuck to the strands. He wore a white apron, which was smeared with bones and blood, and his glasses were completely fogged up.

'Marvellous, you arrived just at the right point. It's time to press the base to extract all the juice.' Peter rolled up his sleeves, produced a gleaming new press that resembled a potato-masher, only much larger, and asked me to hold the pot steady.

'Where's Tanya?' I asked, wondering what I could use to clamp my nostrils together while I performed this task – would a paperclip do? Or would that hurt too much? Peter was too busy trying to find the right way to use his press to answer. 'Where's Tanya?' I enquired again.

'She left about twenty minutes ago,' said Peter, still fiddling with the press. 'She was trying to sell some champagne to the Russian boat owner you met.'

I headed down to the port and left Peter to finish our supper – he still had the larger fish to add to his bouillabaisse and then, if Peter was doing things authentically, once cooked he would remove them and serve the fish and the soup separately.

I was a little anxious at the thought of Tanya alone on the boat with Alexis, and I half walked, half ran to the marina. It was early evening and all the locals had emerged to parade along the front, so my progress was slowed by a menagerie of their pets – various jumper-wearing pooches and even a hairless cat being led on a jewel-encrusted lead.

I reached the harbour and anxiously scanned for signs of Alexis's silver boat. It was so low in the water it could easily have been hidden between two of the larger ships in port. But by the time I reached the end of the promenade, I'd still not located it. I jogged back down the row of yachts and then stood with my hands on my hips looking out to sea. Where had it gone, and more importantly where had Tanya gone?

My eyes followed a trail of disturbed water, and at the far end of the marina, I finally saw Alexis's boat. Its large engines were just cutting in as the sea opened up before it. The front of the boat reared from the water like a serpent ready to strike. It skipped over a couple of large incoming waves and the silver hull merged with the sea. For a couple of minutes all I could see was a tiny flashing red light on its stern, which winked a final goodbye and then disappeared.

While I was watching the silver boat vanish over the horizon, Tanya was busy closing a deal to sell two crates of champagne. As instructed and according to our agreed terms of supply to millionaires, she'd marked up the price by a multiple of five and agreed a time for delivery. She'd then toasted the deal with a glass of furiously bubbling pink champagne.

And this is how I found her, glass at her lips, back at the Saint-Antoine ensconced around a table with the two Englishmen who'd complained about their dirty planes on our first day in the bar. Once again they were dressed in lurid coloured shirts that fitted a little too tightly against their ample bellies. Jean-Claude was playing chess on a nearby table, with his glasses pushed high on his forehead and an expression of concentration on his face. Tanya passed him a flute of champagne and made space for me at the table.

'We were running a bit short for our trip to Majorca,' ventured one of Tanya's new clients.

'It's a short hop, but Ralf Schumacher's having a party and we thought it's worth stocking up and making the trip,' explained the other as they rose to leave. 'We'll see you on Friday to collect.'

I poured myself a glass from the remains of the bottle and relaxed in the sun. 'Come on,' said Tanya. 'Alexis is waiting.'

I pointed to the empty berth where the silver boat was usually docked. 'Alexis is at sea and I thought you were too.'

★

The champagne sale was the biggest single deal of our summer so far and the profits more than covered the cost of our flat for the rest of the week, so any sales on top went directly into our savings. To date, La Vie en Rosé had worked really well outside the Saint-Antoine. There had been enough interest from regulars to keep us busy, and we'd pulled in plenty of additional customers from the street. Our hopes were high for the remaining five days, and at the end of our time in Cannes we'd resolved to return to La Cadière d'Azur to pick up Tanya's coat of many colours and see in person the phone-a-phobic Madame Bérard.

But our final few days didn't progress as expected. Gradually our trade began to tail off and the regulars who'd been showing such a keen interest in rosé returned to their old drinking habits and ordered pastis. Tanya and I insisted the smell of bouillabaisse clinging to our clothes was putting people off, but Peter denied it. 'It's because they've already tasted every wine we have, so they now have to buy,' he argued, probably correctly.

The atmosphere also began to shift subtly. After our first week we'd decided that half of the customers in the bar were one step from heaven – like our friendly fisherman, Fabrice – and that the other half were only one step from the gutter (in fact some of them frequently fell into the gutter). But as the fierce heat of the July sun beat down on Cannes, drunkenness increasingly became the rule in the Saint-Antoine.

Late in our second week we watched as a large four-wheel drive pulled up by the kerb, obscuring our view of the fading sun. It was covered in the same dirty sand that had so upset our plane-owning English clients. The driver of the car entered the *tabac*, and the moment he was out of view, a small, grey-haired man shambled from inside the Saint-Antoine. His hair was full of gel and was combed over his scalp. He wore a loose-fitting shirt and trousers and a rough pair of plimsolls. Checking the owner was still absent, he inscribed obscenities with his finger on the dirty car door and then loped back into the bar, casting us an unpleasant sideways glance. In an apparently unrelated incident, the next morning when I was doing a stock-take I noticed that six bottles of rosé had gone missing.

Increasingly we had to rely on Jean-Claude's support. He exerted an almost magical authority over his clientele. He wasn't a big man and so he couldn't intimidate them physically, and he wasn't as chatty and involved with his customers' lives as John Murphy, but he had a quiet presence. Somehow he'd managed to establish a moral authority over everyone who came into the Saint-Antoine. He'd created an atmosphere in which the bar was like a home to the regulars but also welcoming to strangers, and for that people respected him.

The more our sales declined, the more supportive Jean-Claude became. He'd ferry glasses out to our corner of the terrace, pat us supportively on the back and invite us to play chess and dice. His son, Igor, was also helpful, bringing friends along to try rosé and telling us how the clientele on the Côte d'Azur changed with the months. The *juilletistes* – people who came in July – were apparently the best customers. They had money to spend and could take holidays whenever they wanted. By contrast the *aoû-tiens* were skinflints who just liked the idea of coming on holiday to Cannes. They never had any money, and their idea of a good night out was to eat a sandwich and drink a beer on the seafront. 'You'll struggle to sell much wine in August,' warned Igor.

At least the increasing rowdiness of the Saint-Antoine made our entrance every day ever more spectacular. It was usually only 10 a.m. when we arrived, but we were still greeted with a chorus of drunken catcalls. '*Bonjour*, Monsieur Le Rosé. *Bonjour*, Madame Le Rosé. *Bonjour*, Peter Le Rosé.' We didn't even have to try and attract people off the street – the regulars at the bar did it for us, almost physically accosting pedestrians and dragging them towards us. 'They're selling the best rosé in France,' they cheered, or was it jeered?

By the final Friday we were hardly selling any rosé to the regulars. We'd had fun and they'd had fun, but it was clearly time to move on. We just had to wait for our English plane owners to pick up their crates of champagne and then we'd shut La Vie en Rosé in Cannes.

It was a far from quiet last day, though. As usual the sun was unsparingly hot. It melted the ice in our buckets in minutes, and the physical exertion of continually replenishing it had us all dripping with sweat. The nearest table to us was filled with a collection of the more unsavoury customers at the Saint-Antoine, including the shabby individual who'd written graffiti on the car and a woman with blonde peroxide hair whose flabby face was permanently fixed into a look of disgust. Since we had no customers, I took a couple of bottles of rosé over to them and asked if they would like a *dégustation* – a treat only ever turned down by the Saint-Antoine's rosé specialist.

There was a grunt of assent from around the table, so I poured a taste of the first wine into each of their glasses. They knocked it back like a shot of vodka and I topped them up with the second wine, which was dispatched in a similar fashion. With the *dégustation* finished, I asked whether they would like a glass. To my surprise, they all said yes and I spent the rest of the morning in a relay between our ice buckets and their table, taking bottle after bottle to them and watching as their movements became heavy and clumsy. At 2 p.m. the blonde woman with the saggy, dispirited face made to leave and I presented her bill. There was a slight fuss as she first claimed not to have any money and then pretended that she was surprised to have to pay, but eventually she handed over a crumpled note.

I thought nothing of it, but as I turned away, people began whispering. With each step I took towards our serving area the whispers became louder. By the time I sat back down in the shade there was a full-blown argument going on at the table I'd just charged. It was conducted with typical Gallic flair – all fist-waving, exaggerated gestures and curled lips. And there was no doubt the source of their ire was me – did I not know that in France when you offer someone a *dégustation* it's free? How could I be so ignorant? Where's Jean-Claude? We'll get Jean-Claude to tell him. And so it went on, protestation after protestation as to why their morning's drinking session should cost them nothing.

They knew I was listening and they knew I understood. Their objective was to instigate some sort of mob rule because when there were rumours of free drink flying around, the Saint-Antoine became a very clubbable society. More and more regulars gathered outside bemoaning the fact that our rosé wasn't free. Quite how so many people who had been paying for their drinks all week and who could see a blackboard full of prices behind our heads became so convinced so quickly that all our wine should be free was beyond us.

It was akin to a minor political protest, with perhaps twenty people standing around our bar shouting their objections. A passer-by could have been forgiven for thinking that we had done something grievously wrong. The ringleader was the shabbily dressed car graffiti artist. He choreographed the whole affair, dragging people back into the fold when they threatened to lose interest. It was obvious what everybody wanted – in front of Tanya, Peter and me, there were ten bottles chilling in ice, and if wine was free in La Vie en Rosé, there would be one big fête for the next hour or so.

'If you've finished drinking, you owe us twenty euros,' said Peter in his best French to the ringleading graffiti artist.

The crowd went silent, waiting for the outcome. And then, whether it was because he was drunk or simply to impress the gathered throng, the graffiti artist's mask slipped. We'd watched him shamble around the bar all week, listened to him slur away with all the other customers and not for one minute had we suspected.

'You cannee even speak the language, so donnee lecture me,' he answered in a Scottish brogue. 'A taste of wine in France is free.' He threw a €20 note at us and retreated in what he thought was triumph.

And that was that. It was 3 p.m. on a sunny day in Cannes and we'd normally have stayed open until ten that evening. But after our disagreement with our fellow Brit we were shut out of the society of the bar.

Igor came over with three consolation glasses of pastis. 'Don't worry, it had to happen eventually. This lot will do anything for a free drink – they were just testing to see if you'd break.'

Until that afternoon in Cannes I'd always hated pastis. And my first glass of the cloudy yellow liquid highlighted why. The initial sip stripped away all moisture from the roof of my mouth. My tastebuds were then assailed by the overwhelming flavour of aniseed. Seconds later my body's natural defence mechanism kicked in and flooded my mouth with warm saliva.

But with Igor ferrying glass after glass of pastis to us, I had no choice but to drink up. By the third glass I'd actually convinced myself that I liked the cloudy yellow liquid – it had certainly taken the edge off the earlier argument and the Saint-Antoine once again seemed a friendly place. The fisherman Fabrice came and joined us at our table, and Tanya surreptitiously slipped his dog, Howard, sips of her pastis. Peter couldn't have been happier. His tastebuds needed no acclimatising to the drink, and he smoked a cigar in the sunshine telling anyone who cared to listen what a wonderful time we'd had in Cannes.

Darkness fell and still we sat and sipped our never-emptying glasses. By now every object I looked at had a hazy outline. It was like watching a TV channel that was slightly out of tune.

Needless to say, we'd all completely forgotten that we had one further deal to conclude before we packed up for good

– selling our champagne to the plane-owning Englishmen.
And we were just about to leave when a tiny Citroën pulled
up outside the Saint-Antoine. Inside we could see four large
men with their knees hunched up against their chins. The word
'Crew' was emblazoned in large letters on the front door of the
car.

One man got out. He was dressed in a crisp white shirt,
the shoulders of which were crested with epaulets with three
golden stripes sewn on to them. His trousers were black, his
shoes shone, and under his arm he carried a pilot's hat. We were
all too drunk to notice that his shirt was characteristically tight
around the belly.

He coughed politely. 'I am here to pick up the champagne.'
The three of us looked straight through him, unsure who he
was and what he wanted. 'I am here to pick up the champagne,'
he repeated, and because it seemed like the sensible thing to
do, I stumbled to my feet and retreated to the storeroom in the
Saint-Antoine. With Peter's help I squeezed the two crates into
the boot of the car, finding room amid the wheeled suitcases.
The Citroën clunked into gear and struggled away up the hill,
leaving Peter and me standing in the street trying to pierce the
cloudy yellow fog in our brains and make sense of what we'd
just seen.

'But I thought he owned the plane,' mumbled Tanya. 'What
was all that talk about him insisting on a glass of pink champagne before every take-off and landing? And what about Ralf
Schumacher's party?'

We turned back towards the Saint-Antoine to collect our
belongings. The neon light on the fascia projected glowing
golden strips down to the pavement, the bar was thronged with
regulars who shifted in and out of focus, and the glasses of pastis
they held tightly in their hands looked luminous in the bright
lights. Rowdy conversation spilled on to the street, filling our
ears with a hubbub of undecipherable words. And amid it all, at

the back of the bar on the raised dais, I could see Jean-Claude calmly playing chess.

'Half of them are one step from heaven ...' began Peter.

16

The King and Queen of Saint-Tropez

Early the next morning we said farewell to the Saint-Antoine and drove once again to La Cadière d'Azur. We traipsed into the Hostellerie Bérard and asked to see Madame Bérard. Despite our half-closed eyes the receptionist recognised us. She confirmed the shop was still available for rent and said that Madame Bérard was busy. We offered to wait but the receptionist confirmed that she had our number and promised we would receive a phone call.

Back outside in the street, we squinted in the bright sunshine. There was a queue outside the *boulangerie*, the terraces of the two bars were full of assorted customers, and a couple of market traders were just setting up their stalls. The butcher pulled up the iron grille in front of his shop and chalked up his daily specials on the blackboard. Another day was starting in La Cadière d'Azur, the self-professed Provençal village, and we all instinctively knew that Madame Bérard was not going to call us. 'It's more of a pastis place really,' said Peter, beginning to acknowledge the truth.

As we wound our way down the hill from La Cadière, Tanya began to sing to herself. The tune was 'Do You Know the Way to San José', but as she'd done the previous summer, she changed the last two words to 'Saint-Tropez'. Peter started to whistle along, drumming the steering wheel with his fingers at the end of each chorus.

The thought occurred to me that San José might at this precise moment be preferable – we were on the road again, with a boot full of rosé and nowhere to sell it. I am sure I wasn't alone in periodically reflecting what life might have been like in Aix. By now we would have rented a flat and shipped our belongings from England. Each day we would have had the luxury of making our way to the same bar and serving the same customers – our own regulars.

Instead, we were living out of a suitcase and wandering from bar to bar. Despite the beauty of our surroundings, it was a slightly soulless existence. Getting to know the regulars was an enjoyable but ultimately futile exercise. By the time we'd established a friendship we had to move on and start all over again. The feeling every time we worked in a new bar reminded me of starting a new school. There was a sense of anticipation and also fear that things might not work out, that the staff or the customers might object to our presence.

And if I analysed the bars we'd worked in so far, it was only in Uzès that we'd managed to create the life we'd dreamt of back in England. Nîmes had been a struggle, if an ultimately rewarding one, and even Cannes, where we had sold plenty of rosé, hadn't quite felt right. The atmosphere in the Saint-Antoine was normally friendly and warm, but observing such a high level of drunkenness on a daily basis was ultimately depressing.

'Well, do you know the way?' asked Tanya, drawing me from my thoughts. In fact it was more or less impossible not to know the way to Saint-Tropez. The port, which is the size of a small town, is as well signposted as Paris. On *autoroutes, routes nationales* and minor roads across the south, it is the one place to which you can always pick up directions. Marseille, Montpellier, Nice, who needs them? Deep in the past some long-forgotten head of a government department must have decided that Saint-Tropez was a priority destination – perhaps he'd spent a nice holiday on Plage de Pampelonne in his youth.

Setting aside the lure of the gentle light and bobbing hulls, we had two good reasons to return to the port. We were still keen to run a rosé festival at one of the beach clubs, and although Eric Omores, the person I'd been put through to at Nikki Beach's Miami headquarters, had been out of touch, he'd at least considered the idea when we spoke in May.

We also had some unfinished business from the previous summer. Throughout our quest for France's palest rosé, people had mentioned the name of Régine Sumeire and a rosé called Petale de Rose. But in our mad rush across the country, we'd never found time to visit her vineyard. Near the end of our quest, we'd found a bottle of her rosé in a shop. Unfortunately the rosé that experts across France had confidently predicted to be one of the palest in the country was a rich pink, not as deep as a clairet or the dark blush wines of America, but nowhere near as pale as the Corsican *gris* we'd discovered.

Nevertheless people kept mentioning Régine's name. When we returned to London and told friends about our trip, they smiled and said, 'So you'll have met Régine Sumeire, then.' It was infuriating. For reasons I was determined to find, our quest to find France's palest rosé remained incomplete until we had visited this final vineyard.

And so we weaved our way through the hills, periodically catching glimpses of the sea through the branches of the bushy canopy of pines. We passed through the sun-stilled villages of Gassin and Ramatuelle, where the silence was only stirred by the occasional whir of distant helicopter blades. As we descended towards the coast, an army of lush vines marched in neat rows towards us. Our destination was Château Barbeyrolles, one of only three châteaux on the Saint-Tropez peninsula and the home of Régine Sumeire.

The château, which was more of a large Provençal *mas*,

sheltered underneath a copse of tall pines just kilometres from the sea. In the garden, palm trees curved towards the blue sky, flowers bloomed in well-tended beds, and vines flowed into the distance, breaking against the encircling hills. Lines of roses grew in the shade of the thick stone walls, strategically planted at the end of each row of vines.

Vignerons traditionally grew roses to warn them of the potential onset of a crop-destroying disease – parasites would attack the roses before the grapes, and the vigneron would have a precious few days to respond to the threat. But Régine's roses had another purpose – the petals were predominantly white with fragile pale-pink tips – they were the symbol of her award-winning rosé.

As we were admiring the surroundings, a door at the side of the château opened and a small Scottish terrier came scampering out. The dog was quickly followed by Régine. She had a mobile phone clasped to her ear, and her free hand was raised skywards in exasperation. '*Maintenant, merde. J'ai complètement oublié,*' she apologised for missing an appointment.

As she talked and paced, kicking puffs of sand into the air, we were able to observe her closely. She was a small woman, barely 5 foot 2, with shoulder-length auburn hair. Her face was more distinguished than pretty, dominated as it was by a strong Roman nose. Her skin was the dark brown of someone who'd spent a lifetime in the sun, and its rich colour was highlighted by a light baby-blue knitted top. She completed her outfit with flowing cotton trousers and a pair of sandals.

Régine finished her phone call and invited us inside her office. The papers on her desk were arranged into ordered piles, trays were marked – letters to sign, correspondence in, correspondence out – files were colour-coded, and a whole wall was taken up by a cabinet with hundreds of labelled drawers – marketing literature, weather forecasts, envelopes, paperclips, the list went on and on.

'Now, what can I do for you?' said Régine, struggling to remember where she had put her fountain pen.

I explained about our quest the previous summer, and as she searched in drawers and under pieces of paper, Régine listened as attentively as she could. Just as she'd found her pen – in her pocket – and was ready to talk to us, her phone rang. '*Merde, maintenant?*' She looked at us in despair.

Régine excused herself for twenty minutes, and we stood in the shade of the château and watched more rosé disappear down her drive than we'd sold all summer. Car after car crunched up the track and parked opposite the *cave*, and crate after crate of rosé was loaded into open boots. The clientele was completely diverse – battered Peugeots and bulky Bentleys were parked side by side. Millionaires in beige suits with crisp notes folded in silver money clips bought the same pink wine as men who emptied their pockets searching for their last euro.

'I'd like to hear more about your quest.' Régine swept back into the room wearing a new outfit – a black dress and matching black-and-white shoes. 'Would you like to stay for lunch?' Seeing our surprise at her formal attire, she explained that she had a meeting at her other château, near Hyères, that afternoon. 'Come on, let's get some food.'

We sat at a long cast-iron table in the shade of a pine tree, and when Régine's phone wasn't ringing or she wasn't dashing back into the kitchen for the forgotten salt or pepper, we told our story. Régine poured some cold Petale de Rose, a delicate, fruity wine, made as she explained from a simple slight pressing of Grenache, Cinsault and Mourvèdre. The crickets sang in the background, a gentle wind stirred the branches of the trees, and we helped ourselves to slices of dried ham, aubergines and courgettes stuffed with breadcrumbs, and tomatoes cooked with Provençal herbs. By the time we'd reached the pudding of *tarte tropézienne*, a rich sponge cake filled with custard, we'd exhausted our tale, but we still hadn't found out the significance of Régine's Petale de Rose.

'Tell me,' said Peter, 'why did everyone tell us to come and see you? Your rosé is wonderful, absolutely wonderful, but it's not that pale.'

Pushing her *tarte tropézienne* away, Régine invited us to follow her. She seemed to enjoy the suspense of not answering our question and as we crossed in front of the château, she stalled us by stopping to examine the vines, peeling away dead leaves and plucking grapes that she judged were not maturing properly. Hidden away on the far side of the property, we discovered that Régine was in the process of building a new *cave*. A concrete shell had been constructed, and workmen were busy fitting doors and wiring the electrics. As always Tanya had her camera at the ready and began to take a few photos. Régine waved a finger at her. 'If people see my *cave* like this, they will think that I am disorganised. You mustn't show those to anyone. Come on, this way.'

Régine led us up some steps into a large, newly painted room, in the centre of which was a wooden press. It resembled the old hand-operated presses we'd seen in Champagne the previous year. Two wheels about 3 or 4 metres in diameter were laid on their side and mounted one on top of the other. A round hole had been drilled in the centre of each, and through this a thick wooden pole had been threaded, which was grooved like a screw. At harvest time the grapes would be placed in between the two wheels, and with the help of about five or six men to operate the mechanism, the upper wheel would be pressed down on to the lower wheel and the juice of the grapes would be extracted. But what did it have to do with France's palest rosé? How could I fake an appropriately enthusiastic reaction to what, after all, was just a press?

Régine smiled munificently as if she were about to deliver a great bounty. 'In 1985, eight years after I bought this château, vignerons were all making their rosé by maceration – bleeding the juices from the grapes over a period of hours.' She paused to allow time for us to appreciate the significance of her words. 'Instead of copying them, I experimented and used this press to create a rosé by direct pressing without any maceration.'

'Which means,' said Peter, 'that this vineyard and this press made the first ever pale rosé.'

The previous year we'd discovered all about the growth in rosé consumption and the trend for paler and paler rosés. The palest wines we'd discovered were almost inevitably made either by a direct press or a very quick maceration. Using either method, the secret to controlling the colour of the resulting rosé was to limit the amount of time the juice of grapes spent in contact with the skin. And at last we understood – although Petale de Rose wasn't that pale, it marked the point some two decades ago at which vignerons had started to experiment and make ever lighter rosés. Without Régine, Provençal lunches would have been a poorer experience, and without Régine, we'd have never been challenged to find France's palest rosé.

'*Merde*,' said Régine, looking at her watch. 'I've forgotten another appointment, you'll have to excuse me.'

'I feel as if we've just met the Queen,' said Peter, as she disappeared inside the château.

Down the road at Nikki Beach, the day was just getting under way. As had happened on our previous visit, a bouncer dressed in a karate suit met us at the entrance and disdainfully took the keys to Peter's BMW. We stepped on to the wooden planks that lay across the hot sand, passed through the small hut that guarded the entrance and smiled with delight. We were back, and once again it was like entering a parallel world, one in which there were only two colours in the spectrum – the bright white of everything and everyone in Nikki – the sun loungers, the parasols, the staff uniforms – and the intense azure blue of the sky and the pool.

We were greeted by the *plagiste*, the man with the weighty and lucrative responsibility of allocating sun loungers to people. His fingers resembled a portable cash till – around each digit he'd wrapped notes of every denomination, starting with green €500 notes on the little finger of his left hand and working all the way down to €5 on the little finger of his right. Each note was folded in half and then bent round a knuckle, and judging from the lack of space between fingers, he was strolling around with nearly €10,000.

Although we were not prepared to pay extra to guarantee a good sun lounger, we did have one advantage. As the *plagiste* led us into the distance towards the far corner of the club – 'People could die of dehydration on their way to the bar from here,' commented Peter – I asked whether we could see the manager later in the day. The *plagiste* checked his stride – suddenly he didn't quite know where to place us. Were we visiting celebrities who didn't need to tip to get a good lounger? Pushing my luck, I continued, 'I'm a friend of Eric Omores from your Miami office and he suggested I talk to the manager.' The *plagiste* stopped, frowned and then led us back from where we'd just come, reluctantly pointing to a king-sized mattress right next to the pool.

All around the edge of the water, long-limbed girls and loose-limbed boys kissed and petted, wrapping their arms round each other and intertwining their legs, so that anyone brave enough to take a dip had their exit blocked by a mesh of tangled flesh.

'Eric's here. I'll get him to come and see you later,' the *plagiste* said as he handed us our towels and went off in search of bigger-tipping clients.

As I pondered what Nikki's Miami marketing guy was doing in Saint-Tropez, I noticed that the *plagiste* was having difficulties with his next clients – three middle-aged and over-made-up women. They'd spotted our position by the pool and were complaining loudly in heavy Russian accents about the sun loungers they'd been allocated. Given their dress sense, I was surprised they'd been allowed in at all. They'd clearly spent all morning trying to accessorise but instead they'd managed to look like children let loose with a dressing-up box. They'd teamed their all-too-revealing swimming costumes with garish wraps and branded baseball caps (worn reversed like teenage skateboarders). They had bracelets on their ankles, rings on their toes and handbags the size of bin liners. More and more cash was pulled from the depths of these sacks and gradually the three women made progress, mattress by mattress and euro note by euro note to their desired location.

Back by us, the all-white colour scheme had been given an interesting twist. Yellow and blue ribbons had been wrapped round the parasols and draped over ice buckets, and a Brazilian flag flew by the entrance to the restaurant. Although we'd eaten over an hour ago, lunch at Nikki was only just under way. The chef at the sushi bar was busy gutting raw fish and moulding mounds of rice. People draped themselves on low benches, idly dipping their hands into ice buckets which were pleasingly filled with bottles of rosé. We ordered some drinks and waited for Eric, unaware that one of the biggest parties any of us had ever attended was about to kick off.

Just as Peter was about to go for a swim – a task that involved negotiating his way past the ongoing game of Twister by the pool – a drumbeat started in the distance. It was quickly overlaid with another, quicker beat and then another and another and finally the air was pierced by a series of shrill whistles. Samba dancers surged through the restaurant wearing tassels instead of bras and G-strings you could floss with. Plumages of multicoloured feathers rose into the air from ornate headdresses bedecked with flowers and jewels.

Stopping in front of each table, the dancers gyrated to the music, their buttocks and busts rising and falling in perfect time with the beat. As the music quickened, the dancers pulled diners and sunbathers to their feet and the area around the pool transformed into an impromptu dance floor. Much to my disappointment, one girl forgot to put on her bikini top and did the samba semi-naked in the sunshine, matching the almost unbelievably quick drumbeat by allowing her body to quiver like a plucked string. And as the music finally faded, she returned to her sun lounger with one final insouciant flick of her bottom.

The dancers disappeared, only to be replaced by a team of Brazilian martial-arts specialists. And as they karate-kicked fruit from the top of people's heads and vaulted over improvised obstacles, more and more rosé flowed into the club. Magnums replaced bottles, only to be ousted by jeroboams. By late afternoon the clientele had graduated to methuselahs and the waitresses had to serve the wine by hoisting bottles on to their shoulders and bending on to one knee to pour.

Still the Brazilian music beat on. The samba dancers made another appearance, models pranced through the club displaying skimpy bikinis for sale, and yet more rosé was drunk. People began to gather around the main bar – a circular raised wooden structure sheltering under four white sails, which had been hoisted into the sky to provide shade. As the music reached a crescendo, a siren momentarily silenced the club and staff members leapt up on to the bar and sprayed champagne like victorious Formula One drivers.

Throughout the afternoon I'd been trying to ignore the party raging around us and locate Eric. From his voice on the phone, he'd sounded like a European who'd learnt to speak English fluently in America and I'd built up an identikit picture of him in my head as a recent immigrant to the States. And because of the gentleness of his phone voice and the fact that he'd never returned my calls, I pictured him as a rather effete and ineffectual marketing and PR man. The type of person who thought everything was a good idea until he had to ask his boss. So I'd circled the restaurant without success looking for a skinny man making a mess of whatever he was in charge of.

But just as we were about to join the main party, a tall, broad black man came over. He was dressed in flowing white clothes and open-toed sandals. 'You must be Jamie,' he said in a soft voice. 'I'm Eric.'

I stumbled to my feet and shook his hand, muttering something about how we'd spoken on the phone.

'Yes, you wanted to run a rosé festival, and I never got back to you.' He smiled a broad, friendly grin and took his dark glasses off. 'I was a bit busy at the time – my wife was just having a baby. Anyway, come and sit down and we'll talk.'

We made our way over to a table and listened as Eric told us about the Nikki Beach empire. According to Eric, the clubs had started in Miami nine years ago, when the first Nikki had been set up on the Caribbean coast of the US. The idea was to try and recreate the Saint-Tropez beach clubs in the States. The experiment had worked and Nikki was now a global brand and there were clubs in eight different beach resorts.

'Tell me, what price do you pay for your rosé?' asked Eric, changing the subject. I went through our price list and he nodded appreciatively. 'You know we only sell rosé at our bar – no red or white – it's the drink of the moment. As I said to you on the phone, it's a phenomenon.'

Across at the bar, the party was getting ever more raucous. Ice buckets the size of baths held enormous bottles of pale rosé which glinted in the sun. Girls in bikinis clasped glasses to their toned stomachs, and older men supported their drinks on hairy paunches. A saxophonist leapt up on to the serving area and plugged his instrument into the central sound system of the club. Standing high above people's heads on his improvised stage, he raised the intensity of the rhythm, almost goading the crowd with his music. And people responded by dancing, drinking and swaying ever faster. As the sax hit its top note, a girl pulled herself on to the bar and clawed at her skimpy white top until it came away, allowing her to twirl it in triumph above her head. The sax played on, and more and more revellers leapt up on to the bar and cast away their tops. I'd seen pictures of debauched parties at other Saint-Tropez beach clubs – of naked boxing matches and improvised pole-dancing around parasols – but these photos had dated from the 1960s and I'd assumed the whole atmosphere was more restrained now.

I looked back at Eric, who wasn't showing the slightest bit of interest in the unfolding antics. 'I can't jeopardise my relationships with the local vineyards and so it will be difficult to let you run your festival now. But your prices are good, so maybe later in the summer. Keep in touch,' he said, as we shook hands and he slipped away to the back of the restaurant, ignoring the topless cavorting at the bar.

I didn't know whether to be jubilant, despondent or relieved. At least it wasn't a no, but it wasn't a yes either. And then there was the question of whether we were up to the task – La Vie en Rosé only had a couple of magnums of rosé in stock, so where would we source the fifty or so jeroboams we'd seen consumed, not to mention the methuselahs?

Shortly afterwards the siren went again and the staff grabbed more magnums of champagne and sprayed them everywhere. But as the sun dropped from the sky, almost imperceptibly the beat of the music gradually slowed, the saxophonist disappeared, and people began to talk and drink rather than dance. The revellers sat on their sun loungers in the late-evening sun cradling the remains of their rosé, perhaps wondering how they'd been whipped into such hysteria in the middle of a sunny afternoon. For a couple of hours the beach club had resembled a late-night rave, not a lazy Saturday on the Côte d'Azur.

And as I watched people fishing for the keys to their Ferraris, I began to think about something Eric had said to us – 'Our days have a special rhythm which we have to manage very carefully.'

The Brazilian samba dancers and martial-arts experts had been part of an organised show, but were there other performers as well? Had the first girl to dance topless by the pool been a plant? And what about the girl who'd clambered on to the bar and ripped off her top? Hadn't she moved like a professional dancer? It had been some party, but had it all been carefully manipulated?

As we left, I saw Eric sitting at a table at the back of the bar. On the other side of the table was another black man. His knuckles were covered in jewels, his ears glinted with diamonds, and a special mouth brace really did give him a million-dollar smile. All day we'd heard rumours that the rapper P Diddy was in the club, but as Tanya, Peter and I tried to get a closer look, our way was blocked by a man as broad as the three of us. It was only as we reached the exit and I reflected on Eric's starry connections that I finally realised he wasn't a marketing man from Miami but the owner of the whole Nikki empire.

17

Les Marchands de Tapis

There was no sign of Peter's car amid the gleaming row of Ferraris outside Nikki Beach. Apparently a battered fifteen-year-old BMW didn't fit in with the club's image and had to be deposited as far away as possible. We handed over our receipt for the keys and watched as the valet disappeared into the distance. After a twenty-minute wait he finally returned with our dust-covered car. Leaping quickly from it, he held his hand out for a tip and immediately scanned for a more luxurious and lucrative ride.

'I've got a little secret to tell you,' grinned Peter, as he wrestled with the convertible roof, which was refusing to fold away. 'I'm actually rather glad Eric said no for now.'

I winked at Tanya – the disdain with which Peter's car had been treated seemed to have had a disproportionate effect on our companion. 'Why? We could run a great rosé festival here,' I persisted.

'It's not that. I've fixed us up with another beach club,' said Peter enigmatically. 'We start in a week.' He refused to explain any further until we'd solved the problem of the broken hood, which was beginning to rile everyone at Nikki – first we had the cheek to turn up in a substandard car and now we had the chutzpah to stand around trying to fix it. What would the neighbours think? God forbid that anybody at Club Cinquante-Cinq should hear about it.

We were blocking in a couple of Porsches and a gleaming Lamborghini, and all around us electric hoods whirred snugly back into their casings. Any delay – let alone a five-minute one – was clearly too much for the super-rich and one by one they began hooting their horns. I think Peter quite enjoyed the spectacle. He'd had problems with the hood before and solved them within minutes, but now he was pacing around the car like a professor trying to solve a mathematical equation, pondering each solution with the excessive deliberation of a bad actor. Finally, when he'd created enough mayhem, he nodded to me, delivered two precise punches to the fabric and together we slammed the hood back into its container. The moment we left the car park, a convoy of low-slung sports cars spun past in clouds of dust.

As we bumped up the dirt track away from Nikki, Peter explained about our next bar. While we were in Cannes, he'd caught the train up the coast and treated himself to a luxurious lunch on the beach in Juan-les-Pins. He'd got talking to the owners and had suggested a rosé festival. 'It's a beautiful place, you eat with your toes curled into the warm sand, there's a pontoon stretching into the sea, and a perfect little corner for us to set up our bar. I didn't tell you because you had your hearts set on Nikki, but believe me, you're going to love this place.'

There was something thrilling about the thought of La Vie en Rosé on the beach. The whole concept was somehow wonderfully decadent, working just metres from the soothing hush of the breaking waves and watching the sun's daily journey across the deep-blue sky.

'Marvellous,' said Tanya, doing her best to imitate Peter, 'absolutely marvellous.'

Even I, the natural pessimist of the group, was excited. At times I'd doubted whether it was possible to make a living from selling rosé. The amount of time and effort it took to sell just a glass of wine to a Frenchman never seemed commensurate with the reward of a few euros. But if the beach club in Juan-les-Pins was anything like Nikki, then we had a real opportunity. A week's rest and then two weeks in Juan-les-Pins would take us through to mid-August, and the real challenge after that was to try and find a viable permanent location for La Vie en Rosé.

Just before we turned off the dirt track that led away from Nikki back on to the main road, we encountered what appeared to be a miniature sandstorm. Dust was spiralling into the still air and then slowly drifting back to earth. Each particle sparkled in the late-evening sun, and as we entered the centre of the cloud, we heard the guttural spluttering of expensive engines. Peter turned and beamed at us and then waved nonchalantly out of the window as we passed a Ferrari and a Porsche stranded in the middle of the track. The offending rut in the road wouldn't have troubled a kid on a tricycle but it had more than effectively beached two super-cars.

We used the week before our rosé bar started in Juan-les-Pins to register with estate agents. Property on the Saint-Tropez peninsula and most of the coastal strip was hard to come by and far too expensive for our limited budget, so we hunted inland in the central Var. Our test for whether an area was a possible candidate for La Vie en Rosé was whether the area smelt and felt suitably southern. Tanya was the ultimate arbiter – could she detect a memory of the Mediterranean in the sun-baked air? Did wild herbs grow by the roadside? When did the cicadas start and finish singing? We were convinced that a line could be drawn on a map to the north of which La Vie en Rosé would founder. A rosé bar was a romantic idea and it needed a resplendent, sensuous backdrop.

I'd decided that the cost of buying an existing bar was prohibitive – the going rate was three times the annual turnover of a business and it was just too risky an option. I'd even managed to persuade Tanya that, at least to begin with, we should try and find a property where the ground floor had the potential to be used for commercial purposes. We could then live above the premises and supervise the conversion into La Vie en Rosé. The only drawback of this approach was the French licensing law that prevented us from opening a bar within 50 metres of any existing licensed premises.

It was a pretty specific set of requirements but it still perplexed every estate agent we met. The moment we introduced ourselves, euro signs waltzed into their heads and did a tango with their common sense. Doubtless we were seen as part of a procession of English people who'd walked into their offices with bright eyes and bulging bank balances. And so instead of shaking their heads and saying that they had nothing for us, they decided to show us everything on their books. For me, it was a particularly worrying approach because Tanya was like a love-struck teenager when it came to falling for French property. At any given moment, however inappropriate, risky and expensive the project, she might set her heart on a bar. The French estate agents even had a name for such behaviour, labelling properties with the words 'coup de coeur' – literally meaning a 'blow to the heart'.

Estate agents dragged us from Lorgues to Draguignan and from Cotignac to Aups, and regardless of our stated desire for a conversion opportunity, we were shown failing bar after failing bar. How places where the only clientele appeared to be members of the family could possibly be turning over €500,000 a year and be up for sale at €1.5 million was a mystery. They were largely charm-free places and nothing even threatened to make Tanya's heart flutter.

As an alternative to bars, we were shown various hairdressing salons with the potential for conversion. Half of these salons were not even on the market, but there seemed to be an unspoken rule that you could always persuade a *coiffure* to sell up. The suggested prices were once again hugely inflated – the salon owners insisted that we were buying a business and applied the 'three times the turnover' rule when they named a price. Until now I'd always assumed that the stories about the difficulties of buying property in France had been hugely exaggerated, but in the town of Barjols I changed my mind. There, with a perfectly straight face, the owner of a *salon de chien-toilettage* asked us to pay an uplift in price in return for handing over his client list of dogs.

Discussing poodles with a penchant for rosé was light relief when compared with our efforts to understand French planning legislation. When we saw a property, we inevitably enquired about extensions and alterations only to discover that any work we proposed was likely to be illegal and yet at the same time perfectly acceptable. Typical of this was our experience in Cotignac. We suggested putting a roof terrace on a small property, allowing us to create the outside space that was key to the success of our bar. 'The *préfecture* of the Var turns down all new applications to create roof terraces,' the agent informed us, 'but that doesn't matter as long as the *mairie* approves. Look around you – all the properties in this town have roof terraces and they're all illegal, so why shouldn't you have one?'

'But what about the *préfecture*? What if they find out?'

'Then you'll have to take it down, but that will only happen if you are denounced, and if the *mairie* approves, you won't be denounced.'

To the French, it was a perfectly logical and sensible way of doing things. To us, it was a crazy proposition – why would we spend thousands of euros on converting a property into a bar only to receive a visit from an official on opening day telling us the work we'd done was illegal? *Dénonciation* was part of life in France – if a man bought a smart new car, there was always a chance it would trigger his neighbours to phone the taxman and have his business affairs investigated. Every estate agent we met assured us they were on friendly terms with local officials and that they could ensure the misfortune of *dénonciation* didn't happen to us, but we remained sceptical and property-less.

There were short-lived moments of success. In Draguignan, an agent showed us a *pâtisserie* with a small terrace located in a leafy square. The shop had just closed down and the property had only been on the market for a week. It had potential and our adrenalin began to flow as we talked about how many tables we could fit on the terrace. Later that evening we were still excited enough to take one more look before going to sleep.

The neighbouring business was a busy bar-cum-nightclub. The interior was shielded from view by a heavy black curtain, and the main clientele appeared to be soldiers from the local barracks. We were naïve enough to consider going in for a drink, but just as we were approaching the entrance, the curtain parted and a young man came scampering out, desperately pulling at his trousers, which were gathered around his ankles. Moments later a woman dressed in her bra and knickers stumbled into the square shouting abuse at her fleeing client. Since serving rosé to soldiers before they nipped into a brothel wasn't quite our market, we moved on.

Finally, on our fourth day of property-hunting, we saw something that just might be suitable. We'd made our way east towards Juan-les-Pins and visited an estate agent in Grasse, in the hills above Cannes. We entered the office and waited as the agent, a middle-aged woman with poorly dyed blonde hair, continued her phone conversation.

Pinned to the wall were pictures of various properties. All of them − regardless of size or position − had the word '*piscine*' or '*piscinable*' stamped across the particulars. While Peter, Tanya and I were debating how a pool could be constructed in a gardenless flat, the estate agent continued her conversation. From what I could understand, it was about the menu for supper that evening. By the time she reached dessert we'd come to the enlightened philosophical conclusion that provided you were prepared to knock down walls, entire rooms, even the whole building, every property was *piscinable.*

Eventually the agent finished on the phone and introduced herself as Christine. After looking at our creased, crumpled and dirty clothes, she made a quick judgement that we were not worth her time and accelerated the speed of her French to an unintelligible velocity. She wore her watch with its face up-turned on the inside of her wrist, and she repeatedly glanced down at the time as we spoke. The phone rang again, her voice slowed, and she signalled that we should wait, no doubt hoping that we would lose patience and leave. Eventually, more because she wanted a cigarette than out of any desire to be helpful, she offered to show us a property.

It was in the village of Cabris, just five minutes away at the end of a chicane-filled mountain road. We clambered into a small Peugeot and ruefully fiddled with the broken seatbelts. Christine controlled the car by the novel method of placing the palm of one hand in the centre of the wheel and making a vigorous circular motion – like she was polishing a table – to change direction. After each bend she released the wheel and it spun back into place. This one-handed style allowed her to take drags on her cigarette before addressing each curve in the road. The journey to Cabris was completed with lethal speed and by the end of it I have to admit I was impressed. There had been a few near-misses with oncoming traffic, but we'd entered and exited each bend with perfect precision and had I been wearing a blindfold, I would have sworn the road was straight.

With a burning cigarette wedged between the gold signet rings she wore on her fingers, Christine led us through Cabris. The village was built on the edge of a mountain. To one side, houses clung to the steeply shelving landscape, and on the other was an open plateau where there was a large green, which rather incongruously played host to a cricket team. Next to this slice of England was a gravel area complete with a bar and a sign saying that only members of Cabris's boules club would be served. Further towards the centre of the village, we encountered a small square with a fountain, two cafés and a restaurant. It was the middle of the afternoon and customers were scarce.

Christine led us up through the village, past the pharmacy and the post office, until we couldn't climb any further. Whatever the state of the property, it clearly wasn't going to be ideal for passing trade.

'Well, here it is.' We were standing outside a large terrace house at the top of the village. The pavement was narrow and there was no area to use for outside space. It looked like another wasted trip. Christine stubbed out her cigarette and opened the door, revealing a narrow corridor leading to a steep wooden staircase, which creaked as we climbed. Upstairs, there were two bedrooms, a bathroom and a sitting room. It was surprisingly spacious. The floor was tiled a warm terracotta colour, and as Christine threw open the windows, bright light swept across the room. Her whole demeanour had changed from the woman we'd met in the office half an hour earlier. She bustled around the property showing us fireplaces, electric sockets and storage space. Unfortunately her new wide smile cracked her heavy make-up and mascara and blusher began to run down her cheeks.

If we'd been looking for a house in the south of France, I think we would have considered the property, but I couldn't see how we could turn the downstairs into a bar.

Christine had, however, saved the best feature of the house until the end of the tour. She led us back down the stairs and opened a set of double doors at the rear of the property. 'This is why I brought you here.'

We walked out into the bright sunshine on to a terrace that was perhaps 10 metres square. There were window boxes full of shrivelled plants, and the paving stones were cracked and uneven. But it didn't matter. Reaching for our sunglasses, we looked out over a deep valley dotted with villas and dominated by a large lake. Fingers of water crept between the foothills of mountains, and fields of lavender climbed towards their jagged peaks. Away to the north was the Gorges du Verdon, and to the south the sea. 'On a clear day you can see Corsica,' said Christine, trying to hide the note of triumph in her voice. Leaving us to the view and to talk about the possibilities, she went away to shut up the house.

On her return, we had a list of questions prepared – whose permission would we need to turn the house into the bar? Did she know a local builder we could talk to about the costs of the conversion? How many other people had been to see the house? Was the property likely to reach the asking price?

Ignoring our questions, she took us back into the sitting room. 'There is one more thing to show you,' she said, reaching down and pulling at a hatch in the floor. Taking a torch from her bag, she pointed the light down into the cellar, illuminating the smooth brick of a wine *cuve*. 'If you want, you could have this cleaned up and use it for your *vrac*,' continued Christine. 'If not, you take the *cuve* out and use it as storage.'

The air coming up from the cellar was cool, musty and hardly inviting, but Peter took the torch and clambered down a rickety stepladder. 'Imagine how many litres of rosé we could store in this,' he called up excitedly.

'What about the price?' I asked Christine again. 'Is it negotiable?'

'Estate agents in France are called *les marchands de tapis*,' said Christine, increasing in confidence at the prospect of a sale, 'and with carpet salesmen everything is negotiable.'

She explained that she had the right connections in Cabris and that it wouldn't be a problem to convert the back terrace into a bar. Sensibly I refrained from asking whether it was legal – at some stage we just had to make the leap and trust that with the right local support we could do whatever we wanted.

'While we are on the subject of alterations, is it *piscinable?*' called Peter from the depths of the cellar. All we could see of him was his wispy white hair and his hands clinging to one of the bottom rungs of the stepladder.

'You could always use the cellar as a plunge pool,' advised the now all-too-familiar Christine, with another make-up-cracking smile.

As we wandered back through the village, we learnt that two buyers had already seen around the house and they'd both expressed an interest. The owner was keen on achieving a quick sale and if we put in an offer now, then we stood a good chance of securing the property. 'If you want, I could have the *compromis* drawn up today,' Christine offered as if it were the most natural thing in the world.

In France signing a *compromis* meant we had to put down a 10 per cent deposit, and then after a cooling-off period of seven days had elapsed, it would commit us to completing the purchase of the house. It wasn't a decision to be taken after just one viewing and Christine knew it. Seeing our enthusiasm waning, she took out her business card. 'You must go away and *réfléchir* – reflect – and only when you are ready should you call.'

Reflecting proved to be an uneasy experience. I began to think about all the choices and coincidences that had led us to this point. The temptation was to plot a straight line of causation, seeing progress in every action we'd taken, and nothing but good coming out of our dogged persistence through the hard times in Aix and Nîmes. The house-cum-bar in Cabris was the natural outcome of everything we'd done. Wasn't it just what we wanted? Hadn't we spoken about this moment all summer?

But then there were the doubts, the more intelligent side of me that recognised that everything was pure coincidence – after all, we'd only seen the property thanks to Christine's nicotine craving. And how could we commit our lives to Cabris when we'd just spent an hour in the village? Wasn't it crazy to even consider it?

Then again, weren't these the very uncertainties that we wanted in our lives when we left London? How could we turn away now? Before I'd had the chance to even begin working through these conflicting emotions, and little over an hour after we'd left Cabris, the phone rang. It was an excited Christine. She'd apparently spoken to the *mairie* and there would be no problem in us converting the ground floor of the house into a bar and using the terrace as an outside seating area. Given this and the time we'd had to *réfléchir*, she wanted to know whether we were ready to sign a *compromis* yet. Did she have to remind us that there were other people interested? We might lose the property unless we acted now.

Despite being accustomed to London's cut-throat estate agents, we were surprised by the speed and directness of Christine's approach. Her insistence that she was about to receive an offer from another party was obviously a ploy, but it still had the necessary impact. We stopped the car and sat at a picnic point overlooking the bay of Cannes. Low cloud had begun to roll in over the sea and a light drizzle started to fall. It was still warm enough for us to dress in shorts and T-shirts, but all the smells of the south were masked by a layer of dampness. Had we been sitting in brilliant sunshine, with our spirits lifted by the sun on our faces, it's quite possible we would have been tempted to put in an offer. As it was, we delayed.

The next morning Christine phoned again. I took the call and immediately noted the edge that had crept into her voice. Once again she asked whether we'd had time to reflect. When I answered no and suggested that we needed at least a week to think about the idea, she began shouting rapidly in French. It was difficult to keep track of her anger, but she was apparently upset that we'd shown such an interest in the property – were we liars? If not, why wouldn't we sign the *compromis*? She'd made an extra effort to speak to the *mairie* – didn't we know that this wasn't part of an estate agent's job in France? In the end I held the handset away from my ear so that Tanya and Peter could hear the exasperation in her voice.

While Christine continued to berate me, we held a quick whispered conference. I hastily judged that we were in agreement that however nice the property was and however good the prospects for a conversion, the transaction didn't feel right. How could we buy something from somebody so desperate to sell? There had to be something wrong. And so when Christine eventually quietened, I was able to tell her that we'd reflected and that we wouldn't be making an offer on the property. I didn't even have time to thank her for her help before the line clicked dead.

But later that evening, with Peter out hunting for supper, Tanya and I had our first real row of the summer. Tanya had apparently wanted more time to persuade me that the property was the right choice, but in our hurried huddle I'd assumed her reaction to the bullying estate agent was the same as mine.

According to Tanya, I was backing away from our dream of setting up our own rosé bar and creating problems when there were none. Hadn't I known that there were going to be risks when we left London? Was I really naïve enough to think that we could just come to France and set up a bar with relative ease? So far she'd listened to my words of caution and respected my insistence that we didn't have enough money to buy an existing bar, but in Cabris we'd just seen the type of property I'd been talking about for the last month. It didn't matter if I didn't like the estate agent – at some stage I had to commit, and today had been an opportunity for us to take a step forward. Didn't I want to be settled and happy? Why had I told Christine we wouldn't be making an offer?

Anxiety drove harsh words from our mouths. I wished that I had an answer for Tanya and that I could explain why I was still unprepared to commit but instead I met her persistent questioning with shakes of my head and exasperated gestures.

When Peter returned he must have wondered what had happened. He'd left an apparently happy couple, but now as he unpacked delicacy after delicacy from his shopping bags, Tanya and I barely spoke. 'Stuffed artichoke, anyone?'

18

La Pinède

In the pine-filled centre of Juan-les-Pins, a plaque on the wall outside the nightclub 'Whisky a Go Go' read, '*L'élégance, la bonne éducation et un comportement sans faille sont les conditions d'admission dans notre club.*'

'Elegance, a good education and bearing' – it could have been a slogan for the whole town. Before we opened La Vie en Rosé, we had a couple of days to get to know the place. There was the odd architectural wart like the glass-panelled casino that some misguided planner had approved, but otherwise things remained redolently genteel – the perfect antidote to our turbulent time with estate agents.

Cocktails could be taken in the Beau Rivage, where the prices were the only thing to have changed since Scott Fitzgerald and Hemingway put pen to paper on its terrace. Glorious arched windows and curved balustrades overlooked the sea, and the staff in pinched and starched uniforms appeared straight from a film set.

Our favourite part of the town was the square next to Whisky a Go Go. Through the interlocking branches of the trees, the Mediterranean appeared like a brilliant blue jigsaw. Corners of buildings and yacht masts jutted into the picture, and each individual piece of sea was fringed with brittle green pine needles. A seemingly endless game of boules clattered in the heavy shade, outlasting the light and enduring as darkness draped itself over the water. Teenagers arrived on mopeds with chattering engines, the neon lights of the surrounding restaurants were switched on, seafood was piled high on mountains of crushed ice, and holidaymakers and locals were decanted on to the narrow streets, promenading to the irregular thud and clank of the boules.

Below this central square was the next venue for La Vie en Rosé – La Pinède. Beach clubs stretched for miles all along the seafront, and in the height of summer sun loungers were booked so far in advance that being in possession of the right one carried the cachet of a Wimbledon debenture, particularly since subtle variations in the amount of space allocated between the mattresses at the different clubs had a disproportionate impact on price – a red mattress on one side of a roped partition could cost double an orange one on the other side. The view was identical, the service the same, but that extra iota of space – like travelling club on a short-haul flight – was judged to make all the difference.

And there was a recognised hierarchy among the clubs, with La Pinède at the top. Viewed from the promenade above the beach, there was nothing to distinguish it. There was an iron arch over the stairs, which supported a sign engraved with the name of the club. Two palm trees rose from the centre of the restaurant area, and from the uppermost reaches of their narrow trunks flowed a fountain of tropical greenery. In the gaps between the tight rows of yellow parasols, handbags and sun creams lay scattered in the sand.

Other clubs had invested in sturdy wooden sun loungers and built kinks and curves into their pontoons, and we'd visited some that insisted on their waitresses wearing skimpy shorts that clung to the curves of their bottoms. La Pinède, Peter assured us, was too long established to need such gimmicks. But he wouldn't allow us in to see for ourselves. Peter had agreed the precise time and date of arrival with the owner and insisted that he didn't want to put any pressure on her by arriving early. And so for our first few days in the town we'd had to content ourselves with the enticing view from above.

Finally, a week after we'd left Nikki Beach, we set out from our small hotel to deliver our wine. Throughout the summer the southern streets had become ever more traffic-clogged, but we'd encountered nothing like trying to enter the centre of Juan-les-Pins. For an hour each morning the genteel resort I'd come to know was transformed. All the roads fed into a one-way system leading towards a small roundabout right by the sea. Nearly every car that entered the town had to pass through this bottleneck — tourists hoping to get a good spot on the beach, traders setting up jewellery stalls on the front, vans dropping off clothes to boutiques and the refrigerated lorries delivering food to the restaurants. We joined this clot of traffic at 10 a.m. By ten thirty we'd progressed 50 metres, by eleven another 50, but then we stopped. The vans had reached their destinations and their drivers flicked on warning lights and pretended to be oblivious to the grid-locked cars snarling on the seafront.

A full hour and a half after we'd embarked on the kilometre journey from hotel to beach club, we reached our destination. In local fashion we doubled-parked and put on our hazard lights, determined not to go round the town's one-way system again. The idea was for all three of us to ferry the wine as quickly as possible across the pine-filled square and down into the beach club.

Had it not been for Peter's obsession with the game of boules, it would have taken two minutes. We'd heard about the three different forms of the game the previous year: pétanque, which was played from a standing start over distances of no more than 10 metres; Provençal, played between 15 and 20 metres; and Lyonnais, played over such long distances that larger boules were necessary – but until now we'd never seen anything other than the traditional pétanque.

Oblivious to the weight of the two boxes of wine he was carrying and the gathering traffic, Peter stood mesmerised by the alien form of the game unfolding in the square. From the distances involved and the style of play, it became clear that Provençal rules were being played. The competitors – four young men – were half the usual age of the archetypal boules player, and instead of the faded caps and scuffed sandals we were accustomed to, they wore the latest branded sports kit. As they prepared to throw, they rocked back and forth on their heels like triple-jumpers at the start of their run-ups. Each thrower then took three springing leaps, releasing the ball in midair. Despite having to integrate all the different movements, they managed to be incredibly accurate, cannoning opposition boules out of the way over distances of 20 metres.

Tanya and I stumbled towards the beach club with our boxes of wine, depositing them at the top of a set of steps that led down into La Pinède. Turning round, we found that Peter was now using his cases as a seat. 'I'll take the rest of the wine into the club if you take the car back. It might stop all that hooting,' said Peter, gesturing towards the road as he lit a cigar and leant back in his impromptu chair.

'He's protecting La Pinède like it's a newborn baby,' muttered Tanya. 'I feel like we're never going to be allowed to see the inside.'

As we drove away I glanced in the rear mirror. Aside from a queue of irate drivers, I noticed Peter busily transforming his wine cases into a chaise-longue. His activities attracted the attention of one of the *boulistes*, and by the time we'd inched through the traffic to the far corner of the square Peter was rocking back on his heels and preparing to throw his first Provençal boule. A building obscured the outcome but I thought I heard a heavy clack and a gravelly cry of 'Marvellous'.

Somehow the wine made it into La Pinède's fridges in time for us to start serving in the late-afternoon sunshine. The sand was immaculately raked, the sun loungers – or *matelas*, as the French called them – spaced wide apart, and the restaurant tables as well dressed as any on the Champs-Elysées. The area allocated for La Vie en Rosé was inside a small pergola at the back of the beach club. It was built from the distressed wood so common in Provençal *brocante* markets, and banana plants grew up the supporting struts. We laid a table across the front of the hut, spread our pink tablecloths, pinned posters to the wall, filled ice buckets with rosé and prepared to trade. The sun shone through our bottles of wine, casting a spectrum of gentle pinks against my white beach shorts, and looking out across the beach club past the restaurant and over the *matelas* towards the pontoon stretching into the bay of Cannes, we could see a large captive clientele baking in the sun.

Hopefully they couldn't wait to try our wine, but first Claudine, the owner of La Pinède, who'd been sitting in the shade watching us set up, had to give the final go-ahead. It was difficult to place her age – she looked as if she was in her early forties but she had the calm demeanour of an older woman and a wry, worldly smile. She wore her short dark hair high on her head, and her clothes were simple yet expensive. Gold bracelets jangled from her wrists, and her prescription sunglasses rarely left her dark eyes. Her constant companion was a large wooden board with about fifty metal clips attached to it. Under each clip was a pile of receipts, and staff members were continually coming over and handing her chits. It was an ingenious way of keeping track of people's expenditure – the board represented the beach club and each metal clip a sun lounger.

Spotting that we were ready to serve, Claudine unfurled herself from her shady corner and came to inspect La Vie en Rosé. I was wearing my ankle-length white beach shorts, which had been so out of place in Nîmes but seemed perfect here, Tanya a simple pink sundress, and Peter a freshly ironed bright-pink polo shirt with khaki shorts. We couldn't have looked smarter and the bar had never looked better.

But Claudine paced in front of us like an army sergeant major. She straightened a couple of the posters, smoothed tablecloths, wiped water from the floor where some of the ice had spilled and for a moment I thought she was going to adjust Peter's collar. While the inspection was in progress, we faced forward like new cadets and tried to keep straight faces as we wondered what else Claudine could find fault with. After a final repositioning of our wine glasses, Claudine gave a little nod and then called her husband, Ives, over.

When I'd first set eyes on Ives, I'd assumed he was the old *plagiste* – the new one was very much in evidence with wrap-around shades and spiky blond hair – who'd retired to a more gentle support job. He was as scruffy as Claudine was smart. His thinning white hair sprouted in all directions from his scalp, he wore a crumpled white shirt, left open at the chest, and a pair of baggy white trousers. He shuffled rather than walked, and in our short time in the bar I'd watched him repatriate lost sunglasses and shift sun loungers and tables for tricky clients. He rarely asked another member of staff to do anything, preferring to arrange things in his own unobtrusive way. Now he stood opposite us, grinning at our rosé bar. '*Ça marche,*' he said, and a small satisfied smile spread across Claudine's face.

I am not sure quite how or when we became good at selling rosé, but suddenly on this sunny afternoon in Juan-les-Pins everything came right. As salespeople, we were transformed from the shy, stumbling English people who'd stepped into Place aux Herbes in Uzès. Instead we were confident and competent rosé professionals. Wine flowed freely from our bar. If a client asked about a particular rosé, we could tell them the grape varieties used, the length of the maceration, even the colour of the vigneron's eyes.

We served people in swimming trunks with seawater dripping from their sodden hair, women with so much collagen in their lips they could barely fit glass to mouth and men with bellies that testified to a love of gastronomy. Without exception they tried to establish their superiority over us, either maintaining that our rosé was poor or saying that a particular wine was slightly corked.

Earlier in the summer we'd have backed down and sheepishly offered them something else to try, but now we persuaded and cajoled. And because the language we were using was right, and because after such an unusual combination of experiences – the trip to the rosé laboratory in Vidauban, the near-impossibility of persuading a Nîmois to have a glass of wine, and our alcohol-soaked days in Cannes – we were prepared for nearly every eventuality and we gradually gained their respect.

Our greatest triumph was persuading the wine waiter to try some Bordeaux. He was the alpha male of La Pinède's staff and strode around the restaurant with a proprietorial air. On our arrival he'd immediately inspected our wines. One of the bottles had a label proclaiming it to be '*biologique*' and we were given a brief lecture about the impossibility of producing a totally organic wine. 'At some stage the vigneron always adds chemicals,' he'd chided us. But this was nothing compared with his reaction to the fact we had three Bordeaux rosés on our list. 'Bordeaux vign-erons trade on the reputation of the region,' he explained. 'Most of the wines are all marketing and no substance. They laugh at Provençal wine in Bordeaux, so why should I drink their sub-standard cast-offs? I'll give it to the chef to put in the *daube.*'

But during the course of the afternoon we talked to him about our vignerons and why we'd chosen them, and about how well clairet accompanied food. It was like persuading a Scot to support England at football, but gradually we accomplished it and when we poured him a glass, he frowned, shook his head and eventually admitted, '*Ça, c'est pas mal.*'

In our rare quiet moments we got to sit back and relax. It was a long way from a London office. The waves fell gently on to the sandy beach, parascenders trailed behind speedboats, and the sun dipped towards the villa-dotted hills above Cannes. As a solicitor, I would have been writing a list of a hundred things I had to do before I could go home. Typically I'd avoid all phone calls and then panic that I'd missed an important message. Finally I would have phoned Tanya to tell her she should have supper alone. Instead I replenished the ice and restocked our buckets with wine. It wasn't intellectually stimulating, but neither was inserting a missing semi-colon into a legal agreement, and the view was a lot better.

As the afternoon came to an end and people left the beach, clutching handbags, straightening wraps, applying lipstick and calling out to stray children, our bar filled. The staff at La Pinède packed away the *matelas*, balancing them on their heads in the style of African washerwomen. They watered the plants and washed the sand from wooden walkways and pulled out rakes to groom the beach for the following day. And amid all this activity we poured glass after glass of wine to the throng that had gathered around La Vie en Rosé.

At the Saint-Antoine, Igor had warned us about holidaymakers who frequented the Côte d'Azur during August – *les aoûtiens* – saying that they were notorious for not having a penny in their pockets. It seemed that he had never been to La Pinède. No one asked for a price, looked at their change or hesitated for a second when their glass was empty before asking for another. At six o'clock Ives shuffled over to our bar and put his arms round the backs of the remaining customers, urging them to drink up. We folded away the table, put the rosé in the fridge, thanked Claudine and stumbled out into the pine-filled square somewhat bemused at our instant success.

19

The Foie Gras Festival

Four more days of successful trading followed. The clients of La Pinède shared our view that after a day lazing on the beach, rosé was the perfect drink. We sold out of François Crochet's Sancerre and a couple more of our wines, and our blackboard became crisscrossed with a satisfying number of '*fini*' annotations.

At breakfast on the fifth morning I was scooping slices of ripe melon into my mouth and Tanya was trying to avoid dripping juice down her dress as she bit into a plump peach. The sun was just peeking above the roofs of the houses and we felt the first warm rays on our skin. As usual Peter was beginning his day with a cigar and an extraordinarily strong cup of coffee. He paced up and down in front of the table, sat down briefly, decided it was uncomfortable and resumed prowling around the small hotel garden. Tanya flicked through the property pages of *Nice-Matin*, and I began peeling a kiwi fruit. We had the whole morning to relax – or so I thought – before we headed down to the beach and opened La Vie en Rosé. Pushing my plate away, I prepared to return to our room.

'Good, you've finished. Now come over here,' said Peter impatiently. It was only just 10.30 a.m. but on a table in the shade he'd set up a small tasting. There was a bottle of pink wine and three glasses. 'Don't worry, you only have to have a sip,' continued Peter as he poured. 'It comes from a very special vineyard.' The colour of the wine reminded me of a Sancerre rosé we'd tasted the previous summer – it was more golden orange than pink, and the technical French term for it was *pelure d'oignon*, or onion skin.

Peter gave each of our glasses a vigorous swish to release the flavour of the wine and explained about the vineyard, which was in Languedoc Roussillon, near Belesta-de-la-Frontière. Château de Caladroy was built in the twelfth century. Its grounds contained a chapel and an old schoolroom, and for centuries it had defended the frontier against Spain, sheltering a whole community within its walls. But since 1989 it had been empty, and there was now a proposal to convert most of the buildings into a luxury hotel. 'It will be a shame if it happens, but they still make bloody good wine,' said Peter, holding up his glass.

Tastebuds are vulnerable things first thing in the morning, but the Château de Caladroy wine was remarkably smooth and unlike any rosé I'd ever tasted. It was slightly more viscous than a normal wine and reminded me of a Muscat in the way it coated the back of my throat with a delicious sweetness.

'Wonderful, isn't it?' said Peter, finishing his glass and helping himself to a little more. 'It's called Rivesaltes Ambré and is made from letting the juice from a white grape oxidise over a period of four years. The colour comes from the fact that the barrels have previously been used for red wine.'

All summer Peter had been trying to find a rosé to accompany foie gras. It was his Holy Grail. In Champagne he'd tried to persuade us that a light rosé *saignée* was the perfect match. Unfortunately for Peter, we'd checked with a local vigneron and ascertained that although buttery aged vintage champagne was a frequent companion, foie gras was never eaten with rosé. Ever since, Peter had been determined to prove otherwise, asking in nearly every vineyard we visited. The responses had ranged from polite rebuffs to total incredulity, but now he thought he'd found the answer, hence his overexcitement and frantic pre-breakfast pacing.

'Don't you think it would go well with foie gras?' continued Peter. 'Apparently there's a farm up in the hills that we can visit and buy in bulk. They even do lunch. And then imagine it – a foie gras and rosé festival.'

I had to admit that in Château de Caladroy he'd found a wine so decadently sweet that it would perfectly accompany foie gras, but there were plenty of reasons to say no to this latest scheme. Travelling into the hills behind the Côte d'Azur was becoming increasingly dangerous – a series of fire warnings had been issued recently and every morning the local paper printed a colour-coded map showing the various regions in Provence and the risk level. On a sliding scale of colours, yellow meant a negligible risk of fire and black meant that the police advised against travel. Adding to the problems, the squadron of lumbering Canadair fire-fighting planes had been grounded. During the summer they were usually a common sight on the coast – belly-flopping into the sea and climbing slowly away with a cargo bay full of water – but due to a crash in Calvi, each and every plane was undergoing a safety inspection. As a result this wasn't a sensible time to go into the wilds. But Peter wasn't to be denied, pointing out that the area he wanted to travel to was only rated orange by the paper. And as for my suggestion that we purchase the foie gras from the local deli, Peter simply raised one bushy white eyebrow. If La Vie en Rosé was going to serve foie gras, it was going to serve the best.

'But Rivesaltes Ambré isn't even a rosé,' I persisted.

'Nonsense. There's no such thing as a technical definition of a rosé,' countered Peter. 'If it's pink, or nearly pink, it's a rosé.'

In the end Tanya settled the matter. Due to our lack of success with estate agents we'd been discussing pursuing a different approach and hiring a professional to find a bar for us. Glancing up from the paper, she announced that there was a property-search agent based in the town nearest to the farm. It meant paying an extra set of fees but hopefully we'd increase our chances of success.

'Marvellous,' said Peter, 'we'll meet him for lunch at the foie gras farm.'

Peter put on a fresh shirt in preparation for the lunch and chatted excitedly for the whole car journey. At the beginning of the summer he'd ordered foie gras at every opportunity. Whether a chef sautéed it, stuffed steak with it or served it as a carpaccio, Peter didn't mind – he'd grin and enjoy every mouthful. But just recently I'd noticed that he'd become more discerning. Foie gras was on offer at most restaurants but typically it was poor quality and arrived in great slabs, and so Peter had learnt to wait until he discovered a menu that had the correct 'feel'.

The last occasion he'd eaten foie gras was a week ago at a restaurant called the Chèvre d'Or in Cabris. The menu had read, '*Notre foie gras marbré aux abricots, gelée de Muscat, corolle de pousses de betterave,*' which loosely translated meant that their homemade foie gras was marbled with apricots and served with a Muscat jelly and beetroot shoots. When the plate arrived, it looked beautiful. There was a tiny circular slice of foie gras surrounded by a tracing of Muscat jelly. It was accompanied by a glass of Sauternes and a basket full of white toast – only one side of the bread had been toasted, and with the care of a mother putting a cherished child to bed, the triangles of toast had been tucked snugly under a white napkin. Unusually there was total silence from Peter as he ate, then when his plate was clean, he turned to us and declared the starter to be 'sensational'.

Now, as we bumped up the track towards the farm, he was

salivating again. To our right, we could see large pens full of ducks and a couple of donkeys loose in a field. In the yard in front of the farm, perhaps a hundred golden ducklings darted this way and that like a school of fish. A large mongrel lay in the shade watching this activity with a sleepy lack of interest, occasionally pawing at his nose to disrupt flies.

The farmhouse was a low wooden building that reminded me of the fondue restaurant in Aix where we'd initially come up with the idea for La Vie en Rosé. The sloping roof hung over the terrace, providing much-needed shade to a long communal dining table. At one end, a young French couple were already eating a starter of smoked duck breast and we took a seat next to them.

'You must be the Iveys.'

We turned and saw a man, about the same age as Tanya and me, holding four glasses of pink champagne. He wore a loose-fitting beige suit; his hair was collar length and flecked blond by the sun. His nose and ears were too big to allow him to be classically handsome, but he had brilliant cheeky blue eyes and a wide, full mouth with which he was grinning impishly at us.

'Well, you're looking for a rosé bar, so pink champagne's appropriate. My name's Thierry, the property agent.' He spoke in fluent but heavily accented English and, as we quickly learnt, had a penchant for English colloquialisms. 'Down zee hatch,' he said, taking a gulp of champagne.

'*Salut*,' we replied.

'Unusual place,' said Thierry, reading the menu. To begin with, of course, there was foie gras, but in a bewildering number of varieties – *foie gras entier de canard, foie gras entier de canard mi-cuit* and *pâté de foie gras*. This was then followed by one of two salads – smoked duck or duck liver – and then a choice from three main courses – *civet de canard, canard à l'orange* or *magret de canard au poivre*. 'Looks like it's duck for lunch, then,' continued Thierry with a toothy grin, as he sipped on his champagne.

Even our resident foie gras expert, Peter, couldn't decipher all the different varieties and so Thierry took over, explaining with delight how the whole process worked. 'First you buy some male ducklings. Never female, they talk too much. Quack, quack, quack.' He winked at Tanya. 'You should hear my wife. You see those ducklings over there? Have you heard a quack yet?' Tanya shook her head. 'Told you so, all male. It takes them four months to feed them up to the right size and then it's time for the table.'

According to Thierry, we should all be ordering the *foie gras entier mi-cuit*. This was the whole liver of the duck removed and chopped in two and then pasteurised. It was the freshest and best version of the delicacy. Next in quality was the *foie gras entier*, which was sterilised rather than pasteurised, allowing it to travel better. Then there was the *pâté de foie gras* – an inferior version in which the liver was combined with salt, starch and various other ingredients. 'It's what you get in most restaurants,' confided Thierry.

We ordered, and began to discuss our search for a bar. Thierry gulped his champagne and declared that there was no need for anything as prosaic as a pen and paper – he would remember everything. As we went into more detail about the rosé bar, his smile grew larger, spreading right across his face. 'You English are crazy, but it's good, I like crazy. I am crazy as a coot too.' He started waving his arms above his head and rolling his eyes in a bizarre imitation of a lunatic, or was it a coot?

Before we could ascertain which, the foie gras arrived. It was dusted with cracked peppercorns and served with a glass of golden Muscat, rough country bread and a pot of sweet apricot jam. All the trimmings of the restaurant in Cabris had been dispensed with – the bread toasted on one side, the beetroot shoots – but the food was still luxurious as well as hearty. Peter and Thierry heaped great chunks of the delicacy on to pieces of bread and munched contentedly away. 'It's a very interesting combination,' said Peter between mouthfuls. 'The cracked pepper contrasts really well with the sweet jelly. I'd never have thought it would work.'

Our plates were removed and quickly replaced by large salads of smoked duck. Thierry selected an oaked white wine to accompany the food and then began his sales pitch, explaining how he hoped to reduce the price of any property he found by at least 20 per cent and as a result his fee of 15 per cent was actually a bargain. Once again he rolled his eyes elaborately, gestured wildly with his arms, took gulps of wine and punctuated his sentences with big, toothy grins.

By the time we'd finished the salad I felt he was doing us a favour by accepting such a small percentage. Looking around the table, I could see that all of us were agreed that we should hire him – after all, where else were we going to find someone as crazy as us? But Thierry was briefly too carried away with his own genius to allow us to agree to his terms. As steaming plates of *magret de canard au poivre* arrived, he decided that he wanted to help us with our festival later that afternoon. 'If I can't get twenty per cent off the price of the foie gras you're going to buy, then don't hire me to find you a property,' he said as he scooped a slice of dripping pink duck breast into his mouth, wiping the juice from his lips with his napkin, which he'd tucked into his shirt like a cravat.

At Thierry's suggestion, we opted for several large tins of the *foie gras entier*, which he advised would cope better with the heat on the beach than the *mi-cuit* version. He disappeared inside to conclude the deal and I looked at my still half-full plate. Despite my best intentions after a summer in France sharing a table with Peter, I'd gained two extra chins and a balloon of a belly. It was time for a diet.

Moments later Thierry returned. 'Told you so,' he said, skipping back on to the terrace. 'Thirty-five per cent off. If you give me a couple of days, I'll see if we can do the same with a property.'

★

Back in Juan–les–Pins, La Vie en Rosé opened at 3 p.m. We'd decided to trade as normal until six-ish and then once people were showered, changed and ready to leave the club, we would serve glasses of Rivesaltes Ambré with a small foie gras canapé. We'd priced this luxurious combination at €10, and Peter was adamant that it would prove a success. 'Think about it – the pink-tinged sun setting over the bay, casting a gentle channel of light towards Cannes, and a wonderful *amuse-bouche*.'

Before the festival started, we had another busy afternoon to enjoy. The beach club was completely full, and we strolled among the sun loungers with our bottles of wine offering the recumbent clientele a taste of different wines. Taking rosé out on to the pontoon – with the glittering sea in the background, the gin palaces crossing the bay and the immaculate blue sky – I was struck by how ridiculous our lives had become. Children aspire to be footballers, actors, even astronauts, but even the most precocious young imagination would struggle to invent a job like ours. It was an escapist adult fantasy, and the pontoon, with its rows of yellow umbrellas bobbing amid the rolling waves, encapsulated the idea in a single image. La Vie en Rosé was real, but at times it seemed no more than an indulgent dream – surely at some stage we'd rub our eyes and wake up back in London.

Fortunately at La Pinède there was rarely an opportunity for such worries. An Irish family was having a late lunch in the restaurant, and once they'd finished eating – at about five o'clock – the thought of a couple more hours in the sun proved too much. Instead they crossed to our rosé bar and with their well-lubricated and all-too-lyrical Irish tongues whiled away the rest of the afternoon. Handing his teenage son a couple of hundred euros to spend on parascending, Pascal and his wife, Siobhàn, started to work their way through our wines, chatting to us about their millions as they did so. Within half an hour we'd received a detailed breakdown of their property portfolio

– the eight-bedroom château just outside Saint-Rémy, the holiday villa in Antibes and the Caribbean bolthole. 'The thing about property, Jamie, is that it only goes up in value. Take the château in Saint-Rémy – we paid two million euros for it, and how much do you think it is worth now?'

I poured two more glasses and waited for the answer. 'Over four million euros, Jamie.' After an hour we'd officially become friends of the family, which meant that we were invited to stay in the château and that Siobhàn had no reservations talking to Tanya about the provenance of her diamonds – South African blue were the only ones she'd touch. At six, when the majority of the beach club had showered and changed, our two new best customers were still standing – although barely – at the bar. Their faces were puffy and red from the sun, and they'd tried rosé from about ten different vineyards before settling on several bottles of their favourite.

Meanwhile Peter had prepared for the foie gras festival – he'd returned to the hotel, washed, swept back his hair and put on a shirt, chinos and brogues. Then he'd prepared three trays full of foie gras-based nibbles according to a strict ratio of one for him and one for the clients. The Rivesaltes Ambré was on ice and all we awaited before we started trading was Claudine's approval. She straightened the tablecloth, arranged the *amuses-bouches* into a more orderly fashion and then gave a little nod. I think her only regret was that she couldn't remove our Irish customers, or at least make them stand up straight.

To Peter's beaming delight, a large number of the clients of La Pinède had waited to enjoy the party. The sun was falling from the sky, and just as Peter had predicted, people's faces were bathed in a warm amber glow that precisely matched the colour of the wine.

As people lined up for a taste, there was plenty of quibbling about whether Rivesaltes Ambré was or was not a rosé, and Peter's thesis on the subject developed all too rapidly: 'All grape juice is white, and all rosés – apart from champagne – take their colour from the red pigment in the skin of the grape,' boomed Peter with authority. 'Well, it's the same with Rivesaltes – the juice of the grapes is white and it takes its colour from the pigment left in the barrel by a previous fermentation of red wine. It must be a rosé.'

I opened my notebook to keep track of sales and began to pour the Rivesaltes. As I did so, a heavy drop of rain thudded into the paper, smudging the ink into a wet circle. Glancing skywards, I ripped out the page and started again. There were two more warning thuds and then a volley of bulbous drops shot down from the sky, leaving dents in the sand. Out at sea, the sky was still clear, but a heavy bank of clouds had crept towards the coast from the mountains. One half of the beach was still illuminated by the sun, but the other half was suddenly cast into shadow. Our customers looked nervously upwards, watching the inexorable progress of the weather front. As yet we were on the very fringes of the storm, but barring a sudden change in the wind direction, it would be upon us in minutes.

Tanya and I began handing round glasses of Rivesaltes Ambré, but there were few takers. The entire beach fell into shade and rain exploded into the sand, creating a miniature battlefield. Siobhàn and Pascal still clung to the bar, but as lightning flashed across the sky, even they retreated. Only Peter remained motionless, staring at the heavens. Water dripped from his hair and glasses on to his soaking shirt, which was now matted against his chest.

'Come on, there's always tomorrow,' said Tanya, leading him to shelter.

20

The *Compromis*

It was still raining the following morning. At La Pinède, we found Claudine and Ives sheltering at the rear of the restaurant. The sun loungers were stacked away, and a channel of water flowed through the sand to the sea. Despite the grey skies and the lack of customers, Claudine was still sitting with her prescription shades on flicking through a big pile of receipts. Ives showed us the back page of the paper. The weather map for the whole of the south of France was covered with dark clouds, and there was an editorial about a predicted week of severe storms. Apparently a warm wind from the Balearics was hitting cold air over the mountains of Provence, leading to heavy rain across the region.

What should we do? We still had just under a week of our planned stay in Juan-les-Pins left. Claudine raised her glasses, revealing her gentle hazelnut eyes. '*C'est à la tête,*' she consoled us, advising us we just had to take it on the head, the French version of 'on the chin'. Ives sighed '*en soufflant*' – like him we should deflate for a while.

It was easier said than done. We'd spent a large proportion of the week's takings stocking up for the foie gras festival and we still had a fridge full of canapés that were fast going off. La Pinède had promised to be one of our most successful locations of the summer, but now it looked like La Vie en Rosé would be shut for the rest of our stay in Juan-les-Pins. Making matters worse, there were only three weeks left until September, we hadn't organised any other temporary locations for La Vie en Rosé, and our hopes of finding somewhere permanent rested with an eccentric property finder. It was hard not to conclude that our experiment of running France's first rosé bar was going to end in failure.

The next days brought no change in the weather. Gutters regurgitated water, and the terraces of restaurants remained empty. Chairs were stacked on top of each other and chained together, and awnings were wound back so that they dripped on unwary pedestrians. Holidaymakers wandered the streets using newspapers as impromptu umbrellas, unaware that the print was running down their faces like mascara. According to the news, 113 campsites were evacuated due to flooding, thirty-three trains were brought to a halt between stations, and all the cash machines in Montpellier had ceased to work due to fallen power lines. There were pictures from Nîmes of cars flowing down the streets and people being rescued in rubber dinghies.

In the short breaks between the storms, we watched as diggers tried to clear drainage ditches of debris, but once the rain returned, the channels flooded and the streets ran with water again. Dogs sheltered in doorways and looked lazily skywards, wondering when it was all going to end. A wedding party sat snarled up in the centre of town as hailstones slammed down on the roofs of their cars. At the head of the procession, the bride and groom sat together in a 2CV that must have once been white. The paintwork was stained brick red from driving along roads flooded from overflowing rivers, and the ribbons hanging limply from the aerial dripped muddy water over the bonnet.

Streams of cars hooting their horns to celebrate a wedding was a relatively common sight in France, but intriguingly everyone seemed even more excited than normal. Winding down their windows and keeping their hands planted on their horns, the well-wishers cried, '*Mariage pluvieux, mariage heureux,*' which translated meant a wet wedding led to a happy marriage. 'If that's true, there are a lot of content couples in England,' said Peter.

Amid the thunder and lightning, the only good news was a phone call from Thierry. He'd found a property that might suit us. It was called the Auberge des Sangliers – apparently on cold nights wild boar sheltered in the lee of its walls – and consisted of a former bar that had fallen into disrepair. There was living accommodation and even a separate small cottage included in extensive grounds. It was located outside L'Isle-sur-la-Sorgue, on the fringes of the Luberon National Park, and had once been a regular stop for motorists because of the scenic view. A family disagreement led to the closure of the bar several years ago, and a dispute over ownership meant it had only just come on to the market. The seller had yet to sign on with an estate agent and Thierry advised us to come and see it at once. 'You should be prepared to stay in the area for several days: you'll need to see the property a few times if you are going to make an offer,' he concluded.

To me, the *auberge* represented one last chance. It had to be good value, capture our hearts and offer the opportunity for a viable business, otherwise I would voice the fear that had dogged me all summer – La Vie en Rosé was a mistake.

With the rain still falling, we eventually decided to leave Juan-les-Pins. The beach was a mess of washed-up flotsam, and furrows as wide as rivers had been cut across it by the floodwater flowing into the bay. If, as the forecasters predicted, the storm continued for the next few days, we'd be doing little else but sitting and watching the grey clouds and the steely sea. It was a sad way to leave La Pinède. As we said our farewells, Claudine produced some photos from fifty years ago. We could identify

each of the pine trees that fringed the club, but where the restaurant was now, there was only a beach hut and a couple of
empty deckchairs. According to Claudine, every fifteen years
the town auctioned the rights to run beach bars, and auction by
auction the number and size of the bars had grown.

Kissing us goodbye, she slipped us the number of her daughter, who had just started working in a vineyard near Vidauban.
'If you need some more wine, just drop in.'

As I turned away from La Pinède for the last time, I saw Ives
begin the laborious task of raking the sand.

We met with Thierry in L'Isle-sur-la-Sorgue and then headed
east into the hills. The rain had briefly stopped and the sky was
once again a familiar lush blue. We put down the hood of the
car and enjoyed the warm air gusting into our faces. On either
side of us were cliffs painted varying shades of green by the
pines and wild olive trees. Deep in the bushes wild boar were
rooting for food, and high above hawks floated on the thermals.
We skirted Fontaine-de-Vaucluse, where an underground river
erupted from the ground and cut a deep gorge down the valley.
This village was one of the area's main tourist attractions and the
surrounding roads were full of coaches. We drove on, winding
ever upwards towards the sky.

After another ten minutes there was a faded sign by the
roadside – L'Auberge des Sangliers. We turned right and drove
between two stone obelisks planted on either side of the road.
The middle of the track was overgrown and we could hear the
brambles scraping against the undercarriage of the car as we
continued to climb. After a couple of sharp bends the property
came into view. The highest floor was built at road level, and
the two lower stories fell away down the hillside, with the back
and bottom of the house opening up on to a meadow. The
building was constructed from irregularly shaped stones, and the
five windows at the front were each guarded by a set of blistered

shutters with the red paint flaking away from the wood.

'Well, here we are. You might think there's no passing trade, but people used to stop here for a drink either before or after visiting Fontaine and you can see why,' said Thierry, as he led us to the far end of the house, where, on the same level as the track, there was a terrace surrounded by a balustrade. Beneath us in every direction was a canopy of trees, with their branches billowing upwards, hiding the land beneath. Away in the distance, through the almost tropical haze created by heat and the recent rainfall, past faded purple fields of lavender, I could see the white peak of Mont Ventoux. To the south, the wooded slopes of the Luberon dived towards the sea. Most impressive of all was the distance I could look without seeing another house. Even the roads were hidden by the vegetation. The only thing spoiling the panorama were sets of rusty chairs and umbrellas sodden from the recent rain and speared through the heart of various rickety tables.

The setting reminded me of another place in the Luberon we'd visited by accident the previous year. We'd followed a wedding party into the hills and enjoyed a *fête champêtre* – country picnic – at the Auberge des Seguins. That spot was even more isolated: a mountain stream fed the swimming pool, and there was nothing but the bare cliffs for company. If a business could survive there, then one might prosper here. Strolling on to the terrace, we tried to imagine what it would be like as La Vie en Rosé. The faded umbrellas could be replaced with sturdy white ones; we would need a new set of wooden tables and a couple of large blackboards to mount on the wall.

'The owner's not here today, so we are free to have a good look around,' said Thierry, as he removed a key from his pocket and slid open a set of glass doors that led from the terrace to the bar area. Rows of long wooden tables were strewn across the room, with benches poking out from them at irregular angles. The fireplace was large enough for Peter to walk into and start poking about, showering himself in ash, and a collection of antlers and tusks hung from the wall. It might have been a little eerie but for the rich swathes of light admitted by the windows. Behind the bar, there was an old ice-cream freezer, rows of empty optic-holders, a large poster showing a cartoon of a girl in shock as her skirt was blown into the air by the wind, and a rusty trophy, which had fallen on its side like a felled tree.

'It shouldn't take too much work to get this place ready for business,' said Peter, wiping dust from one of the tables.

In one corner of the room, a stone staircase corkscrewed down to the lower floor. According to Thierry, below were three bedrooms, a bathroom, a living room and a kitchen. The first thing we noticed as we descended was the clutter. There was enough miscellaneous furniture to supply a *brocante* market – chests of drawers, wardrobes, faded black-and-white photos and some more curious pieces, including a headless mannequin dressed in a school gown, a book open on a music stand entitled *The Victims of Neron*, and an old bike with the severed head of a doll in its pannier. Most macabre of all was an ornate bowl full of dead dried scorpions. 'All houses built near stone have a scorpion problem,' advised Thierry, as he led us through the different rooms, crying, 'Scorpion!' at every subsequent opportunity to try and make Tanya jump.

Despite the curious taste in collectibles, I really took to the house. The living area was spacious, the bedrooms light, and the French country kitchen conjured images of hearty stews on cold winter evenings. Copper pots and pans hung from hooks in the ceiling, jars of dried herbs lined the shelves, and there was an old cooker that resembled an Aga and a fireplace set at waist level so that the coals could be used to chargrill food.

'There is just one more thing I need to show you,' added Thierry, as he led us outside. The meadow was alive with the sound of birds and insects celebrating the return of the sun, but over the distant hills dark clouds were once again gathering.

'It's good weather for mushrooms,' said Thierry, as we followed him round to the side of the house towards a copse of perhaps a hundred olive trees. '*Girolles, cèpes,* even truffles – you should get a good crop up here,' he continued, as he led us into the middle of a maze of contorted old trunks until we came to an old stone cottage. It was little more than a hut with one window and a door.

'We can't go inside today because there is still a tenant and I don't have the key,' Thierry apologised. 'Unless ...' Pulling himself up on to the windowsill, Thierry fed his hand behind the shutter and unlatched it. Levering himself through the window, he reappeared moments later at the door. 'Used to be a burglar in London,' he joked. 'That's how I learnt my English. In the clink–clunk.'

Inside, the cottage was completely open-plan. On the ground floor was a small sitting room, kitchen and dining room, and above us on a mezzanine level was the bedroom. 'Make a perfect holiday apartment,' beamed Thierry, still clearly delighted with his illegal entry.

Tanya had turned away from the cottage and was wandering amid the olive trees, picking the leaves and crushing them between her palms. I was worried that the bowl of dead scorpions, the headless mannequin and the unknown tenant had put her off the place.

Catching up, I held her hand. 'Well, what do you think?'

'I love it. I absolutely love it.'

The words were enough to make me want to take a leap of faith.

A day later Thierry received a phone call. The owner of the property – Madame Chevalier – wanted to meet us to find out how serious we were about the prospective purchase.

'Do you know anyone with children?' Thierry asked as he arranged the date and time of our visit. 'Madame Chevalier never stops talking about families. It might help your chances if you brought some kids along.'

'You want us to pretend we've got children?'

'No, but seeing that you are good with children just might help.'

And so Thierry, Claire, Rosie and Tristan joined us on our next visit – Claire to offer a second opinion, and Rosie and Tristan to win the heart of Madame Chevalier.

The negotiations took place in the kitchen. Tristan almost immediately located a live scorpion and began chasing it around the room, whereas Rosie sensibly decided that insects with forked tails didn't appeal and wandered out into the meadow. Madame Chevalier was a frail, dark-haired old woman with deep brown, almost black eyes. She wore a loose-fitting dress made from material that looked suspiciously similar to the curtains in one of the bedrooms. We shared a bottle of wine and talked about the possibility of buying the property. The main complicating factor was the tenant of the cottage, who still had two years left on his lease, but Madame assured me with small taps of her fingers against mine that the problem wasn't insurmountable.

'I do so want to pass the house on to a family,' she sighed, and pushed her chair away.

Standing up, she glanced out of the window at Rosie, who was almost hidden by the lush grass. A mop of light-brown curly hair periodically popped into the open and then just as quickly disappeared, accompanied by a peal of giggles. 'Tistin can't find me,' cried Rosie. Sensing our attention, she leapt up and ran round in a circle, holding her hands out like aeroplane wings.

When Madame returned to her seat, her heavy make-up was smudged across her face. She poured us all some more wine. 'We've had a lot of interest in the property, and the price is very good,' she said as she lit a cigarette and held it to her lips with an unsteady hand. 'I can't wait for ever.'

Realistically there were probably too many uncertainties for us to even consider making an offer. As well as the tenant, we didn't know whether the building was structurally sound, and we had no idea how we would attract customers to such an out-of-the-way spot. And yet as much as I wanted my head to take over, I couldn't shake the feeling that it was the right place for us. The size and space of the property was beyond anything I thought we could afford, and with a little imagination the terrace could once again be converted into the most idyllic place to have a drink. Romantics that they were, Tanya and Peter had completely fallen for the place, their conversation seldom straying from how it could be made into a successful business. There was talk of converting the cottage into a *gîte* to supplement our income and even offering food in the winter.

Thierry was equally enthusiastic about his find. For the price, he viewed it as a really good investment. Even if our business failed, provided we did a little bit of renovation, he assured us it would sell for more on the open market. And although the French didn't typically worry about surveys, he offered to get a friend who was a builder to have a look at the house and check it was sound.

Losing patience, Madame Chevalier opened the drawer at the end of the kitchen table. Inside were a serrated knife – traditionally kept there for the head of the family – and a thick white document. 'Either I sell it to you now or I look for another buyer,' she said defiantly, pushing the legal document towards us.

My natural reaction would have been to get up and leave. Twice now when we'd been close to buying a French property, the owner had tried to close the deal too quickly. Whether it was through an excess of caution or not, it made me feel totally uneasy. I knew that Tanya loved the *auberge*, and after our experience in Cabris I also knew she'd be disappointed if I didn't commit. However, I was desperate to ensure that our French adventure ended happily, and throughout the summer

I'd been plagued by the thought of us losing our savings on a poorly thought-through property investment and being forced to return to London.

Without Thierry I would have risked another row with Tanya and insisted on a couple of days to think the transaction over, but thankfully he was there to reassure me, explaining that a *compromis* only committed us to buying the property following a seven-day cooling-off period. This started to run after our signature of the document. If we decided to pull out after seven days, then our deposit would be refunded. 'Sign the document, and in the meantime I'll do some more investigation,' he urged.

When we'd left London, I don't think either of us had ever dreamt we'd end up in such a property, and now with the single stroke of a pen it was a possibility. We just had to be brave enough to ignore our nerves and go ahead. And so with Thierry's assurance that the document followed the standard format, Tanya and I signed.

Madame Chevalier picked up the pen and I did likewise. 'We'll also need the signature of the co-owner, my daughter, Christine.' Madame waited calmly at the table as a pair of high heels clicked down the stone staircase and Christine entered the kitchen. Tanya, Peter and I glanced at each other. The highlights had been redone, and the cigarette was absent, but it was the same Christine who'd shown us around the house in Cabris.

'I hope you have had plenty of time to reflect,' she said, as she signed her name in large loopy letters and gave us a lopsided smile.

'What's the matter?' said Thierry to me, as we emerged into the sunshine. '*Vous avez mangé une guêpe?*' Seeing my confused face, he translated: 'You look like you've eaten a wasp.'

21

The *Station d'Epuration*

We agreed to meet with Thierry again in a week's time back
at the Auberge des Sangliers to decide whether to go ahead
with the purchase. In the meantime we booked into a hotel in
L'Isle-sur-la-Sorgue. The town was split in two by the tumbling
waters of the Sorgue. Islands of land could be reached by bridges
which curved gently towards the sky. In places, the waters of the
Sorgue were channelled into a series of narrow canals that drove
heavy iron waterwheels draped with lush vegetation.

The sound of running water was a constant companion – the
slow, repetitive chop as the blades dipped into the shimmering
surface, the gentler noise of the constant shower of droplets from
the wheels and the rush of the river over the series of manmade
steps. The canals flowed into the farthest streets, ducking underground only to emerge again outside the front doors of houses
and earning the town its soubriquet, the Venice of France.

L'Isle-sur-la-Sorgue was also renowned for antiques, and
lining the banks of the river were hundreds of dealers selling
anything from marble baths for thousands of euros down to
rusty old hotel keys for a couple. Every Sunday there was the
largest *brocante* in the south of France, and twice yearly one of
the biggest antique fairs in the world spread across the surrounding fields. Leading away from the antique shops were narrow

cobbled streets full of pretty boutiques brimming with clothes, perfumes and local delicacies. The central square was dominated by the Gothic church – Notre-Dame-des-Anges – and on the inside of its vaulted ceiling, golden angels swooped against a clear blue sky. The surrounding buildings were wonderfully run-down. Faded pastel paints advertised businesses from different eras – the bed-makers and cobblers had long since been replaced by bars and restaurants, but you could still read the past by the writing on the old sun-bleached façades.

Back near the canal, we busied ourselves by trying to organise a rosé festival for the week. After we'd been dismissively '*allez-ed*' a couple of times, we found a bar called L'Assorti. A small terrace had been built by the side of the water, and the outside of the bar was decorated with kitchen paraphernalia inventively used to spell its name. The 'A' consisted of a combination of forks, the 'S's were formed by knives, and the 'O' was a kitchen colander. Isabelle, who must have been about our age, had designed the whole fascia and she was keen to try our idea, particularly when she discovered that her mother lived in the same street in Montpellier as Claire and had recently met Tristan and Rosie outside their apartment.

It was late August and after the week of rain the weather had finally settled. Each morning we awoke to a clear blue sky and, outside, would feel the warmth of the sun on the back of our necks. By midday we'd set up our ice buckets full of rosé on the terrace of Isabelle's restaurant. We borrowed a large umbrella for shade and stood waiting to trade. Whether it was L'Isle-sur-la-Sorgue itself or, with the school holidays drawing to a close, just the time of year, the clientele was noticeably different. The average age of our customers was at least twenty years older than we had experienced on the Côte d'Azur, and the price of our wine was a far more sensitive issue. There also seemed to be a preponderance of Scandinavians, and whereas for us pale rosé epitomised the south of France, for these northern Europeans it was the darker rosés. After tasting all our different wines, they almost inevitably opted for the clairets from Bordeaux.

Despite the idyllic background of the gently turning water-wheels and the constant flow of customers, I spent most of the week worrying. Two years ago I could have been sanguine about the future. When we'd set out on the trip to find France's palest rosé, I'd seen it as one final life-enriching jaunt before Tanya and I settled down to our careers and perhaps having a family. But during the course of the trip I'd fallen for the good life. I liked to think that I wasn't just a dreamy romantic who couldn't see past the sweeping fields of lavender and the sun-enriched smells of pine and herbs but of course they influenced my thinking, as did the lifestyle on offer in the south – the reliance on good local produce, the markets and the pride of people, whether a vigneron or a farmer, in the land they worked.

At first the language had proved a real barrier: I was hampered by my schoolboy reluctance to make a fool of myself. But in the middle of our summer trading rosé something had changed and suddenly French words, even sentences had come flowing from my mouth. I still got plenty of things wrong, but at least it was usually funny. Recently I had thought I was having a conversation with a street vendor about the storms – *les orages* – and was presented with a bag of oranges. The same day I lost my mobile phone – *portable* – and when I asked after its whereabouts was handed a glass of drinking water – *l'eau potable*.

If, for whatever reason, we couldn't make a life for ourselves in France and we had to return to England, I hoped I could be comfortable with myself. But when I looked at what we'd accomplished in the past two years, it occurred to me that in some ways the path we'd chosen might be irreversible. We had travelled so far and invested so much in our belief that we could create a different life – how could we suddenly relinquish our ideas? They were about more than geography.

But given a week to wait and analyse my feelings, doubts once again crept into my mind. Was part of me still tied to the past? In the purely physical rather than the emotional sense, weren't all our decisions reversible? Perhaps this was why selling our flat in London hadn't worried me – after all, how much was the property market going to change in a year? Had I been deluding myself all along into thinking I was an adventurer? It was a disturbing thought. When it came to the moment to take the final decision about the purchase of the *auberge*, would I be able to shed my upbringing?

Thanks to Thierry and some fortuitous timing, we'd stumbled on a location that exceeded all our expectations. If there were other similar opportunities, they'd eluded us all summer, and we couldn't survive by relying on the generous bar owners to host our festival for ever. But what if the *auberge* was in the wrong location and La Vie en Rosé failed? There were so many uncertainties that not for the first time since leaving England I longed for a regular career and a regular income – even though my life might be more one-dimensional, our futures would be more secure.

But then there was Tanya to think about. Her hand gestures, her expressions and her way of living were more Gallic than English, and the longer she spent in France, the more apparent this became. How could I deny her her dream?

While we waited for news from Thierry, she retreated into herself, and there was even the odd fractious moment between us. Her anxiety turned her into a perfectionist – our blackboard had to be spotlessly clean, the tablecloths washed, ironed and immaculately arranged, and the stock checked and rechecked.

As the days passed, I became more uncertain and even Tanya began to have some doubts. She talked about missing her friends and above all her family. It was the same conversation that had sparked our row before we left London in late April and once again I found it hard to deal with – to go ahead with the purchase, I needed to believe that living in France would make Tanya happy, but at exactly the moment I wanted reassurance, she was wavering.

However much we tried not to involve Peter in our disagreements, it was hard to mistake the tension between us. As usual his advice was refreshingly direct. Gathering us both together over a glass of wine, he announced, 'Bugger all the worry – everything will be fine with the *auberge*.'

But on a couple of occasions I caught Peter deliberately spilling salt so that he could throw it over his shoulder, and the evening before we were due to meet with Thierry and hear the results of his investigations, Peter even tried to lure a neighbouring black cat to the restaurant by leaving out titbits.

Exactly a week on from our previous visit to Auberge des Sangliers and with just a couple of hours left to pull out of the *compromis* and get our deposit back, we climbed back through the Luberon hills towards the property. Our progress was hampered by the small tractors of the vignerons chugging between field and *cave*. Their orange sirens were revolving, and they pulled trailers full of grapes. The *vendange* had started once again and another year in the fields was about to end.

In some vineyards, enormous mechanical harvesting machines straddled the vines, swallowing the grapes and then regurgitating them on to an ever-growing pile in the trailer behind. In others, the harvesting process was much slower. Teams of workers were bent double in the vines clasping secateurs and working their way methodically down the rows, pausing only to call for a fresh bucket or to sneak a quick cigarette. The reward for all their labour was the quality of the wine. Grapes picked by machine-harvesting were often bruised, which meant that fermentation began not in the carefully controlled conditions of the *cave* but in the fields. As a result, more chemicals had to be added to keep the wine stable, and as we knew all too well from occasionally overindulging on *vrac*, the result for the unwary drinker was a very heavy head in the morning.

'I almost wish that we could help with the harvest,' I said, as we passed a group of labourers sharing a picnic in the shade of an olive tree.

'But last time your back hurt so much you said you'd rather work in an office for the rest of your life than do the *vendange* again,' replied Tanya.

'I said almost.'

We arrived at the Auberge des Sangliers ahead of Thierry. There was no sign of Madame Chevalier and so we uncorked a bottle of our favourite pale rosé – from Château la Dorgonne – and sat on the terrace enjoying the view. Despite our best intentions, it was hard not to discuss how we'd alter things – perhaps a small awning projecting over the glass sliding doors, some pots planted with baby olive trees and moving the bar area outside into the sunshine so that we could enjoy the view as we worked. Without knowing it, we were beginning to talk like the owners of the property and there were still unanswered questions about the intentions of the tenant and the structural integrity of the building.

'Madame Chevalier was right,' said Tanya, looking out across the meadow. 'It's a great place to raise a family.'

'What the devil are you doing here?' Thierry had crept around the back of the terrace and leapt out from behind the balustrade. 'Don't you mind me,' he continued, revelling in the attention his arrival had caused and pouring himself a large glass of rosé, 'you just continue chitter-chattering.' I still marvelled at how we'd put our future in the hands of such an eccentric, but thankfully behind the bluster and the natural comedic talent, there was an active brain and I think genuine concern for us.

'It's been a busy week, twenty-four-seven, and there's some good news and some bad news. First the good. I can find nothing wrong with the property. I've had a builder look at it.'

Thierry paused dramatically. 'He puffed and he puffed and he didn't blow the house down. So I think it is OK. And the bad news—'

'It's the tenant, isn't it?' interrupted Tanya.

'Well, there is no formal agreement with the tenant, but I've spoken to him and he's says he'll go with Madame. I believe him.'

'It's Christine, then?'

'*Non*. It's not her.'

'So what's the problem?'

'Ah,' he said, tapping his head, 'it is a little — how you say? — counter-intuitive. The problem is there is no problem and that worries me. I've been to the *mairie* and they've shown me all the documents relating to the land and everything is perfect, too perfect. The price is too cheap and that makes my gut throb.'

Ignoring another misplaced cliché, Tanya led Thierry through the options. 'So, if you'd actually found something wrong, you would have advised us not to buy?'

'Yes.'

'And although you've found nothing wrong, you're still advising us not to buy?'

'*Voilà*,' said Thierry, finishing his wine. '*C'est le* Catch 22.'

Back in the car, we had a bottle of pink champagne chilling in an ice-box. When Thierry had pronounced that the house was structurally sound and that as far as he could tell there were no problems, I'd almost left my seat to go and fetch the champagne. Now these celebrations seemed a long way off.

'So what are our options?' I asked.

'Well, you can do nothing, the seven-day period will expire and you'll be committed to going through with the purchase of the house. Or you can exercise your right to pull out. If you do pull out, I think the property will sell very quickly at its current price. It's your decision, but my gut-throb is never wrong.'

'Never?'

'Well, perhaps sometimes.'

For a while there was silence. The heavy chirp of the cicadas was the first thing to pull me from my thoughts. I concentrated on the repetitive chorus trying to bring calm to my mind. A hawk drifted on the wind, swiftly gaining and then losing altitude before finally diminishing to a brown spot in the deep-blue sky. White butterflies danced haphazardly among the wild flowers that fringed the terrace and I began counting their number. What if there were thirteen?

'Shall we vote on it?' I ventured tentatively. 'I think we need a unanimous decision. All those in favour of buying the property.'

Tanya raised her hand almost immediately. Peter followed but I hesitated. After a week of worry I thought I'd finally banished my inner demons. Driving up to the *auberge*, I'd been convinced that it was right to go ahead with the purchase. Although our summer selling rosé had not been a great success, we'd learnt the trade. We knew the correct mark-ups to apply, we could describe all our wines in detail and deal with difficult customers, and so I'd concluded it was time to back ourselves. But with Thierry's words of caution all my doubts returned. There was the advice from Guy and Bauduin that France was no place to be starting a new business, and to add to our problems, the *auberge* was in such an isolated position it would be difficult to attract customers.

Eventually I returned to the one question that had entered my head the moment Thierry delivered his verdict – if a problem existed, how bad could it be? Surely there were moments in life when you just had to go for it. I couldn't be afraid of the unknown and so because the south of France had finally claimed me – the scents, the smells and the sleepy cobbled streets – I slowly lifted my hand.

I was about to declare the motion passed when Thierry also held his hand up. 'One for all and all for one,' he declared. 'We are the Four Musketeers, *non*? Anyway, my gut is feeling much better.'

By nature I am a worrier. I'll lie awake all night turning a problem over in my mind. Before I left my job with Horatio Hanson, I'd spent many sleepless hours listening to the regular breathing of Tanya and trying to work through the potential consequences. Although to our contemporaries back home it might have appeared a rash decision, I reassured myself that our summer running La Vie en Rosé had been a calculated gamble.

In contrast Tanya is passionate and intuitive. Her decision-making is based on a spur-of-the-moment sense of what is right and wrong. Until now our two different personalities had served us well. I'd certainly learnt that life couldn't be reduced to a series of logical decisions and I'd become happy to trust her instincts. But almost the moment I'd raised my hand and com-mitted us to buying the *auberge*, it had begun to feel wrong.

Over the next couple of days Peter and Tanya were jubilant and I pretended as best I could to be as excited. It was a busy time – there was money to transfer, a mortgage to arrange, forms to sign, and friends and family to be informed, and it was hard not to be swept away with the rush to start our new life. But even as I smiled and toasted Peter and Tanya with champagne, one question kept bothering me – why had the Auberge des Sangliers been so cheap? All sorts of nightmare scenarios concerning the mysterious tenant played in my imagination – would we arrive to find him squatting in the property with twenty-three friends? Would he ever really leave, or would he just haunt our lives, for ever present as a fleeting shadow in the woods?

The Fourth Musketeer, Thierry, was also troubled. When we'd parted he'd taken me aside and assured me that he would continue his investigations. 'I am like your Miss Marble, I never give up on a mystery,' he'd said, before disappearing down the track hooting his horn and sending a flock of birds zigzagging into the sky.

For two days we heard nothing from him, but then I received a phone call. The whispered voice he affected was that of a hero on the run from relentless pursuers. 'We must meet. Be at the L'Assorti in one hour,' he gasped.

I can recall the precise details of the meeting. I remember the clearness of the water as we sat talking, so clear that I could pick out the white-tipped edges of the stones lying on the riverbed and the spiky whiskers of the trout that darted downstream. In the background, the waterwheels churned continuously and the ducks strove against the current, their labours illuminated by the bright sun. I remember the sense of déjà-vu as Thierry pronounced that there was good news and bad news, and I remember wanting him to get to the point as he narrated a story about potential corruption in local government.

I watched the water showering from the giant wheel as Thierry continued, telling us about his suspicions that an official wanted to secure the property on the cheap for a friend. To do this, he needed some leverage over Madame Chevalier. Thierry reached underneath the table for his briefcase, clicked it open and produced photocopies of four letters. The most recent was dated a week before we signed the *compromis*. They were officially lodged complaints from Madame Chevalier relating to the government's proposals to build a *station d'épuration* on the boundaries of her land at the base of the meadow. Madame argued that the effect on the value of her property was potentially disastrous, particularly since the prevailing wind came from that direction.

'What's a *station d'épuration*?' I asked Thierry.

'I am afraid it's not a good thing. Not a very good thing at all.' He grimaced. 'It's a sewage farm.'

After the initial shock had receded, Thierry remembered the good news. 'Well, it's more like less bad news,' he confessed.

Ordering us all another drink, he explained that in his opinion we should definitely refuse to pay the balance of the purchase cost. The site near the Auberge des Sangliers was one of three possibilities identified as suitable for the sewage farm.

Now that we'd agreed in principle to purchase the property, a number of things could happen. Firstly given the natural beauty of the area surrounding the *auberge*, it might be decided that the site was unsuitable for purpose. This was clearly the best result for us. By contrast for political reasons the *auberge* might be identified as the preferred location – since we were foreigners, we'd be unable to mobilise much local support against the project and this was an expedient solution. Alternatively – and in Thierry's opinion this was the most likely outcome – with the threat of the sewage farm in the background we'd be forced to sell at a greatly reduced price to somebody involved with the planning process. Once we'd agreed, all proposals for the *station d'épuration* would be conveniently forgotten.

It was difficult for us to believe that this level of intrigue existed, but Thierry talked as if such machinations were a frequent occurrence. If we proceeded as suggested and refused to pay the rest of the purchase price, there was a possibility Madame Chevalier might take us to court. But according to Thierry, we had a good defence – we'd been materially misled. 'At the end of the day the good news is that you should win and get your money back, including your deposit,' concluded Thierry. 'It may just take a long time. And it will be expensive.'

We finished the wine and tried to rationalise events. Had the tenant caused problems or a major crack had suddenly appeared in a wall, then we could have accepted our misfortune. Instead we'd been undone by deception and greed. Madame Chevalier and her daughter, Christine, had sat around the kitchen table with us sharing a glass of wine. Outside, Rosie and Tristan had been playing in the meadow and yet all the time they'd been withholding a secret. If Madame Chevalier really loved families as much as she professed, why was she prepared to see ours grow up in the shadow of a sewage farm? We reviewed the words and phrases she'd used, to see whether there'd been any clues we'd missed; we analysed her facial expressions and moods, but in the end we just couldn't comprehend her behaviour. For the second time in a week we voted on a show of hands. This time it was an easier decision and once again we were unanimous – we'd refuse to pay the outstanding money.

Once Thierry had left, and our mock bravado about quickly finding another property had faded, we were left with the reality of our uncomfortable position. We'd enjoyed another summer but at its end we had little to show for our hard work. The typically British attitude would have been to continue as planned and accept what had happened as a major but not final blow. However, it hurt too much for that. In the short term the thought of traipsing around more towns and villages looking for our dream bar was too dispiriting. And then there was the question of the deposit. Losing money equivalent to 10 per cent of the purchase price of the *auberge* severely limited our ability to buy anywhere else. To get this sum back, we faced a long court battle. It was also hard not to feel a little let down by the French. Rationally I knew we'd been unlucky, but both Hervé at the beginning of the summer and now Madame Chevalier had deliberately deceived us and it was all too easy to become suspicious of everyone we met.

September was just a day away and with autumn approaching Peter had been taking an increasing number of calls from his wife, Jenny. Each time he promised he'd be returning to England shortly while refusing to give an exact date.

Our rosé festival on Isabelle's terrace was also coming to an end. It had only ever been an ad-hoc arrangement and we were taking up space she could use for diners. 'We're going to be homeless and jobless,' concluded Tanya, 'so it must be about time we went to stay with my sister.' She was right – once installed at Claire's, we could regroup and reconsider our options. It was the conversation I'd been waiting all summer to have. Would we continue our life in France, or after two wandering summers, was it time to finally settle in England and raise a family? Tanya could teach drama, and Horatio Hanson might have me back, provided that is I chose the right combination of colour-coded cards and gratefully accepted the proffered pickled-herring sandwich.

On our final day of trading in L'Isle-sur-la-Sorgue, just as in Uzès, we were befriended by an accordion player who serenaded our customers with the tune 'La Vie en Rose'. But despite the happy scene, the sun, the waterwheels and the thriving bar, it sounded more like a lament.

22

Rosé en Marché

The morning sun eased on to the narrow streets of L'Isle-sur-la-Sorgue, peeking through gaps between houses and falling over the rooftops on to the pastel-coloured walls. It swept from the *boulangerie* to the *tabac*, awakening stores with the first blink of bright light and spotlighting the girls at the *parfumerie* as they raised the iron grille. By the time we'd finished breakfast even the bar opposite was bathed in sunshine and open and ready to admit the first customers of the day.

As was her habit, Tanya turned to the weather map at the back of the *La Provence*. Another good day was forecast, but by the end of the week the return of the mistral was predicted – driving cold air down the Rhône Valley to the sea and gusting between buildings until the power of the wind made the streets shriek. It was the mistral that had finally driven us from France at the end of the previous summer, and its return heralded the onset of autumn. The trees were already turning a golden red, and horse chestnuts were falling to the ground.

From the courtyard of the hotel we watched a steady procession of people heading towards the centre of town. It was Sunday morning in L'Isle-sur-la-Sorgue, the market was opening, and the locals were keen to beat the tourists to the fresh produce. Old women clasped large wicker baskets in their withered hands, men wobbled by on rickety bikes with panniers tied above the front wheel with worn leather straps, and children tailed their mothers, enjoying the honour of carrying shopping bags as big as themselves. The bar across the street had quickly filled and people were sharing baguettes and drinking glasses of rosé. At this time of the morning the clientele was normally *chasseurs* enjoying some bread and wine after the hunt — the habit was so culturally ingrained it even had a name *casse-croûte*, literally meaning 'breaking of the crust' — but in this case the customers were more likely to be market traders grabbing a moment's respite before their work began.

The previous evening we'd made the seemingly inconsequential but ultimately fortuitous decision to leave the car outside L'Assorti. The plan was to load the remaining wine into the boot and then head off. Peter was going to drop us at Claire's house before beginning his drive back to England.

As we walked towards L'Assorti, we listened to his plans to explore the Atlantic coast of France on his way home. Unsurprisingly his itinerary was heavily biased towards gastronomy — stopping off at Maronne to the north of Bordeaux for oysters, allowing his palate to meander through the *crêpes* and *galettes* of Brittany and the heavy cream sauces of Normandy until he finally reached Calais. 'If there's time, I'm going to search the Loire for pale rosé. There's Rosé d'Anjou and the golden rosés of Chinon to discover. Who knows what I'll find, and who knows what will happen to you two?' he finished with a grin.

All along the river were rows and rows of market stalls. Brightly coloured parasols and awnings obscured the shopfronts and blotted out the views of the water. A crowd of people pressed between the stalls, their arms forming natural arches for us to pass under as they paid and received goods from the traders.

The familiar frontage of L'Assorti — decorated with knives, forks and miscellaneous kitchen equipment — was blocked out by a stall selling freshly squeezed orange juice. Opposite the bar and in front the terrace was another trader, this time specialising in Corsican produce. Different dried meats – from *saucisson de sanglier* to cured pork sourced from chestnut-fed pigs – were laid out on small chopping boards. A serrated knife was provided with each delicacy, and prospective customers could help themselves to tastes. Completing the triangle of stalls was a vendor offering leather goods – wallets, belts, handbags and jackets. And stranded in the middle of the traders with a steady flow of people breaking to either side of the bonnet was Peter's car. Even if we could edge past the pedestrians and persuade the leather salesman to temporarily move his stall, two large white vans – hosting a travelling *fromagerie* and a *boucherie* – blocked our route to the main road.

There was little else to do but explore the market. Heading away, we window-shopped along the canal towards the hundreds of *brocante* stalls. Here the crowd was at its thickest and as people paused to look at goods, our pace slowed to a shuffle. But even this was too quick for Peter. He paused and examined nearly every object we passed – reclaimed wooden doors and shutters, wrought-iron wine-carriers, heavy old sets of boules turned ochre orange by rust, battered watering cans and chipped mirrors. Removing his enormous glasses and twirling them in the air, he haggled away, oblivious to the fact that he was blocking the way.

The crowd began to tail back on to the bridges as Peter vacillated over the purchase of two pictures of a poker-playing monk. In one, the monk was depicted with a frown on his face and a handful of low-scoring cards. In the other, he wore a big grin as he regarded a royal flush. Negotiations had started at €500 for the pair, a price that Peter had described as preposterous. Within ten minutes the queue of people on the bridge had doubled but this figure had halved. From visits to Peter's house in England, we knew he was an insatiable collector – not only were the walls full of paintings, so was the cellar, and the place had become so cluttered that his wife, Jenny, had banned him from buying any more art. Trying to do her a favour, Tanya and I eased Peter away from the stall by asking advice – during the course of the summer we'd missed the weddings of several friends and we were keen to buy some presents, but the market was full of such a mismatch of objects that it was hard to appraise value.

Amid worn Pernod Ricard glasses and jugs we'd discovered a set of Perrier tumblers. Peter was still casting covetous glances over his shoulder as we began to negotiate. The glasses were retro in design and given the price of €20 each were presumably manufactured a long time ago. We held them up and examined their quality, noting the glass was a little worn and scratched. Having accepted that this was inevitable with antiques, we were about to make a purchase. 'You can buy six of those for ten euros in the supermarket,' warned Peter, finally banishing the pictures from his mind.

Metres away, we found something else suitable – a stand full of old Peugeot Frères coffee-grinders. They were made from polished wood with an iron grinding mechanism. Beans were placed in an opening at the top, and there was a small drawer at the base to collect the ground coffee. Importantly each of the grinders on sale came complete with a catalogue showing the date of its production – usually at the beginning of the twentieth century.

'That's the 2CV of grinders,' said the salesman as we examined his wares. 'What you need is the Mercedes,' he continued, presenting us with a larger, more ornate model. Perhaps it was the homely smell of freshly ground coffee, in any event the grinders seemed the perfect wedding gift and under Peter's supervision we purchased two.

By midday the crowds around the *brocante* stalls appeared to be thinning and we made our way back to L'Assorti, hopeful that we might now squeeze the car out. We managed to persuade the leather-goods trader to temporarily move his stall, but there was still a long queue at the *fromagerie* and the owner refused our request. And so we waited, ordering a glass of rosé and sitting on the terrace of L'Assorti watching as people made their way home.

Telling the locals from the tourists was easy – the former carried bags sagging with fruit and vegetables, while the latter stumbled past clutching various antiques – gramophones, ancient maps of the world, old signs from train stations – which they were struggling to get back to their hotel, let alone home. An American couple staggered towards us buckling under the weight of a shutter no doubt reclaimed from some derelict farmhouse. It was blistered, battered and rotten, but the couple looked delighted with their purchase. Tanya smiled. 'People will buy almost anything in a market.' Her smile broadened. She'd had what proved to be her best idea of the summer.

Following Tanya's instructions, we took the hood off Peter's car and spread our pink tablecloths over the interior and across the bonnet and boot. We then arranged all our remaining rosé inside the car – ten bottles of champagne from the long, vine-packed slopes of Rilly-la-Montagne, twenty-four bottles of Sancerre from Maimbray, a village where the hills were so steep that grass was allowed to grow between the vines to prevent soil erosion, twelve pale Provençal rosés from the late-harvesting Luberon vineyard of Château la Dorgonne and a dozen miscellaneous clairets from Bordeaux.

The owner of L'Assorti, Isabelle, watched with interest as we crowned our display by placing a large magnum of rosé on the bonnet of the car. Ever creative, she rolled up some of our posters – the ones depicting a blue sky and blazing sun over the Luberon hills – and pushed them through the neck of empty wine bottles. She dotted her new creations artistically amid our display and covered the windscreen with the remaining posters. '*C'est joli*,' she declared.

Now we were ready to put Tanya's plan into action. People were already stopping and looking curiously at the pink folly that had materialised in the middle of the market. We chalked up our prices on the blackboard and began to work, crying out alternatively in French and English, '*Voulez-vous goûter un peu de vin rosé?* Would you like to taste some rosé?' A crowd quickly gathered, and while Tanya and I handed around small tastes of wine, we dispatched Peter to keep an eye out for the *police municipale*. Although we weren't aware that we needed permission to start trading in the market, this was France and almost inevitably we'd require numerous different papers. If Peter spotted the police, we'd clear up quicker than a sunglasses salesman on Oxford Street.

Whether it was good luck, a good pitch or a combination of the two I'm still not sure. Peter's car resembled a giant pink picnic basket and pedestrians couldn't help but take a look. We sold bottle after bottle, charming the English, guiding the Scandinavians towards the clairet and outwitting the French by discussing grape variety and vinification in such detail that they had to concede we had some expertise. After the worry over the Auberge des Sangliers it was enjoyable just to be trading again and feeling the weight of coins build up in our money belts. Tanya was at her effervescent best, passing on hotel recommendations to tourists, swapping anecdotes from our summer with the locals and completely outselling me.

After just half an hour Peter came panting back to the car clasping a painting in either hand. His breath came in heaving gasps and it was a couple of potentially crucial seconds before he was able to speak. 'The *police municipale* are on their way,' he said, pointing through the crowds. Two officers, one male and one female, were heading towards us. My immediate impression was that they were more concerned with their appearances than police work. They both wore designer sunglasses, their hair was gelled, their collars starched, and their boots were polished to a reflective sheen. The two of them measured their stride so that their legs moved in unison in the manner of ballroom dancers rather than law-enforcement officers.

As they glided closer, Peter hurriedly removed the posters from the windscreen and whipped the tablecloth from the bonnet. It wasn't until he started to clear the interior of the car that he realised Tanya and I weren't helping. 'Come on,' he urged, 'help hide the stuff.'

But rather than aid Peter we stood with amused expressions on our faces as he twitchily stuffed tablecloths into the glove compartment. The police strutted closer, checked their appearance in the car's wing mirrors, ignored Peter's clumsy attempts to obscure their gaze and moved off.

'You two were remarkably cool,' said Peter, as he looked under the seats for our remaining stock.

'It's all gone,' clarified Tanya. 'We stopped trading five minutes ago, long before the police arrived.'

'Every last bottle?' queried Peter.

Tanya and I nodded in unison.

'Congratulations,' said Peter, as he unveiled his new purchases – the two paintings of the poker-playing monk intended as the perfect homecoming present for his wife. While Tanya joked with Peter about his lackadaisical attitude to lookout duty, I did some quick calculations.

We'd spent all summer worrying about the location of La Vie en Rosé, trying to work out how much casual trade we would attract from the street. We'd looked at bars in the centre of busy cities such as Cannes and in touristy villages like Cabris, and we'd considered paying thousands of euros to lease or buy one of various properties. And yet none of the locations we'd seen could compare with the flow of people in the heart of a French market. Thanks to Tanya's idea, we'd just enjoyed our busiest and most profitable half-hour of the summer.

The market traders began to pack away and as the sea of

awnings and parasols receded, the hills of the Luberon valley once again became visible above the rooftops of L'Isle-sur-la-Sorgue. The sky was a lush blue and the light so bright that a spectrum of colours reflected off the rocky slopes, creating a shimmering haze. We relaxed and enjoyed one final drink before departing. And as I sipped on the pale-pink wine I finally came to an obvious conclusion. It was one that should have occurred to us long ago.

'It does make you think,' I said, broaching the subject.

'That we might not even need a bar,' continued Tanya, counting the pile of crumpled notes in her hand.

'*Rosé en marché*, it sounds marvellous,' said Peter, pausing as he puffed on a freshly lit cigar, 'absolutely marvellous.'

23

Lourmarin

Just two weeks later Tanya and I rose early, filled the back of the car with wine and bumped down a gravel track. It was the morning of our first proper market. We passed through the misty outlines of an olive grove before turning on to the main road. To our right, the long, dark silhouette of the Luberon hills emerged into the early-morning half-light. Ahead was the village of Lourmarin. The spire of the village church peeked through the cloud, its outline becoming clearer and clearer as the first rays of the sun dissolved the darkness.

We drove on past the village, taking the road that plunged through the Luberon, curving its way towards the regional capital of Apt. As I swung Peter's ancient BMW round the hairpins, vineyards gave way to rocky canyons and light once again to shadow. We passed old stone houses, trapped between high cliffs, as we circled ever upward. The pines and cypresses of the southern side of the valley ceded the rocky earth to lush-leaved oak, and the early-morning mist evaporated, revealing a light-blue sky and a ripe moon visibly reluctant to leave the stage.

Arriving at a junction, we opted for the more picturesque route, turning left towards the village of Bonnieux rather than continuing straight on through the hamlet of Buoux. A cedar forest – a favoured spot for hunting *cèpes* as autumn approached

– scrolled across the car windows and then the landscape dipped away, revealing the far side of the Luberon. In the foreground was Bonnieux, perched on a rocky outcrop. Behind it, on the distant hills, we could still make out the lights of the other ancient sentinel villages of Gordes and Goult, and beyond them, looming over everything, was the white-capped giant, Mont Ventoux.

We rattled through the narrow cobbled streets of Bonnieux, wincing as our bottles of wine clinked against each other in the back. The shutters in the *boulangerie* were already up and we could see the first customers huddled inside, clasping their baguettes under their armpits like military batons as they handed over their change.

The temptation to stop and buy some breakfast was strong, but we headed out of the village on the narrow road that ran along the hillside. The slopes here were gentler, and on either side of us rows of vines climbed and dived with the landscape. We passed Château de Mille, the oldest vineyard in the Luberon, where a few days ago we'd enquired about buying some rosé, only to discover that as well as the oldest vines in the area, it was also home to the most ferocious Dobermann in the valley.

Finally we came to a series of small roundabouts, the road widened, and the traffic thickened. We'd arrived in the outskirts of Apt. Ahead of us, the market traders would already be setting up and we were about to join them. I half listened to Tanya chatting nervously about the day ahead, while I ran through a mental checklist of what we had to do – find a place in the market, get the car as close as possible to unload the wine and then start trading. Fumbling in my pocket, I reassured myself that I'd brought along a corkscrew to open the wine for tasting. But what if things went wrong – if we couldn't find a place or we couldn't get the car close enough to unload the wine? We usually visited markets at about midday when they were already a thriving, bustling, multicoloured tented village. I had no idea about the logistics of setting up. How did so many people cram their wares in such an orderly fashion into such a small space? Was there an unwritten set of rules that every other trader was familiar with? We would have to wait and see. For now I reassured myself that for the last week things had been going rather well for us.

The events surrounding our failed purchase of the Auberge des Sangliers already seemed a distant memory. Our recovery had been surprisingly quick and complete. On our way to Montpellier to stay with Tanya's sister, Thierry had called and insisted that we come and see another property. It was to rent rather than to buy, but the renovation work had just been completed, and he was sure we would be as 'pleased as a punch' with it. Peter had immediately performed a rather hazardous U-turn just outside the town of Beaucaire, and we picked up the keys from a local agent. Within the hour we were viewing our new home.

The property turned out to be an old *mas* about 3 kilometres from the village of Lourmarin, on the south side of the Luberon valley. It was surrounded by a field of mature olive trees, which had been beautifully tended and neatly cut back to ensure a good crop. A row of cypresses lined the potholed drive, and the surrounding fields hosted rows of vines heavy with swollen red grapes. Through an arch at the front of the *mas* we could see an old well and a fishpond. This part of the house had already been converted into a *gîte*. Instead it was the area at the back of the *mas* that was for rent. We followed the track that curved round the property, looping round a long-derelict *cochonnière*, or pig house. Parking next to an old olive tree at the rear of the main house, we climbed up on to the terrace and looked back at the view.

The dark-green colours of the Luberon seduced us. Rocky canyons were formed where the wooded slopes of the competing hills folded into each other, but otherwise trees covered all the high ground. Behind the *cochonnière*, another row of angular cypresses rose upwards, blending in with the verdant backdrop. Only their tips stretched higher than the smooth line of hills to be silhouetted against the blue sky. In the distance a donkey brayed, and its call was immediately answered from much closer by a cockerel. We peered round the side of the house. 'You'll have fresh eggs,' said Peter, pointing at a pen full of chickens, 'and early mornings.'

Pushing open the door to the *mas*, we discovered the interior had been entirely refurbished with local materials. We entered a double-height reception room with an open kitchen and mezzanine galley. Leading off the main living area was a narrow corridor with three bedrooms, all with windows opening on to a sweeping view.

It was much smaller than the Auberge des Sangliers, but perfect for us. Since we were only renting rather than buying, the decision was easy. We phoned Thierry to tell him we would take it and then walked outside on to the balcony and breathed the warm, herb-scented air. And it was as we were toasting the remarkable change in our fortunes that the phone rang again.

It was Thierry with more good news. Our mortgage application for the purchase of Auberge des Sangliers had just been returned to him. The bank had declined the loan, he explained triumphantly. I sipped on my rosé, looked at the view and entirely missed the significance of what Thierry was trying to explain. 'Good news is like buses, no? You wait for ages and then it all comes along at once.'

'Thierry, I don't understand.'

'There's a clause in the *compromis* that stipulates that if the bank are unable to lend on the property, then the deposit must be refunded. The bank found details of the sewage farm too – that's why they refused the loan. You're getting your money back.'

Two days later we moved into the *mas*. Our beds consisted of an array of cushions, and we ate crosslegged on the floor as we planned excursions to the nearest furniture shops. At night the Luberon hills slipped into shadow and we gazed up at the stars. Back in London, it had been easy to forget what the night sky should look like, but from our terrace we could pick out every constellation. Occasionally we saw shooting stars. To begin with it was so quiet at night that I found it impossible to sleep.

Peter was so enchanted by our new place that, despite exasperated phone calls from Jenny, he extended his stay by a week. We spent our time getting to know the local villages. Shy little Vaugines, sheltering under the mountains, where a moss-covered fountain and sleepy bar hid in the shadows, and castle-crested Cuceron, built on a small hill with a postcard-pretty water-filled basin at its foot. Then there was our nearest village, Lourmarin, which was more brazenly beautiful than the others, enchanting visitors from whichever angle they approached.

To the south of Lourmarin, the foreground was filled by cherry trees, and from the far side of this orchard the old stone buildings of the village rose. A trinity of towers presided over the residents – a belfry, the peaked roof of the Protestant temple and the green-tiled spire of the Catholic church. Each guided the eye ever upwards to the immensity of the hills and the rich blue sky.

From the west the view was dominated by the fifteenth-century château, with its stocky buttresses and foundations built into solid rock. And then there was the vista I liked best. As we approached every morning from the north, the spire of the church and the belfry gradually rose above us and then the rest of the village emerged, revealing itself building by building, almost coquettishly.

After familiarising ourselves with the area, Tanya and I were ready to begin our new life in the markets, but before we could, there was one final thing to do – say goodbye to Peter. We arranged a farewell lunch in Café l'Ormeau, one of a cluster of three bars that seemed to shape the social life of Lourmarin.

The bars were all located on the small cobbled street that threaded itself through the heart of the village. This road wove past a myriad of small boutiques and then performed a gentle wide curve, like the meander of a river, just outside the *tabac*. Here the pavement widened and tables and chairs from the three central bars huddled together in the shade offered by the high walls. Amid the peaceful trickle of water from a fountain, the blue and white livery of Café Gaby, the green and beige of Café l'Ormeau and the dark wicker of Café de la Fontaine competed for customers. Waiters crossed the street carrying plates of steaming food, stopping to kiss friends before serving meals.

Taking a table outside the Café l'Ormeau with Peter, we sat and reminisced about our summer. From the very beginning in Aix things had gone wrong. There had been several dark moments when the whole adventure had appeared futile, but now, at the end of it all, we wouldn't have had it any other way. We had our house in the south of France and the challenge of building up our wine business ahead of us. Nearly a year ago the three of us had sat in a fondue restaurant in Aix, dreaming of creating just such a future. Peter gripped my shoulder tightly and gave Tanya a kiss. 'We did, we bloody did it,' he said triumphantly, before clasping me in a bear hug and kissing me on both cheeks. He smiled at his over-exuberance. 'When in France,' he said sheepishly.

Our *steaks frites* arrived and we watched the trail of sightseers looping through the village, clutching their rucksacks and their cameras, stopping to buy postcards and examine menus. For Tanya and me, it would be wonderful to finally live in one place rather than wandering from town to town. Our challenge now was to meet people and integrate, to become familiar with the various bakers and the barmen, to greet them in the street and perhaps one day to be the people that the waiters paused to talk to before serving the tourists their food. All that was in the future; for now we simply had to learn which shops were open when, which *boulangerie* made the best croissants and which baked the best bread.

As we began to talk about the future, Peter poked at his steak, dipped the odd chip in some mustard and then finally pushed a half-full plate to the side.

'There's one more little thing. You're going to need something to drive, and if you will have her, I'd like to lend you my car,' he said, taking out the keys to his BMW and putting them on the table. 'I think she prefers the warm weather.'

Both Tanya and I started to protest but with a raised eyebrow and a fierce look he silenced us. 'It's only a loan. I'll be back in a couple of months to collect her. Now, let's get the bill – my flight home leaves in three hours from Marseille.'

And that was it. Peter refused to talk about the subject. If we didn't take the car, then he insisted he would just leave the keys on the table.

And so an hour later we dropped him at Marseille airport. I unloaded his suitcase from the boot and waited as Tanya said a tearful goodbye and elicited repeated promises from Peter that he would come and visit us soon. Peter and I then shook hands. He gave Tanya one more farewell hug and disappeared into the modern terminal building, leaving us standing together underneath the row of palm trees that lined the pavement. 'We didn't even get a farewell "marvellous",' I joked.

The next morning we'd woken before the cockerel to drive through the hills to the market. Now with the last of the series of roundabouts successfully negotiated, we parked Peter's old BMW on a kerb near the centre of Apt. Leaving the hazard lights flashing, we headed off to find the *placier*, the man responsible for allocating us a pitch.

The clothes traders at the base of the market were sliding together their metal hangers like builders putting up scaffolding, and the fruit and vegetable sellers were snapping open temporary legs and laying an elaborate network of board around themselves on which to arrange their produce. The mobile *boucheries* and *fromageries* already had their hatches up, and their owners were grabbing a final cigarette before starting the day. Feeding away to our left was a road leading towards the church square where furniture and carpet vendors had started burning incense, confusing the senses by conjuring a Moroccan souk in the south of France. And somewhere amid this vibrant jumble of stalls was the *placier*.

We asked for directions and were pointed towards the government buildings in the main square. Here the traders were standing in huddled groups, drinking cups of coffee that they'd transported from the nearest bar. If we were lucky, in the next year we'd become part of this life, swapping stories in the early-morning light, travelling from village to village – Saturday, Apt's busy streets; Sunday, fighting for a place amongst the *brocante* dealers at L'Isle-sur-la-Sorgue; Monday, the Provençal village of Cadenet; Tuesday, Cuceron and its pretty tree-lined *étang*; Wednesday, the chi-chi and forever trendy Saint-Rémy; Thursday, a much-needed day off; and Friday, back home to Lourmarin.

It was 7.30 a.m. on a clear September morning and the first rays of the sun were falling in warm corridors of light across the market. A grand staircase swept away above us towards the offices of the *sous-préfecture*. Looking up, I saw the red, white and blue tricolour flap lazily in a stray gust of air. Underneath the imposing staircase was the small cubby-hole office of the *police municipale*, where we'd been told to look for the *placier*. It was from here that Apt market – rated as one of the hundred most beautiful in France – was run. There was a window of opaque glass and a flimsy wooden door. I gave Tanya a quick kiss and we knocked and entered.

Les Fêtes du Vin Rosé

Café de la Renaissance
6 place aux Herbes, 30700 Uzès
Tel: 04 66 03 11 82

Murphy's Bar
5 rue Maubet, 30000 Nîmes
Tel: 04 66 26 38 31

Le Saint-Antoine
6 place de l'Hôtel de Ville, 06400 Cannes
Tel: 04 93 39 43 80

Pinède Plage
Square Gould, 06160 Juan-les-Pins
Tel: 04 93 61 07 03

L'Assorti
7 quai Rouget de l'Isle, 84800 L'Isle-sur-la-Sorgue

Carte des Vins

'They are all bloody good' Peter Tate (head sommelier)

Bordeaux

Château de Parenchère, 5 Parenchère, 33220 Ligueux
Tel: 05 57 46 04 17

Château Lauduc, Maison Grandeau Lauduc, 5 avenue de
Lauduc, 33370 Tresses
Tel: 05 57 34 11 82

Despagne, 33420 Naujan et Postiac
Tel: 05 57 84 55 08

Château de Sours, 33750 Saint-Quentin-de-Baron
Tel: 05 57 24 10 81

Champagne

Vilmart & Cie, 5 rue des Gravières, 51500 Rilly-la-Montagne
Tel: 03 26 03 40 01

Champagne René Geoffroy, 150 rue du Bois des Jots, 51480
Cumières
Tel: 03 26 55 32 31

Languedoc

Félicie Plantation, Domaine de Sainte-Marie, 34370
Maureilhan
Tel: 04 67 90 50 32

Château de Caladroy, 66720 Belesta-de-la-Frontière
Tel: 04 68 57 10 25

Mas d'Espanet, 30730 Saint-Mamert-du-Gard
Tel/Fax: 04 66 81 10 27

Loire

Domaine Pascal and Nicolas Reverdy, Maimbray, 18300 Sury-
en-Vaux
Tel: 02 48 79 37 31

Domaine Robert and François Crochet, Marcigoué, 18300 Bué
Tel: 02 48 54 21 77

Provence

Château la Dorgonne, Domaine de la Dorgonne, 84240 La
Tour d'Aigues
Tel: 04 90 07 50 18

Château Sainte-Marguerite, 83250 La Londe
Tel: 04 94 00 44 44

Domaine Saint Jean-Baptiste, 1525 route des Arcs, 83510
Lorgues
Tel: 04 94 73 71 11

Château la Calisse, route D-560, 83670 Pontevès
Tel: 04 94 77 24 71

Château de Roquefort, quartier des Bastides, Roquefort-la-
Bédoule
Tel: 04 42 73 20 84

Domaine Saint-Hilaire, route de Rians, 83470 Ollières
Tel: 04 98 05 40 10

Château Montagne, quartier du Gré, 83390 Pierrefeu-du-Var
Tel: 04 94 28 68 58

Château de Fonscolombe, 13610 Le-Puy-Sainte-Reparade
Tel: 04 42 61 70 00

Château de Rochebelle, 400 chemin des Luquettes, 83740 La
Cadière d'Azur
Tel: 04 94 90 13 37

Château Barbeyrolles, 83580 Gassin
Tel: 04 94 56 33 58

Some of Tanya's Favourite Places to Stay

Abbaye de Saint-Hilaire
route de Rians, 83470 Ollières
Tel: 04 98 05 40 10

Hiding in the countryside to the north of Aix is this renovated old farmhouse. It's been converted into about ten apartments, some of which sleep two people, others up to ten. There's a pool, horse riding, a field of lavender nudging the windows and spectacular views of Mont Sainte-Victoire. Oh, and the farmhouse is built within the lands of Domaine Saint-Hilaire so you don't have to travel far if you run out of rosé.

Hôtel du Général d'Entraigues
place de l'Evêché, 30700 Uzès
Tel: 04 66 22 32 68

We spent one night in this hotel on the outskirts of the old town in Uzès. Bedrooms with terraces have spectacular views of the Tour Fenestrelle; there's a small pool and a large terrace where you can dine under olive trees in the evening. There can be few better bases to explore the town of Uzès, and it is only five minutes' walk from Le Renaissance.

Hôtel la Villa Tosca
11 rue Hoche, 06400 Cannes
Tel: 04 93 38 34 40
Web: www.villa-tosca.com

Clean, comfortable, affordable town-house hotel with ever so funky bathrooms. It's just two minutes from La Croisette, and you can enjoy a nice glass of wine on the terrace of the Carlton with the money you have saved on the room. It's also a short walk from the station, where a Carte Isabelle allows you unlimited travel up the coast for a day – Juan-les-Pins, Antibes, Nice, Beaulieu-sur-Mer and Monte Carlo – it's got to be among the prettiest train rides in the world.

Hôtel Brise-Marine
58 avenue Jean Mermoz, 06230 Saint-Jean-Cap-Ferrat
Tel: 04 93 76 04 36

This was the only affordable hotel we could find on Cap-Ferrat. Unfortunately for us it was full. It's just outside the centre of the village; the terrace is draped with bougainvillea and commands wonderful views over the Mediterranean. There's an old-fashioned beach club a five-minute walk up the road. If you go for a swim, check with the lifeguard for jellyfish sightings first – the waters around the *cap* are unusually warm and, as the unfortunate Tanya learnt, prone to schools of *méduses*.

Hôtel Horizon
100 promenade Saint-Jean, 06530 Cabris
Tel: 04 93 60 51 69

The hotel couldn't be more aptly named. The views from the terrace and the swimming pool are absolutely stunning. To the north are the villa-studded hills of Haute-Provence, to the south the sea, and if you believe the owner's explanation about the curvature of the earth, on a clear day you can see Corsica. If you are planning on visiting Grasse, then Cabris is the perfect stop-off point. It's a ten-minute drive up the road and much more picturesque.

Some of My Favourite Restaurants

La Ferme de Biorne
24310 Lunas, near Bergerac
Tel: 05 53 57 67 26

The same idea as the foie gras farm we visited in Provence, but better. The menu consists of duck, duck, duck and more duck. They'd make a duck sorbet for dessert if they could. The foie gras is fantastic, and the *confit de canard* falls away from the bone. There's even a donkey sanctuary and a large garden to keep children amused.

La Chèvre d'Or
1 place Puits, 06530 Cabris
Tel: 04 93 60 54 22

Continuing the theme, according to Peter this restaurant does the best foie gras in the south of France. Other dishes include *médaillon de veau rosé aux morilles* and *carré d'agneau rôti*. The presentation of every dish was so immaculate that Tanya took a photo of our main courses. Menus start at about €25, but with a complimentary apple sorbet soaked in Calvados between courses, it's well worth the money.

Pavillon Croisette

42 La Croissette, 06400 Cannes
Tel: 04 92 59 06 90

For price and location this has to be the best restaurant in Cannes. Dine under the palm trees on La Croisette, watch the beautiful people parade past, and sip on some wonderfully pale rosé as the sun slips into the water. The menu is full of French classics and creamy risottos. We dined here to celebrate our first day at the Saint-Antoine.

Hôtel-Restaurant Bellerive

Rasteau, 84110 Vaison-la-Romaine
Tel: 04 90 46 10 20

In the middle of the vineyards of the southern Rhône near Orange, the restaurant's wine list runs to hundreds of bottles, listing all the local producers of note. Ask for a table on the terrace and enjoy a wonderfully tender slow-roasted pork compress followed by steak in a rich red-wine and mushroom sauce. If you've eaten too much to move, the hotel has plenty of rooms.

L'Équateur

9 avenue du Port, Les Lecques, 83270 Saint-Cyr-sur-Mer
Tel: 04 94 26 20 02

Moules frites, spaghetti bolognese and enormous salads right on the seafront. The owner, Frank, couldn't be happier singing along to himself as he whisks between the tables and the bar. The best spot for a no-frills lunch on the coast.

Acknowledgements

Peter Tate for his inspiration, humour and love of France. Claire, Neil, Rosie and Tristan for offering us shelter and sharing their stories. My agent, John Saddler, and my publisher, Alan Samson, long may their enthusiasm for a glass of rosé remain undimmed, and for their continued support in America, George Lucas of Inkwell and Michael Flamini of St Martin's. Thanks to Katie White and Mark Rusher at Orion for all their help in promoting and marketing the books, and Lucinda McNeile for all her hard work, turning a blind eye as she passed out the peanuts and above all for being such a good friend.

Ali George for giving his time so freely and not receiving the proper credit in these pages, Annie, John, Jean-Claude, Claudine, Isabelle and their families for making the whole adventure possible and allowing us to share their bars with them, the vignerons who provided us with rosé at very favourable prices, Mike Hawkes for some crucial advice and the following friends and family who helped us along: PJ, Lisa, Amandamoo, Martine, Michelle, Guy, Deborah, Faiza, Pierre, Nick, Kate, Trigger, Alan and of course the Aarvolds.

And finally my thanks to Tanya. Although nominally I am the author, it is of course very much our book.

Find out more about the travels of Jamie, Tanya and Peter at
www.extremelypalerose.com

Index